GIRALDUS CAMBRENSIS

First published 1972
Revised edition 1976

© 1976 Michael Richter

ISBN (o 901833 78 9)

GIRALDUS CAMBRENSIS

THE GROWTH OF THE WELSH NATION

MICHAEL RICHTER

The National Library of Wales
Aberystwyth
1976

In memoriam
Angelika   Arend

PREFACE

This is the first book on Giraldus Cambrensis published for sixty years. Dealing with this prolific writer and historian, whose works consist of several thousand pages, a book this size is not intended to be a comprehensive study. It is both general and specialized, general in sketching the life and times of Giraldus, specialized in analysing more closely two main aspects, his writing on Wales and his involvement in the dispute over the metropolitan dignity of St. David's. All other aspects of his life and works have been subordinated to these two central themes. Although historiography on Wales in the twelfth and thirteenth centuries is notoriously meagre, two particular authors will have to be mentioned on whom this book draws heavily, Sir John Edward Lloyd and Dr. James Conway Davies. I do not always find myself in agreement with them, but their publications proved indispensable.

The book is, in essence, a translation of a thesis entitled 'Normannen und Waliser bei Giraldus Cambrensis', which was submitted in 1968 at Free University, Berlin, for the degree of Dr.phil.. I owe a great debt to the inspired teaching of my superviser, Professor Wilhelm Berges who first drew my attention to Giraldus Cambrensis and whose unfailing advice was both encouraging and beneficial. On this side of the Channel, I received much help especially from Professor R. R. Darlington, Professor C. R. Cheney, and Professor Thomas Jones. For two years, I had the honour to be a Senior Research Fellow of the University of Wales at Aberystwyth, during which time I had the opportunity, both by teaching and further research, to improve on my original text. The present book has appeared, without the bibliography and the index, in article form in *The National Library of Wales Journal*, xvi–xvii, 1969–1972. I am particularly grateful to the Editor of the *Journal*, Mr. David Jenkins, who agreed to issue the articles in book-form and make them thereby more easily accessible both to students and to a wider public.

MICHAEL RICHTER

London, July, 1971

PREFACE TO THE SECOND EDITION

Seven years after the work was first completed as a doctoral thesis, and four years after its last revision for publication in book-form, I welcome the opportunity to issue a revised edition of the text. Over the past years, I have devoted part of my research to Giraldus and his times, and for this reason I have included, at least in the footnotes, references to more recent publications. I am aware more than ever before of the great amount of work which still needs to be done on Giraldus. Some of it I hope to do myself, but I shall gladly welcome any assistance in this rewarding field. How much there can be learned, I experienced in the completion, together with my fellow-editors, of the edition of Giraldus Cambrensis, *Speculum Duorum*. I feel that a full study of the man will have to be preceded by intensive work on the manuscripts of his works and ideally by a new edition of all of them. In view of this, I have resisted the temptation to introduce great alterations into the text. It has been revised stylistically throughout, and I take this opportunity to thank my Dublin friends Fintan Butler and Edward James for their substantial help. As previously, my thanks are due to Mr. David Jenkins of the National Library of Wales, Aberystwyth, for his agreement to undertake a new edition of this book.

MICHAEL RICHTER

Dublin, 14 July 1975.

CONTENTS

		PAGE
ABBREVIATIONS	... ...	xii
INTRODUCTION	... ...	1
GIRALDUS, LIFE AND WORKS	... ...	4
THE CULTURAL AND POLITICAL BACKGROUND: THE DIOCESE OF ST DAVID'S	...	12
I. CHURCH REFORM IN BRITAIN AND IRELAND AFTER THE CONQUEST	... ...	22
THE BISHOPS IN WALES PRIOR TO 1148	... ...	29
BISHOPS BERNARD'S METROPOLITAN CLAIM AND CANTERBURY'S REACTION	...	38
II. THE NOTION OF THE WELSH NATION	... ...	57
THE WELSH WORKS: MOTIVATION AND INTENTION	... ...	61
WALES AND THE WELSH AS SEEN BY GIRALDUS	... ...	66
OTHER OPINIONS ABOUT THE WELSH	... ...	78
CONCLUSION	... ...	81
III. THE FIGHT FOR A WELSH ARCHBISHOPRIC	... ...	83
GIRALDUS' DEVELOPMENT INTO A 'CAMBRENSIS'	... ...	84
BISHOP-ELECT OF ST. DAVID'S	... ...	94
POSTSCRIPT	... ...	127
APPENDIX I THE CORRESPONDENCE ABOUT THE METROPOLITAN CLAIM OF BISHOP BERNARD	... ...	130
APPENDIX II SELECTED DOCUMENTS	... ...	133
SELECT BIBLIOGRAPHY	... ...	136
INDEX	... ...	145

ABBREVIATIONS

ALMA	*Archivum Latinitatis Medii Aevi*
An. Mon.	*Annales Monastici*
Arch. Camb.	*Archaeologia Cambrensis*
BBCS	*The Bulletin of the Board of Celtic Studies*
BJRL	*The Bulletin of the John Ryland's Library*
CSEL	*Corpus Scriptorum Ecclesiasticorum Latinorum*
Cym. Trans.	*The Transactions of the Honourable Society of Cymmrodorion*
EHR	*The English Historical Review*
Ep. Acts	*Episcopal Acts and Cognate Documents Relating to Welsh Dioceses, 1066–1272*
Haddan & Stubbs	*Councils and Ecclesiastical Documents Relating to Great Britain and Ireland*
HCY	*The Historians of the Church of York*
HSCW	*The Historical Society of the Church in Wales*
JEH	*The Journal of Ecclesiastical History*
LC	*Le Liber Censuum*
LL	*The Text of the Book of Llan Dâv*
Mansi	*Sacrorum Conciliorum Collectio Nova*
Migne, *PL*	J.P. Migne, *Patrologia Latina*
NLWJ	*The National Library of Wales Journal*
Proc. Brit. Acad.	*Proceedings of the British Academy*
RS	Rolls Series
SEBC	Chadwick, N. K., ed., *Studies in Early British Church*
Trans. RHS	*The Transactions of the Royal Historical Society*
WHR	*The Welsh History Review*
ZSRG	*Zeitschrift der Savigny-Gesellschaft für Rechtsgeschichte*

INTRODUCTION

THE period conventionally called the High Middle Ages saw the final decisive encounter between the universal Empire and the universal Church which ended with the victory of the Church, although this victory was short-lived. For to this day Europe has been divided into smaller political units which can be called national states. Constitutional historians have inquired widely into the emergence of the separate states.[1] What is lacking, however, is an unbiased analysis of the function of those ethnical elements involved in the emergence of the states which in medieval times were already called by the ambiguous term 'nation'. The present study attempts such an inquiry confined, as it may be, to a small subject. It deals with twelfth-century Wales as it appears in the writings of the most outspoken and controversial son of that country, Giraldus Cambrensis.

If the choice of sources may appear to be arbitrary,[2] the subject itself imposes welcome limitations. Britain being an island, the emergence of states was somewhat simplified, for the lack of possibilities of expansion directed state-building forces towards the island itself. The Norman invasion, however, retarded the emergence of one single state, for this was not achieved in the political field until 1603 (or 1707) and is yet to be achieved culturally. The arrival of the Normans in 1066 provided a new impulse to the creation of the state. This simplification of the issue cleared other aspects as well. In the twelfth century, Scotland finally emerged as one separate kingdom. If Wales did not witness a similarly straight-forward development, the thirteenth century brought at least the unrivalled leadership of Gwynedd. The Norman conquest of England was sweeping and lasting; the resistance in Wales took two centuries to be broken. At the beginning of the thirteenth century, with which our study ends, the result of the Norman encroachment in Wales was undetermined and unpredictable.

---

[1] For an excellent survey see Frantisek Graus, 'Die Entstehung der mittelalterlichen Staaten in Mitteleuropa', *Historica*, x, 1965, pp. 5–65. Although Graus deals mainly with the tenth century and concentrates more on Eastern and Central Europe, his article shows parallels with the present study which can but encourage further research on a wider scale. The present author avoids, wherever possible, terms like 'Nationalstaat' or 'nationalism', as employed by Graus or e.g. Gaines Post, *Studies in Medieval Legal Thought* (Princeton, 1964), esp. ch. x, 'Public Law, the State and Nationalism'.

[2] The political poetry in Wales especially has to be left aside; for an introduction see Glanmor Williams, 'Prophecy, Poetry, and Politics in Medieval and Tudor Wales', *British Government and Administration* (Studies presented to S. B. Chrimes, ed. by H. Hearder and H. R. Loyn, Cardiff, 1974), pp. 104–116.

A history of medieval Europe which does not take account of the impact of the Church cannot be imagined.[1] This institution gave an impulse from outside for the emergence of states. Rome, after the Gregorian reform movement of the eleventh century, seized her chance to influence the establishment of greater ecclesiastical units by granting archbishoprics, thus opening the path, if unwanted at times, towards analogous well-defined political units. Rarely, if ever, was a combination of the powers of crown and pallium more effective than in medieval England.[2] In Wales, from the beginning of the twelfth century, attempts were made to obtain an independent archiepiscopal province which would be largely or completely outside the influence of Canterbury. Since the Normans in Wales took special care to bind the Church closely to them – which was one of the reasons for their ultimate success – it is difficult to overestimate what the consequences of creating an independent Welsh Church might have been. Wales was brought from the beginning of the new Church organisation into close contact with Rome, with the result that the papal curia, according to a *provinciale* dating from the middle of the twelfth century, did not regard the Welsh dioceses as suffragans of Canterbury!

The struggle between Normans and Welsh had many faces; rarely if ever was it to become as fructiferous in the literary field as in the case of Giraldus Cambrensis. As a son of a Norman father and a Welsh mother, Giraldus was subject to the tension between these two peoples all through his life. He attempted to find his place first with the Normans, then with the Welsh, and failed on both occasions. He was insulted by the Normans for being a 'Welshman', mistrusted by the Welsh as a Norman; so, whatever side he took, his descent was clearly to his disadvantage. Such implications are easily overestimated, but it is equally dangerous to brush them aside as meaningless.

Two of the most important works by Giraldus deal with Wales and her people. They have been rightly praised in the past, though without taking into account sufficiently the career of their author. Thus the fact that he wrote them while still trying his luck with the Normans has not been fully appreciated.[3] In the introduction, Giraldus stated

---

[1] For a first sketch of papal intervention in the establishment of the European states see Karl Bierbach, *Kurie und nationale Staaten im frühen Mittelalter (bis 1245)* (Dresden, 1938), esp. pp. 45–140.

[2] C. R. Cheney, *Hubert Walter* (London, 1967): 'never since Archbishop Lanfranc had an archbishop of Canterbury wielded so much power in affairs of the state; never did this happen again', p. 89.

[3] Apart from the unfortunately biased account in Paul Kirn, *Aus der Frühzeit des Nationalgefühls* (Leipzig, 1943), p. 98 there is only Thomas Jones, 'Gerald the Welshman's 'Itinarary Through Wales' and 'Description of Wales': An appreciation and analysis', *NLWJ*, vi, 1949–50, pp. 117–48; 197–222.

that the Welsh were a people different from all others, and the content of the description of Wales fully justifies what otherwise could sound like a *topos*. He mentioned peculiarities in language, law, customs, and especially descent (*natio* proper), common to the Welsh. Here he expressed categories which would be understood, accepted, and shared by his audience. He perceived the Welsh as a *natio* by seeing and describing them better than any of his contemporaries. He was fairly closely acquainted with the country, but failed to identify himself with its people. At this point, the traditional image of Giraldus, be he called 'the Welshman' or just 'of Wales', has to be subjected to a rigorous examination. Attempts to find consistency in his character which would be expressed by such a label become easily artificial and do great injustice to his complex personality and sensitive awareness.

Giraldus took a leading part in the attempt to raise St. David's to an archbishopric. He was not the first person to do so. A careful appreciation has to be made of the achievements of his spiritual predecessor, Bishop Bernard. With regard to himself, an account of what he as bishop-elect did for Wales will be more interesting than a complete reconstruction of his suit in Rome, for which an essential part of the sources has not been preserved. In Rome he became an outspoken protagonist of the Welsh cause and pointed out the disastrous effects of the Norman advance in Wales. By this action, Giraldus attempted to give to the Welsh a unity which would be guaranteed by Rome, while earlier in his life he had clearly described the Welsh as a people different from the Anglo-Normans. Had Wales in 1200 been a unified kingdom, his attempt to be granted the pallium might have met with ultimate success; as it was, he had to admit to the pope: 'Wallia portio est regni Anglicani, et non per se regnum'. Giraldus' fight before the pope against the English king and the archbishop of Canterbury not only made him for some time a genuine *Cambrensis*, but was an important contribution towards Welsh unification.

It is hoped that a study of Giraldus' writings by someone neither English nor Welsh may help to come to a new appreciation of this author. In retrospect he must be called neither Welsh nor Norman but a truly European figure. Thus the interest in his writings by far exceeds the geographical limitations of his subject. It is designed as a contribution towards our understanding of the notion of the nation in the Middle Ages.

Giraldus, Life and Works.[1]

Giraldus de Barri was born at Manorbier Castle, Pembrokeshire, probably in 1146. His paternal ancestors were Norman, his grandfather, Gerald of Windsor, being King Henry I's constable of Pembroke Castle. Gerald of Windsor had entered into one of the leading families in Wales by his marriage to Nest, daughter of Rhys ap Tewdwr.[2] One of their daughters, Angharad, became the wife of William de Barri and mother of four sons, Robert, Philip, Walter and Giraldus. Giraldus thus was born into an influential setting in Wales. In addition to that, the ecclesiastical field was opened to him when his uncle, David fitz Gerald, in 1148, was made bishop of the most important diocese in Wales, St. David's. The bishop provided for the early education of his nephew, had him sent to St. Peter's, Gloucester, and at the early age of fifteen or sixteenth, to Paris for the study of the arts and later Roman and canon law.[3] In about 1174, Giraldus returned to England and shortly afterwards was commissioned by the archbishop of Canterbury to go to Wales to collect tithes in the diocese of St. David's. The energy and ruthlessness with which he set on his task betrayed the academic in him, untouched by the difficulties and compromises of life, and earned him a reputation for thoroughness. Sweepingly, he treated Flemish settlers in Pembrokeshire and Welsh farmers alike. Disregarding customs which had persisted in the church, not only in Wales but elsewhere, he suspended the archdeacon of Brecon just because that man was married and did not want to part with his wife. The post was immediately filled with the appointment by Bishop David fitz Gerald of Giraldus himself.

As archdeacon, Giraldus showed the same vigour, if at times his energy met with less success than he himself pretends. One incident may be discussed because it is a good example of the way Giraldus carefully prepared his image for posterity. It is the famous story about the consecration of St. Michael's church in Ceri, where Giraldus

---

[1] This is only a short sketch. No full biography has been written; for more details see J. C. Davies, 'Giraldus Cambrensis, 1146–1946', *Arch. Camb.*, 99, 1946–7, pp. 85–108; 256–280, and the perceptive study by F. M. Powicke, 'Gerald of Wales', *BJRL*, xii, 1928, pp. 389–410.

[2] Sir George Duckett, 'Evidences of the Barri family of Manorbier and Olethan', *Arch. Camb.*, 5th ser. vii, 1891, pp. 190–208; 277–96.

[3] Dorothy Humphreys, 'Some Types of Social Life as shown in the works of Gerald of Wales' (Oxford, B.Litt. thesis) (typescript), 1936; for Giraldus' legal training see *Speculum Duorum*, pp. lii–lvii.

vigorously opposed Adam, bishop of St. Asaph.[1] The story is so well told, having such a touch of life about it, that the reader does not realize how the narrator obscures the issue. Despite the impression which is given to the reader, Giraldus as archdeacon could not consecrate a church, although he could, and did, prevent the bishop of St. Asaph from doing so. It would appear that the consecration was performed by the new bishop of St. David's, Peter de Leia. Bishop Adam appealed to the pope who in turn delegated the case to the bishops of Exeter and Worcester.[2] At the Third Lateran Council, in 1179, Bishop Adam established his right against St. David's, a decision which was later, by unknown means, reversed by Giraldus.[3]

It has to be doubted whether Giraldus took part in the Westminster synod in the spring of 1176.[4] On that occasion, the canons of St. David's raised the metropolitan claim of their church, an issue which did not concern Giraldus at that time as fervently as it was to do three decades later.[5] Thus it is difficult to accept unreservedly the account which conveys that upon his nomination to the bishopric of St. David's in 1176 he was turned down by the archbishop and the king because he stood out as metropolitan champion. It would rather appear that Giraldus was nominated to the bishopric along with his three other archidiaconal colleagues. Even the fact that he was the late bishop's nephew may not have been without influence on his nomination in an age when such offices were frequently and unobjectedly kept within a family. It did not shake the thirty-year old Giraldus fundamentally that he was not elected bishop, for there were more chances and possibly better ones to come. The office of archdeacon was an ideal starting point for a higher ecclesiastical career.

---

[1] *Opera*, eight volumes, edd. S. J. Brewer, J. F. Dimock, G. F. Warner (Rolls Series, London, 1861–91), i, 32–9. This Adam is constantly confused with Adam du Petit Pont, the philosopher and teacher of John of Salisbury, B. Rashdall, *Medieval Universities*, I, 228, n. 2; Millor, Butler, Brooke, edd., *The Letters of John of Salisbury* (NMT, Edinburgh, 1955), I, p. XVI; but see Humphreys, *op. cit.*, pp. 96–102; Glanmor Williams, *The Welsh Church, from Conquest to Reformation* (Cardiff, 1962), p. 23; also L. Minio-Palmello, 'The 'ars disserendi' of Adam of Balsham 'Parvipontanus', *Medieval and Renaissance Studies*, iii (1954), pp. 116–69, esp. p. 165f.

[2] The decretal is printed by H. E. Lohmann, 'Die Collectio Wigorniensis', *ZSRG, kan. Abt.*, xxii, 1933, 116, and Dom A. Morey, *Bartholomew of Exeter, Bishop and Canonist* (Cambridge, 1937), pp. 129–30.

[3] Op. i, p. 232.

[4] J. C. Davies, loc. cit., p. 96, n. 8 refers to the Westminster synod of 1175, but see Roger of Howden, *Chronica* (RS), ii, p. 92; Mansi, *Sacr. Conc. Coll.*, xxii, pp. 157–8; Giraldus, *Op.* i, p. 41, viii, 218: 'allegatis demum hinc inde pugnis'.

[5] Michael Richter, 'The Life of St. David by Giraldus Cambrensis', *WHR*, iv (1968–69), pp. 381–86.

Giraldus now returned to Paris to complete his training in Roman and canon law, quite successfully as he reports, and once he started to teach, his lectures must have been popular and well attended. In the diocese of St. David's, meanwhile, the cooperation between the chapter and Bishop Peter had become increasingly difficult, especially since the bishop was often absent. Giraldus was recalled from Paris in 1179, possibly by some of his colleagues on their way home from the Lateran Council. There they had again raised the issue of the metropolitan dignity of their church, but they had been unsuccessful, for their bishop had refused to lead the request, on account of the promise he had made to the archbishop of Canterbury on the occasion of his consecration.[1] For some years thereafter Giraldus acted as representative of Bishop Peter in St. David's, but it turned out to be a 'mésalliance'. The bishop did not stop interfering despite the protest of the archdeacon, and, it seems, the chapter. So Giraldus resigned this position about 1182. Although these years of his life are shrouded in darkness, there are reasons to believe that it was then that he laid the foundation of a popularity in the bishopric which was to help his campaign for election to the bishopric after Peter de Leia had died.

Next we find Giraldus in Ireland. In 1183, he crossed over with his brother Philip to visit his relatives who had taken part in the conquest of 1169;[2] there he was offered the bishopric of Ferns[3] which he refused. On his return to Britain he entered the royal household as a clerk, and thus was an ideal companion for Prince John who went to Ireland in 1185. John's irresponsible behaviour caused him to become unpopular with the Irish, and he did not stay long,[4] but Giraldus was left behind and seems to have stayed for almost a year.[5] He took the opportunity to become acquainted with the country as best he could, and collected material for a book which earned him some praise in his time and much scorn by later readers.[6] The *Topographia Hibernica* seems to have

---

[1] Michael Richter, 'Professions of Obedience and the Metropolitan Claim of St. David's,' *NLWJ*, xv, 2, 1967, p. 210f.

[2] *Register of St. Thomas's Abbey*, ed. J. T. Gilbert (RS), pp. 205, 325.

[3] Maurice P. Sheehy, ed., *Pontificia Hibernica* (Dublin 1962), I, p. 139, n. 1.

[4] Mary T. Hayden, 'Giraldus Cambrensis', *Studies*, xxiv, 1935, p. 100.

[5] *Cartularies of St. Mary's Abbey, Dublin*, ed. J. T. Gilbert (RS), I, 171–3. A fuller account of Giraldus' Irish connexions in Mary Teresa Ryan, *The Historical Value of Giraldus Cambrensis' 'Expugnatio Hibernica' as an Account of the Anglo-Norman Invasion of Ireland*, MA thesis (typescript), Univ. College, Dublin, 1967.

[6] 'To write about Ireland and the Irish people Gerald was obviously unqualified', M. T. Hayden, *loc. cit.*, p. 104.

been completed shortly after Giraldus had returned to Britain. Its first version is dedicated to King Henry II.[1] The second work on Ireland, the *Expugnatio Hibernica*, the history of the conquest of 1169, was completed before 1189 and dedicated King Henry's son Richard.[2]

In the spring of 1188 Giraldus accompanied Baldwin of Ford, archbishop of Canterbury, on a five-week tour through Wales where the archbishop preached the crusade. It is likely that Giraldus was chosen as a companion not so much because he was archdeacon of Brecon, but as a loyal supporter of the crown and as a friend of Baldwin; in addition, his influential relatives in Wales may have recommended him. The lasting results of this visit to Wales are to be seen in Giraldus' ensuing literary activities which materialized in the *Itinerarium Kambriae*. This was an account of the archbishop's tour, which Giraldus wrote about 1191 and revised later. He dedicated it to Hugh, bishop of Lincoln, and later Stephen Langton, archbishop of Canterbury. Next he wrote a topography of Wales, the *Descriptio Kambriae*, which may have been completed in 1194 and which is dedicated to Hubert Walter, archbishop of Canterbury; a later version dates from 1215, being dedicated to Stephen Langton.[3]

In the following year Giraldus was in Normandy and witnessed the death of King Henry II. Henry's successor, Richard I, immediately sent him back to Britain to work on the crown's behalf to pacify the uproar which broke out in Wales upon the death of the king. For some years Giraldus continued to enjoy the confidence of the court. Yet quite suddenly, in 1194, he withdrew into private life and took up his studies again.[4] He would have liked to return to Paris, but the political situation making that impossible,[5] he turned first to Hereford, then to Lincoln. There he heard, in 1198, of the death of Bishop Peter of St. David's. Now, a major turning point in the career of Giraldus took place. As had been the case 22 years earlier, he was nominated, together

---

[1] 'Illustri Anglorum Regi Henrico secundo *suus Giraldus*'. The Topographia was newly edited by John O'Meara, 'Giraldus Cambrensis in Topographia Hibernie', *Proc. Royal Irish Acad.*, Sect. C, 4, 1949, pp. 113–78. On the dedications of his works and the problems of literacy in the Middle Ages more generally, cf. Herbert Grundmann, 'Litteratus-Illitteratus', *Archiv für Kulturgeschichte*, xl (1958), pp. 1–65, esp. p. 47 f.

[2] A critical edition of this work has been prepared by A. B. Scott, Belfast, and F. X. Martin, Dublin.

[3] The editor of the *Descriptio Kambriae* in the Rolls Series assumes that a revised edition was made as early as 1197 and dedicated to Bishop Hugh of Lincoln, but this would appear as an attempt to exonerate Giraldus 'the Welshman', cf. *Op.* vi, p. xxxi, n. 1.

[4] This critical phase of his life will be discussed in greater detail below, p. 84 ff.

[5] Howden, iii, p. 251.

with a number of other candidates, to the vacant bishopric. The king, John by this time, refused him again, but on this occasion to no effect. Giraldus was unanimously elected to the bishopric. The plan was that he should go to Rome, receive his consecration from the pope, and revive the question of the metropolitan dignity of his church.

It is important to realize that Giraldus at this stage cannot have known very much about the metropolitan claim. His uncle, David fitz Gerald who became bishop of St. David's in 1148, had at his consecration undergone obligations not to continue with the metropolitan ambitions of his predecessor Bernard, and he had kept his promise. Although it was brought up twice between 1148 and 1199, at the Westminster synod and at the Third Lateran Council, Giraldus on both occasions did not take part in it. It is true that in 1179 he had been informed on the proceedings in Rome by the subsequent bishop of Coventry, Gerard Pucelle,[1] but this information was probably unfavourable to the St. David's claim, and it cannot have gone very deep.

When Giraldus presented Pope Innocent III with his request, he at first encountered unwillingness. He must have had, however, a vague notion about the earlier moves of the metropolitan claim, and therefore he asked permission to search in the papal registers for grants to the church of St. David's. This was conceded, and 'turning to the deeds of Eugenius in France, while the papal chaplain was sitting at his side and observed everything, he quickly found, and not little rejoicing, studied and read these letters . . .'[2]. Giraldus then had found in the papal registers a letter to Archbishop Theobald bearing on his controversy with Bernard of St. David's. Pope Innocent, having been informed about this, commanded Giraldus to look for more papal privileges at St. David's. The search was successful, for Giraldus found some old documents, 'which by careless treatment and negligence had been almost lost and forgotten . . .'[3]. It was only then that Giraldus learned about the vigorous fight of Bishop Bernard for an archbishopric in Wales, and he put all his energy into the effort to achieve what by misfortune had been denied to Bernard.

Crown and Canterbury did their best to counter Giraldus in his proceedings, and after four years they succeeded totally. The bishopric of St. David's was filled with an acceptable person. This was more than a personal defeat for the ambitious Giraldus, because the claim

---

[1] *Op.* i, p. 48f.

[2] 'vertens ad gesta Eugenii in Francia, coram clerico camerarii consedente et totum observante, confestim invenit, nec mediocriter exultans inspexit et legit literas istas'. *Op.* iii, 180.

[3] 'per incuriam olim et negligentiam fere deperditas et oblivioni datas'. *Ibid.*, p. 187.

of St. David's to jurisdiction over the Welsh bishoprics was shelved again, but this time for good. Wales lost one rallying point of joint resistance against the Norman conquerors.

The actual controversy had come to an end, but the artistic use of it in Giraldus's work was only beginning. He had been defeated, and he had submitted to his defeat, but he was not the man to keep quiet about the injustice which had been done to himself and the bishopric, as he understood it. The immense amount of material put at his disposal he ordered, presumably quite early, in the third and most extensive part of his autobiography, the *De rebus a se gestis*.[1] More than a decade later he took up the question again. He completed the six books of Invectives[2] and wrote the dialogue concerning the legal position and the status of the church of St. David's.[3] The later literary activity is mainly concerned with this stormy part of Giraldus' life. There are, however, some stray references which allow us to sketch the rest of his career. In 1204–5 Giraldus was in Ireland,[4] then went to Rome again, as a pilgrim. A few charters betray that he still took some interest in the diocese of St. David's[5] before he went to Lincoln again in 1208. After this his personality slowly fades out of our grasp.

When, in 1215, the see of St. David's fell vacant, Giraldus was urged by the canons to accept this time, but he refused.[6] A native Welshman was elected bishop and accepted by King John who then had to fight for his existence over Magna Carta. The triumph of the Welsh Church without Giraldus shows best how his interests had changed. He seems to have sympathised with the French invasion of England in 1216;[7]

---

[1] *Op.* i, pp. 89–122. Only 19 chapters are preserved in full, of the other 200 (!) chapters we have only the headlines, *ibid.*, pp. 6–18.

[2] It has to be used in the – unfortunately uncritical – edition by W. S. Davies, *Y Cymmrodor*, xxx, 1920. For the genesis of this work see the introduction to Giraldus's *Speculum Duorum*, pp. xix–xxi.

[3] *Op.* iii, pp. 101–373, and for some additions from Corpus Christi College, Cambridge, MS 400, H. E. Butler, 'Some new pages of Giraldus Cambrensis', *Medium Aevum*, iv, 3, 1935, pp. 143–52.

[4] Humphreys, *op. cit.*, p. 43; *Speculum Duorum*, p. xxxi, 44.

[5] *Cartularium Prioratus S. Johannis Evangelistae de Brecon*, ed. R. W. Banks (Cambr. Arch. Ass., London, 1884), pp. 37, 83f. Our Giraldus witnesses these charters as 'magister Giraldus de Barri', Giraldus, archdeacon of Brecon, is his nephew in whose favour Giraldus the elder resigned the position in 1203.

[6] *Op.* iii, pp. 132–3.

[7] *Op.* viii, pp. 301–2, 309, 328. Attention has also been drawn to one of Giraldus' poems, by W. S. Davies, 'Giraldus Cambrensis: 'Speculum Duorum', *Arch. Camb. 83*, 1928 (pp. 111–34), pp. 132–34. The poem is printed, in a corrupt text, from BM Cotton MS. Vit. E v, in *Op.* i, no. xxxiv, pp. 374–77. The complete text, 'Epigramma metricum nuper editum, ex versu vigiliano tamquam themathe carmen incipiens', is preserved in Corpus Christi College, Cambridge, MS 400, f. 115 rv. and begins properly with poem no. xxxiii of *Op.* i, p. 374. Lincoln, where Giraldus was living at that time, was the last stronghold in England of Louis of France in 1216/17.

this attitude, highly compromising in the light of later events, probably accounts for the fact that his last years are shrouded in complete darkness. He died *c.* 1222/3, and the last reference to him comes from the diocese of Lincoln.[1]

The eight hundredth anniversary of Giraldus' birth stirred Wales to no small extent. 'Wales's debt to Giraldus is more profound than that of many other nations . . . It was as a Welshman that he suffered his greatest defeat and personal humilation. Many of his virtues were essentially Welsh', remarked Dr. Conway Davies.[2] '. . . we Welsh can still recognize ourselves as substantially the same people as those whom Gerald describes', is the expert opinion of Professor Thomas Jones.[3] A new stimulus seemed to be given to research into the life and works of the compatriot. But the enthusiasm faded away quickly. An effort to produce an edition of the last of Giraldus' known works still unpublished, the *Speculum Duorum*,[4] came to nothing. An important part of the source material of the medieval Welsh Church, where Giraldus figures so prominently, is after two decades still unpublished.[5]

The picture given above is by no means unduly pessimistic, for it is no exaggeration to say that Giraldus is still undeservedly neglected by British scholarship.[6] He is often quoted but seldom understood. The difficulty is that this figure, controversial as it was in the Middle Ages, casts its shadow on the continuing emotional friction between England and Wales. So Giraldus is hardly seen in his true light, as a European

---

[1] *Rotuli Hugonis de Welles, Episcopi Lincolniensis* (Lincoln Record Society, vi, 1913), p. 9f.

[2] 'Giraldus Cambrensis, 1146–1946', *loc. cit.*, p. 279.

[3] *NLWJ*, vi, 1949–50, p. 219.

[4] Rome, Bibliotheca Vaticana, Cod. Reg. Lat., MS 470. The present author wishes to acknowledge gratefully the permission given to him by Dr. J. C. Davies to make use of photocopies of this MS which are on deposit in the Inner Temple Library, London. The work has now been published: Giraldus Cambrensis, *Speculum Duorum* or A Mirror of Two Men, edited by Yves Lefèvre and R. B. C. Huygens, English translation by Brian Dawson, General editor Michael Richter (Board of Celtic Studies, History and Law Series, no. 27, Cardiff, 1974).

[5] *Episcopal Acts and Cognate Documents Relating to Welsh Dioceses*, 1066–1272, ed. J. C. Davies (HSCW Publications, 1, 3, 4, 1946–8, henceforth quoted as *Ep. Acts*). The third volume, containing the texts for the dioceses of Bangor and St. Asaph, was announced for 1950. The two first volumes give an excellent analysis of the sources, although the translation does not always come up to that high standard. For some reviews see *Speculum*, xxiii, 1948, pp. 297–300; *EHR*, 64, 1949, pp. 100–103; 66, 1951, pp. 611ff.

[6] The single exception is Dorothy Humphreys, *op. cit.*, and recently Eileen Agnes Williams, 'A Bibliography of Giraldus Cambrensis, *NLWJ*, xii, 2, 1961, pp. 97–140.

figure, and is only beginning to be discovered by continental scholars.[1] His popularity in Wales, where the Welsh works are regarded as standard text-books, is only equalled by that of Geoffrey of Monmouth. Both seem to have more in common than has been allowed for in the past, but whereas Geoffrey has been a favourite subject for international scholarship, Giraldus is dwarfed into the position of a national hero; an attempt to examine his position with regard to Wales has yet to be made.

Giraldus' reputation in Ireland is completely the opposite of what it is in Wales. The *Topographia Hibernica* has been called 'a kind of perpetual thorn in the side of Irish nationalist'.[2] The challenge had been taken up by the 17th century writers John Lynch, *Cambrensis eversus, seu potius historica fides in rebus Hibernicis Giraldo Cambrensi abrogata ...*[3] and O'Sullivan Beare, '*Vindiciae Hibernicae contra Silvestrum Giraldum et Richardum Stanihurstum.*[4] Whereas some Irishmen in the present century continued to pour contempt on Giraldus,[5] serious concern with his statements on Ireland begins to bear fruit in excellent new studies. Something similar in Wales is yet to come. It was perceived at an early stage, however, that Giraldus was not all kindness towards the Welsh either. So the first printed edition of his Welsh works in 1585 by David Powel omitted the section which described the unpraiseworthy sides of the Welsh, the *illaudabilia* in the *Descriptio Kambriae*, which was printed for the first time only in 1691 by Henry Wharton.[6] Even the latest edition in the Rolls Series hides one passage particularly unbecoming to 'Gerald the Welshman' in a footnote.[7]

---

[1] Charlotte Ahlenstiehl, *Giraldus Cambrensis*, dissertation (typescript), (Rostock, 1921); Georg Misch, 'Die autobiographische Schriftstellerei des Giraldus Cambrensis', *Geschichte der Autobiographie*, iii, ii, 2 (Frankfurt, 1962), pp. 1297-1479; Paul Kirn, *Das Bild des Menschen in der Geschichtsschreibung von Polybios bis Ranke* (Göttingen 1955), pp. 174-204; Karl Schnith, 'Betrachtungen zum Spätwerk des Giraldus Cambrensis "De Principis Instructione"', *Festiva Lanx* (München, 1966), pp. 53-66.

[2] Quotation in Mary Teresa Ryan, *op. cit.*, p. 15.

[3] Williams, *loc. cit.*, p. 136, n. 59.

[4] University Library, Upsala, Sweden, MS. H 248. For a report see *Ann. Hib.*, vi, 1934, pp. 1-11.

[5] 'We Irish have not much reason to cherish the memory of Gerald the Welshman ... He was a real flesh and blood—this learned, vain, pugilistic cleric, so confident of his merits, so bitter towards his opponents', Hayden, *loc. cit.*, p. 100.

[6] Williams, *loc. cit.*, p. 121 f.

[7] *Op.* vi, p. 225, n. 4. J. F. Dimock comments: 'It may be, we may hope, that when he suppressed this passage in the second edition, he was heartily ashamed of ever having given such cold-blooded, merciless advice of extermination of a whole race', *ib.*, p. xxxi.

Although Giraldus knew well an amazing number of persons in Church and state, the contemporary historians, with the notable exception of Roger of Howden, hardly mention him at all. Posterity therefore knows him almost exclusively by his own writings. Taking Giraldus' works at their face value, some scholars have regarded him as an early specimen of Welsh nationalism. This is an attitude as rash as that adopted by other scholars who felt obliged to dismiss Giraldus altogether for the bias he shows. Yet, once the bias is openly admitted and taken into account, Giraldus emerges as an eye-witness of an important stage of the Norman advance in Wales. As such he cannot be dismissed; instead, his prejudiced account is of high value, as long as it is taken as a purely personal point of view. It has been rightly observed that 'in dealing with the history of a nation it is not enough to record bare events, for these cannot be seen in the right perspective until a study is made of the thoughts and feelings which gave rise to them'.[1] To Wales, the twelfth century was a period of transition and crisis. Professor Glanmor Williams has recently reminded us that it was a time when the Welsh were made conscious of the fact that they had something in common which set them apart from the rest of the population in Britain.[2] The notion of the Welsh nation was slowly, although not steadily, gaining ground. Mrs. Chadwick rightly emphasized that 'patriotism . . . was not a steady and continuous emotion, not felt alike . . . at all periods. It sprang up from time to time in response to various causes, now local, now widespread, at one time military, at another political, or again religious'.[3] Giraldus' share is mainly in the religious side.

The cultural and political background: the diocese of St. David's.

When in Wales, Giraldus was involved first and foremost with the affairs of the diocese of St. David's. There he worked, and his private personal life was linked more closely with that area than with the rest of Wales. It is impossible fully to appreciate Giraldus's activities there without a sketch of the problems which were at stake in South Wales. The next chapter will deal with the introduction of Norman bishops into the four Welsh dioceses down to 1148. What is necessary here is a rough outline of the cultural and political background of Wales down to the establishment of medieval bishoprics.

---

[1] Margaret Enid Griffiths, *Early Vaticination in Welsh with English Parallels*, ed. T. Gwynn Jones (Cardiff, 1937), p. 217.

[2] *loc. cit.*

[3] Nora K. Chadwick, ed., *Studies in the Early British Church* (Cambridge, 1958), p. 10 (quoted hereafter as *SEBC*).

At first sight, the Welsh peninsula conveys the impression of being a physical unity, distinct in its mountainous features from England in the east and severed by the sea from the Cornish peninsula in the south and Ireland in the west. Prehistory and protohistory, however, teach that no *cultural* entity corresponds to the physical appearance. Wales falls into three main cultural areas: (a) the south-east (which roughly emerged in the twelfth century as the diocese of Llandaff), which had links with the country bordering on the Severn Sea as well as with the English Lowland zone, (b) the south-west, which was, from prehistoric times to the Middle Ages and beyond, subject to Irish influence (comprising later, broadly speaking, the diocese of St. David's), (c) the north, which can be regarded as a cultural sub-province of an area comprising the north of England and Scotland, and which in addition, although to a lesser extent than the south-west, was exposed to Irish influence (here emerged the twelfth century dioceses of Bangor and St. Asaph).[1]

Before dealing with the political development in Wales, we shall discuss the establishment of the two southern dioceses, Llandaff and St. David's, as a phenomenon connected with the cultural division of Wales which we have just sketched. The monastic Celtic church was based, in its subdivisions, on the distribution of churches which, by their dedication to a particular 'saint', commemorated the activity of a number of churchmen whom legend and hagiography associated with the fifth, sixth, and seventh centuries. In the twelfth century this Celtic monastic church was, under the influence of Canterbury which followed in the train of Norman military advance, transformed into a diocesan church on Roman lines. The process was not smooth, and of necessity its result was not a faithful reflection of earlier missionary activities and subdivisions. The two medieval dioceses, St. David's and Llandaff, embraced in their territories churches of a plurality of 'saints', both major and minor.

Of the major 'saints', St. David's took the territory covered largely by churches dedicated to *Dewi* (David). In the north, in Cardigan, it incorporated the *Padarn* sphere. Llandaff received what can be called the area of *Illtud* and *Cadoc* churches. The two regions formed relatively distinct units, corresponding roughly with the two cultural areas mentioned above.[2] Matters were complicated, however, in that the bishopric of

---

[1] For the latest detailed discussion E. G. Bowen, *Saints, Seaways and Settlements in the Celtic Lands*, UWP (Cardiff, 1969), pp. 39–47. Professor Bowen generously put the material in proof stage at the author's disposal.

[2] E. G. Bowen, *op. cit.*, p. 82: '(St. David's) this territory possessed a large measure of cultural unity before the limits of the diocese were determined by the medieval bishop ...'

Llandaff (the name of the diocese was *Glamorgan* in the first quarter of the twelfth century) reached out, towards the east and the west, beyond the *Illtud | Cadoc* sphere. It claimed the *Dyfrig* (Dubricius) sphere in the east, which was held by Hereford, and the *Teilo* sphere in the west, which was held by St. David's.[1] A legal process concerning the territory of the bishopric of Llandaff, to which we shall return presently, was started formally in 1119 by its bishop, Urban (1107–33). But the dispute was older, going back, as far as written evidence is involved, to the end of the eleventh century.

We touch here the one major field of Welsh historical records in the twelfth century which yet remains virtually unexplored: the Saints' *Lives*. In the last years of the eleventh century, two major hagiographical works were composed, the *Life of Saint David*, by Rhigyfarch,[2] son of Bishop Sulien of St. David's, and the *Life of Saint Cadoc*, by Lifris, son of Bishop Herewald of Glamorgan.[3] In these two *Lives* the respective saint is shown as having other saints, two of whom are named particularly, as their disciples: *Teilo* (who alone concerns us here), and *Padarn*. Thus the *Teilo* sphere was, by virtue of the *Lives*, claimed by the bishops of St. David's and Llandaff respectively.

At the time when the legal process about the territory of Llandaff started, the *Teilo* area was under the control of the bishop of St. David's. The first move towards a papal decision in favour of Llandaff was made by its bishop shortly before the Council of Rheims in 1119 which Urban of Llandaff attended together with Bishop Bernard of St. David's.[4] Pope Calixtus II confirmed to Urban the territory of his diocese in general terms, but postponed a definite decision.[5] The bishops of

[1] E. G. Bowen, *The Settlements of the Celtic Saints in Wales*, UWP (Cardiff, 1956), pp. 35–43, 56–65; W. Rees, *An Historical Atlas of Wales* (London, 1951), plate 32.

[2] Ed. J. W. James, UWP (Cardiff, 1967); this is not Rhigyfarch's text, but a modified version from the mid-twelfth century. Some features of an earlier version (? Rhigyfarch's own) can be traced, Michael Richter, 'Canterbury's Primacy in Wales and the First Stage of Bishop Bernard's Opposition,' *JEH*, xxii, 1971, pp. 177–89.

[3] Hywel D. Emanuel, 'An Analysis of the composition of the *Vita Cadoci*', *NLWJ*, vii, 3, 1952, pp. 217–27.

[4] *The Chronicle of John of Worcester, 1118–40*, ed. J. R. H. Weaver (Oxford, 1908), p. 14.

[5] *The Text of the Book of Llan Dâv*, ed. J. Gwenogvryn Evans and John Rhys (Oxford, 1893) (henceforth quoted as *LL*), pp. 89–92. A final analysis of the Book of Llandaff is urgently required. Preliminary studies are E. D. Jones, 'The Book of Llandaff', *NLWJ*, iv, 1945–46, pp. 123–57; J. W. James, 'The Book of Llan Dav', *JHSCW*, ix, 1959, pp. 5–22; Ceri Lewis, 'The Liber Landavensis and the diocese of Llandaff', *Morgannwg*, iv, 1960, pp. 50–65; idem, 'Agweddau ar hanes cynnar yr Eglwys yng Nghymru', *Llên Cymru*, vi, 1960, vii, 1963. Dr. Wendy Davies' detailed analysis of *LL* is shortly going to the press. Among preliminary studies should be mentioned especially her 'Liber Landavensis: its construction and credibility', *EHR*, 88, 1973, pp. 335–51.

St. David's and Hereford (from whom Urban claimed the *Dyfrig* sphere) failed to follow various papal summonses to discuss Urban's claim, although Bishop Bernard was a frequent visitor of the papal court when other business was concerned. It was Pope Honorius II, therefore, who gave a decision in 1128 in favour of Bishop Urban,[1] and this was meant to be the final arrangement. But it was revoked almost as soon as given, for now Bernard had come to Rome and somehow convinced the pope that Urban's pledge was not altogether sound. The question was pending again. Honorius' successor, Innocent II, delegated the case to the archbishops of Canterbury, York and Rouen,[2] while still reserving for himself the final settlement.[3] The papal judges-delegate decided in favour of St. David's and Hereford, [4] and, as it happened, this decision was to last. Bishop Urban of Llandaff died in 1133 on his way to Rome before he could protest against the injustice he believed had been done to him. After his death the see of Llandaff remained vacant for seven years, long enough to prevent his successors from taking up the problem again. 'Thus tradition, historical background, and immediate predilections and policy all combined to give a decisive and final victory to Bernard and St. David's.'[5]

Urban's legal process had procured a wealth of material which was gathered in the famous *Liber Landavensis*, composed in its present form after the death of Urban, and most probably written in the third quarter of the twelfth century. Among a wealth of documentary material it contains a number of Saints' *Lives*, precisely of those who were claimed to belong to Llandaff: Samson, Dyfrig, Teilo, and Oudoceus. It is noteworthy that the main saint of Llandaff, Cadoc, is not represented there.

Urban's case aptly demonstrates the enormous change that took place in the Welsh Church in these years. The 'Age of Isolation' was finally broken: Wales was now open in two directions: towards England and towards Rome. As it happened, the settlement of the controversy showed with a remarkable precision which way the Welsh Church was to go in future. While theoretically the decision lay with Rome alone, the outcome of an appeal would always be influenced by the attitude of those persons who had to be involved to compensate Rome's information gap. In this case, the delegates of Rome, the English and Norman

---

[1] *John of Worcester*, p. 28.

[2] *LL*, pp. 66–7.

[3] *Ibid.*, p. 62.

[4] The charter by William of Corbeil, archbishop of Canterbury, confirming Hereford's position, is printed by Mary G. Cheney, *EHR*, 56, 1941, p. 178, n. 1.

[5] J. C. Davies, *Ep. Acts*, I, pp. 189–90; the whole controversy is discussed *ibid.*, I, pp. 147–90; the relevant documents are arranged chronologically *ibid.*, II, 615–33.

archbishops, were not completely disinterested in the outcome of the controversy. They preferred – each for various reasons – to support the former royal clerk Bernard. Thus they took part in shaping the Welsh Church reform. To the Welsh ecclesiastics it would be difficult in future to appeal to Rome and by-pass England.

We have to mention now the political developments in Wales in the decisive late eleventh and twelfth centuries. The division of the country was a different one from the pattern which was set by the 'culture areas' and eventually taken up in the ecclesiastical division of the country.

The Anglo-Saxon invasion of England decisively formed the pattern of the political division of the island in the following centuries. It was a division not necessarily brought about by the physical features of Britain which make the island not more favourable to particularism than many other countries where one political unit was achieved in the course of time. Wales was finally severed from England during the eighth century, the dyke of King Offa of Mercia (757–796) remaining the border with England down to the eleventh century.[1] If encroachment across the dyke took place, indeed, it was not from west to east, as had been the wishful thinking of a whole branch of Welsh literature in these centuries, but from England into Wales. From the time of King Alfred the Great to the days of King Harold, the Welsh experienced varying states of dependence from the English rulers, owing to the ability of individual achievements by English kings.[2]

The Normans, as in many spheres, were the true successors of the late Anglo-Saxon monarchy with regard to Wales.[3] But, as in other respects, the Conqueror surpassed his predecessors. His aim was military conquest, not merely suzerinty. The Norman influence in Wales was exercised in two kinds: the immediate impact of the monarch, and the indirect way though the Marcher Lords. Thus it came about that throughout the twelfth century, Wales was split into three major areas: (a) the area not under the control of the Marcher Lords or the Crown, i.e. Wales proper (*Wallia, Pura Wallia*); (b) the territory held by the Marcher Lords (*Marchia Wallie*); and finally (c) the areas more or less directly held by the English Crown.[4]

---

[1] J. E. Lloyd, *A History of Wales*, 2 vols. (London, 1911), I, pp. 197–201; idem, 'Wales and the Coming of the Normans', *Cym. Trans.*, 1899–1900, pp. 122–79.

[2] A. J. Roderick, 'The Feudal Relations between the English Crown and the Welsh Princes', *History*, 37, 1952, p. 202; cf. Lloyd, *loc. cit.*, pp. 136–8.

[3] The problem of continuity before and after 1066 is aptly summarized by R. R. Darlington, 'The Norman Conquest' (The Creigthon Lecture in History) (London, 1963).

[4] Sir J. Goronwy Edwards, 'The Normans and the Welsh March', *Proc. Brit. Acad.*, 42, 1956, pp. 155–77; see also A. J. Otway-Ruthven, 'The Constitutional Position of the Great Lordships in South Wales', *TRHS*, 5th series, 1958, pp. 1–20.

In South Wales, the subject of our study, the subdivision was into Pembroke and Glamorgan, which had strong bonds with the English Crown, the remains of the old Welsh principality of Deheubarth, which was in Welsh hands, and a variety of areas held by the Marcher Lords.[1] Of the greatest importance for our present study is the fact that as early as the beginning of the twelfth century St. David's in Pembrokeshire had come under the influence of the crown. This area was of considerable strategical importance to the English monarchs, because it was a firm base for conquest from behind the lines. More deeply felt, however, was the influence of the royal representatives on the personnel of the cathedral church of St. David's itself. As it was, St. David's became the intellectual centre of resistance as far as ecclesiastical matters were concerned, against the encroachment of Canterbury, but it could not become more. A brief historical speculation may be permitted. Had St. David's been in the position of Bangor which remained at that time free from Norman control, the metropolitan claim of this see may well have taken a different direction than it actually did. It is significant that Giraldus Cambrensis, when seeking political backing for this metropolitan claim at the turn of the century, went to North Wales, and Llywelyn ab Iorwerth did his best to support a policy which aimed towards the separation of the whole of the Welsh Church from Canterbury.

From the great threefold division of south Wales as a result of the Norman advance we have to pass now to the smaller subdivisions which the Normans found in the whole of Wales on their arrival and which persisted into the thirteenth century. Wales consisted of small territorial units, the *cantrefs* and the *commots*, which had each their own jurisdictional independence. The commote – or a plurality of them – was ruled by an independent lord. At his death it often happened that his property was divided equally among his heirs, each of whom took the full title and all legal privileges.

Thus Wales in the twelfth century was ruled by a host of major and minor lords whose badge of independence was the right to build their own castles and to wage war without requiring anybody's permission to do so. It has been shown recently that this legal position did not apply to the Welsh lords alone, but to the Norman Marcher Lords also. Since the Welsh laws did not confine the right of inheritance to Welshmen alone, a Norman could and did acquire, by military conquest or by marrying into Welsh royal families, the position of a Welsh lord. This is the reason why the Marcher Lords in Wales could build their

---

[1] For a detailed discussion of the stages of conquest L. H. Nelson, *The Normans in South Wales, 1070–1171* (Austin, Texas, 1966).

own castles and could wage war without the King's permission. It was a situation recognised by the Crown as late as the thirteenth century.[1]

The Norman conquerors took over what they found, without essential modifications. But the effect in Wales was diametrically opposed to what it had been in England: England at the time of the conquest had been a centralized kingdom, centralized mainly in financial administration and jurisdiction,[2] whereas Wales had consisted of an agglomeration of small units. 'Historically, the contrast between Normanized England and the Normanized March of Wales was a prolongation of the previously existing contrast between Saxon England and Welsh Wales'.[3] In the territories held by the Marcher Lords the original Welsh *morcellement* remained, whereas *Pura Wallia*, due to the political achievements of the two Llywelyns, overcame this stage and achieved greater territorial unity.

Thus Wales in general, and south Wales in particular, was a field of a multitude of competing forces, all of which to some extent contributed to the eventual military conquest by England. It was a country which had been under the influence of different cultural traditions, and which remained the target of a variety of divergent ambitions. Nor was this all. With the arrival of the Normans the country lost its ethnic uniformity. Welsh and Irish people were joined by Normans, English and Flemings. These immigrants were not integrated into the native population, but kept their distinct identity for centuries. It is one aim of the present study to show that the Welsh were regarded by their neighbours in the east as being different from them, and having features in common which distinguished them both from English and from Normans. This will be dealt with later, but it may be advisable to glance at one ethnic group a little closer now, since they will not feature in the later discussion: the Flemings in south-west Wales.

The *Brut y Tywysogyon* gives under 1108: '. . . a certain folk of strange origins and customs, I do not know where they had lain concealed in the island for such a length of years, were sent by King Henry to the land of Dyfed. And that folk seized the whole cantref of Rhos near the estuary of the river called Cleddyf, after having completely driven (thence the inhabitants). And that folk, as is said, had come from Flanders . . . this folk begged and beseeched King Henry that they might obtain a place to live in. And then they were sent to Rhos, driving thence the rightful inhabitants, who have lost their rightful place from that day

---

[1] J. G. Edwards, ed., *Littere Wallie*, Board of Celtic Studies, History and Law Series, No. 5, UWP (Cardiff, 1940), pp. 54–8.

[2] Darlington, *loc. cit.*

[3] J. G. Edwards, *loc. cit.*, p. 175.

to this . . .'.[1] A number of Flemings had presumably arrived in Britain in the train of William the Conqueror and been settled in Northumbria,[2] until they were transferred wholesale by Henry I to Pembrokeshire.[3] Others would appear to have come directly from Flanders, like the later lord of Dangleddau, Wizo.[4] It can be accepted that the immigration from Flanders lasted for a considerable time.[5] To drive the Welsh from their country appears as a frightening modern method; the place lost within a short time its Welsh character.[6] The measures taken by the king, however, were much less unusual than the lament of the *Brut* suggests; they received the approval of William of Malmesbury;[7] Giraldus, later in the century, gave Henry II similar advice, but he proposed that the measures be applied to the whole of Wales which, he suggested, should be emptied of all its original inhabitants and re-settled by a peaceful people.[8] The Welsh did not submit to their fate but fought the Flemings bitterly; 'during the whole of the twelfth century there was a real guerilla-war fought between Flemings and Welsh in

---

[1] *Brut y Tywysogyon* (RBH), ed. Thomas Jones, Board of Celtic Studies, History and Law Series, no. 16 (Cardiff, 1955), p. 53.

[2] *Florence of Worcester*, ed. Thorpe, II, p. 64.

[3] G. C. Dept, 'Een Vlaamsche Kolonie in Wales', quoted in Paul de Keyser, 'Vlaamsche Waarzeggerij uit de 12ᵉ eeuw', *Ann. Soc. d'Emulation de Bruges*, 76, 1933, p. 40.

[4] R. R. Darlington, ed., *The Cartulary of Worcester Cathedral Priory* (Register I), (London, 1968, PRS, NS, 38) Introduction, p. xxxi–xxxiii and No. 252, p. 134: '. . . Est quidam locus in Walia in illis regionibus (i.e. Pembroke), . . . qui Dungledin vocatur. Hunc locum a tempore Henrici regis ex ipsius dono Flandrenses incolunt, horum princeps quidam nomine Wizo fuit, qui primus ad predictum locum possidendum *de Flandria veniens*, . . .'. Professor Darlington thus could establish without doubt that the Flemings of Pembroke maintained contact with their people on the continent for decades after their settlement in Wales. The present author is indebted to Prof. Darlington for his kind permission to make full use of the *Worcester Cartulary* before it had been issued, and more generally for much kind advice during a year's research at Birkbeck College, London.

[5] Alfred de Beverley': Quorum (i.e. Flemings) *crebra insulam confluencia* et inter Normannos cohabitatio, quosque procedat, sequens aetas videbit', quoted from Henry Owen, 'The Flemings in Pembrokeshire', *Arch. Camb.*, 5th ser., xii, 1895, pp. 96–106, here p. 100.

[6] The place-names in Pembrokeshire of non-Celtic origin are as frequent as in the whole of the rest of Wales taken together, cf. G. B. Charles, *Non-Celtic Place-Names in Wales* (London, 1938). One would, however, hesitate to subscribe fully to Dr. Charles' statement on the relative lack of Flemish place-names: 'To account for this we must probably assume that the Flemish were quickly Anglicised through contact with the English before and after the migration into the county', *ibid.*, p. xxxii. The name Wiston is derived from Wizo, Lloyd, II, 425; Darlington, *op. cit.*, p. xxxi.

[7] *Gesta Reg. Angl.* (RS), II, 365f., 477.

[8] *Op.* vi, p. 225, n. 4; cf. below, p. 77.

Pembrokeshire'.[1] Ordericus relates that the Welsh (*Guali Britones*) were killed by the Flemings like dogs.[2] More than half a century later, the Welsh and Flemings were still hostile towards each other, according to Giraldus.[3]

The Flemish settlers had arrived in Rhos by royal mandate. They settled under the shadow of the Marcher Lords, combined forces with them to fight the Welsh,[4] and by their dependence served them well as a protective shield. To what extent they were subject to the Marchers' jurisdiction is difficult to say. Around 1140 the Flemings were subject to Gilbert, Earl of Pembroke,[5] and this would appear to have been the intention from the beginning. We are able to get a little more insight into the situation by referring to Giraldus' *Autobiography*. He tells how (about 1175) he had been given mandate to collect the tithe of wool and cheese in the diocese of St. David's and was met with the stubborn resistance of the 'Flandrenses de Ros et complices suos'.[6] Giraldus then put the Flemings under the interdict, which however, he had to withdraw presently for the cantref of Rhos at least, through the intervention of the king and the archbishop of Canterbury.[7] Even so he ensured that the immunity would not apply to the Flemings outside Rhos.[8] It may be concluded that the Flemings who lived in Rhos had, on their arrival, received such an immunity. Later on, in the case recorded by Giraldus, other Flemings claimed this immunity merely by reason of the fact that they belonged to a different ethnic group, thus trying to extend the originally territorial immunity, which thanks

---

[1] 'Gedurende gansch de 12ᵉ eeuw was het tusschen Vlamingen en Wallenzen in Pembrokeshire enn echte guerilla – oorlog', P. de Keyser, *loc. cit.*, p. 40.

[2] *Hist. Eccl.*, v, p. 43 'absque omni humanitatis respectu quasi canes interfecti sunt . . .'

[3] *Op.* vi, 102: 'inter hostiles hodie populos, hinc Flandrensem, inde Kambrensem'. Still later he calls the Flemings 'vindices et minaces', *Op.* i, 314.

[4] *Brut*, p. 115 'the Flemings and Normans took to flight according to their usual custom'. In his *Speculum Duorum*, Giraldus refers to a 'miles . . . vir Ernaldus et alii de Flandrensico genere viri robusti', p. 38.

[5] *Worcester Cartulary*, p. xxxiii and No. 253–5, pp. 135–6.

[6] *Op.* i, p. 24. This passage has often been quoted as a proof of a general resistance to tithes in the Middle Ages. But it seems to prove the point made by Giles Constable that 'most known instances of refusal to pay tithes were caused by specific conditions rather than by any objection to tithes in general', *JEH*, xiii, 1962, pp. 172–85, here p. 176.

[7] *Op.* i, p. 28.

[8] *ibid.*, 'quia Flandrenses ubicunque in finibus illis fuerant, tam extra Ros quam intra, eadem immunitate gaudere volebant'.

to Giraldus, could be prevented. This incident also shows the spread of the Flemings. Starting from the cantref of Rhos, they were found later in considerable numbers in Dangleddau, Talcharn, and Penfro,[1] throughout the south of Pembrokeshire.

Giraldus describes the Flemings as 'gens fortis et robusta, continuoque belli conflictu gens Kambrensibus inimicissima, . . . vicissim loco et tempore nunc ad aratrum, nunc ad arma, gens promptissima . . .'[2] It is amazing to realize that this ethnic group was able to maintain its identity for such a long time. They preserved not only their legal position but also their language.[3] Some customs they maintained to the end of the century – Giraldus tells of their vaticinatory method 'quod in armis arietum dextris, carne nudatis, et non assis sed elixis, tam futura prospiciunt, quam praeterita et antea incognita respiciunt'.[4] By this means their ancestors had foreseen the rising of the Welsh after the death of Henry I, and had left the country in great numbers.[5]

In the case of the Flemings we are able to perceive clearly Giraldus' notion of the 'gens'. It is the foreign descent, and connected with it, the language, the customs and finally their exclusive legal position which prevented their integration into the surrounding Welsh population. Due to the protection they received from the Marcher Lords, they were able to continue an existence along their traditional lines. Both were natural allies against the common enemy, the Welsh. Crises came with the lack of strong government in England, then the Welsh hostility would become palpable.[6]

---

[1] Giraldus presumably has this cantref in mind when speaking of 'illi de Angulo, qui licet habitantes in provincia de Penbroc, tamen quia Flandrenses erant, et similiter cum Rosensibus sicut et illi de Dugledu, ad immunitatem quaerendam sumptus fecerant, simili libertate gaudere volebant', *Op.* i, p. 28.

[2] *Op.* vi, p. 83.

[3] Higden, *Polychronicon*, ii, 158: 'Flandrenses vero, qui occidua Wallie incolunt, dimissa iam barbarie, Saxonice satis proloquuntur', does not necessarily apply to the 12th century (so, however, Charles, *op. cit.*, xxxii). Giraldus unam biguously attests at the beginning of the thirteenth century the contrary: 'quod miles quidam modestus et prudens de partibus illis, cui nomen Ernaldus, cognomine Rheting, patri vestro (i.e. Giraldus's brother Philip de Barri) Flandrensica lingua . . . apud Haverfordiam dixit', *Speculum Duorum*, p. 36.

[4] *Op.* vi, 87, cf. Keyser, *loc. cit.*

[5] *Op.* vi, 88.

[6] *Op.* i, 24.

I.—CHURCH REFORM IN BRITAIN AND IRELAND AFTER THE CONQUEST.

It has been disputed whether politically the Norman Conquest of 1066 had a revolutionary impact on England.[1] In the ecclesiastical sphere – with all due respect to the reform of the late Anglo-Saxon Church[2] – a similarly wide range of opinion could not occur. Here the conquest brought 'a reorganisation of the English Church to bring it into line with the normal standards of the Church as a whole'.[3] This does not apply to the English Church alone. In Wales the changes were even greater.

The first archbishop of the Conqueror, Lanfranc, had to start with what was left of the old Augustinian model of English Church organisation which had divided the island into the two provinces of Canterbury and York. He had to give to the bishops dioceses with fixed boundaries, to subdivide these into archdeaconries and the smaller administrative units, and to secure strict subordination of his suffragans. Lanfranc's design was as far-reaching as that of the Conqueror.[4] He 'could not stop short of a general authority over the whole of the British Isles: anything less would have done violence to the early history of the see as it was understood at Canterbury, and to the large geographical and historical conceptions which lay behind these claims'.[5] In the short run he succeeded, but archbishops after him had to concede the breaking away of first York, then Ireland, and finally Scotland. These three issues have to be dealt with separately in order to appreciate more fully what happened in Wales under Bishop Bernard. For it can be shown that Bernard's case was not an isolated one, but that it occurred in a manner which reveals a close affinity with the church reform movements in the above mentioned areas. Each movement, except that of York, started from a comparable position, and the churchmen who led these controversies learned from each other. This will be readily appreciated once one recalls that bishops in particular and higher ecclesiastical

---

[1] Sir Frank Stenton, *Anglo-Saxon England* (Oxford English History, II, Oxford, 1947, 2nd ed.); R. R. Darlington, 'The Norman Conquest'.

[2] R. R. Darlington, 'Ecclesiastical Reform in the late Old English Period', *EHR*, 51, 1936, pp. 385 ff.

[3] Z. N. Brooke, *The English Church and the Papacy* (Cambridge, 1931), pp. 119–20.

[4] 'he knit the English Church into an organic whole, with its nerve centre at Canterbury', M. D. Knowles, in: R. R. Darlington et alii, *The English Church and the Continent* (London, 1939), p. 34.

[5] R. W. Southern, *St. Anselm and his Biographer* (Cambridge, 1963), p. 135.

officials in general formed a closely knit layer of society. These people met frequently, be it at the king's court, at Church councils, or even at the papal curia. They were aware of what was going on in the country, and had ample opportunity to exchange their views. We shall examine the metropolitan controversies in Britain as a whole, and then go into more detail with regard to Wales. We hope to come to a closer understanding of the situation as it existed in the Middle Ages by these means rather than by treating the Welsh case on its own.

One of the means of bringing the suffragans into a state of dependence upon their metropolitan was by forcing on them a profession of canonical obedience which had to be given by the bishop-elect before his consecration and would apply to the metropolitan and his successors.[1] The Canterbury professions, as they are conventionally called, are a major key to the problem of Canterbury's claim.[2] At what time they were adopted in their twelfth-century form is not certain. They appear, however, to form part of a standardisation of procedure in episcopal elections which came to England as early as the reign of Edward the Confessor.[3] There is evidence from a later stage that the profession of the bishop-elect retained some importance even after the consecration, since it was demanded that the profession should be read before the respective bishop twice annually.[4]

Archbishop Lanfranc managed to secure a profession from Thomas, archbishop-elect of York, in 1070. Although this was restricted to Lanfranc personally,[5] it set a precedent dangerous to the independence of York. Technically speaking, Lanfranc could claim that he was following ancient customs, since in the preceding decades York had been held several times jointly with the bishopric of Worcester, an undoubted suffragan of Canterbury. With the next archbishop of York, Gerard, the problem was evaded since he was translated there from Hereford. The following archbishop received his consecration only

---

[1] Michael Richter, 'Professions', *loc. cit.*, p. 199.

[2] *Canterbury Professions*, ed. by Michael Richter, with a palaeographical note by T. J. Brown (Canterbury and York Society, vol. lxvii, 1973).

[3] The *Pontificale Romano-Germanicum* includes another element which soon came to be applied in English episcopal elections: 'Decretum quod clerus et populus firmare debet de electo episcopo', English specimens of which have been edited in *Canterbury Professions*, pp. 113–17. For the *Pontificale Romano-Germanicum* see M. Andrieu, *Les* Ordines Romani *du haut Moyen-Age*, I, *Les Manuscrits* (Louvain, 1931), p. 510, and the edition by C. Vogel and R. Elze, *Le Pontifical Romano-Germanique du dixième siècle, Le Texte*, I (Studi e Testi, vol. 226, Città del Vaticano, 1963). The pontifical in use in England was based on a type like BM MS Add. 17 004; for the 'decretum' ibid., f. 121r.

[4] *Canterbury Professions*, pp. lxxx-lxxxi.

[5] Donald Nichol, *Thurstan, Archbishop of York, 1114–1140* (York, 1964), p. 36f.; *Canterbury Professions*, pp. lviii-lxviii, 28.

when Canterbury was vacant after the death of Anselm. The question came to a crisis under Archbishop Ralph. Henry I joined forces with Canterbury, threatening that he would not allow Thurstan to stay in his province in case he would be consecrated by anybody but Ralph. This was to no effect: Pope Calixtus II personally consecrated Thurstan at the Council of Rheims on 19 October, 1119. The four following years were for Canterbury a decisive stage.

Ralph had foreseen that Calixtus might consecrate Thurstan and had therefore, being unable to attend the council in person, written a letter in which he discussed the relations between the two archbishoprics. It is most likely that the English bishops who came to the Council, William of Exter, Ranulf of Durham, Bernard of St. David's and Urban of Llandaff[1] knew about this letter if they had not actually taken part in its composition. For they went to Rheims straight from the king's court.

The intention of Archbishop Ralph, expressed in a lengthy letter of almost thirty pages in print, can be summarized in one single sentence: Thurstan and his predecessor could not be regarded as archbishops according to the notion of the Roman Church; they were rightly subordinate to Canterbury. Some of Ralph's phrases may be quoted: 'How can anybody call himself metropolitan or archbishop who has no suffragans? They say he has as suffragans the bishop of Lindisfarne, that he has that of Glasgow. They have to admit, however, that in former times the archbishop of York had neither Lindisfarne nor Glasgow as suffragans. Which bishop then has the archbishop of York ever installed; which suffragan was ever consecrated in his province? ... They say that Gregory decreed that the bishop of York should establish bishops who in future would be under his jurisdiction. The lord bishop of York may well have twelve bishops, or thirteen, or as many as he creates and consecrates, but he should kindly leave those to Canterbury which Canterbury has installed ...'.[2] Earlier on Ralph had mentioned that somebody could be styled archbishop only if he had created suffragans, which, after all, was implied in the term itself.[3] He could point out that archbishop Thomas (I) had made a profession to Lanfranc and ended his letter with the bold statement that the archbishops of York had always been subject to Canterbury and had always given a profession. This was a situation which should be acknowledged and enforced by the Roman pontiff.

---

[1] *John of Worcester*, p. 14.

[2] *Historians of the Church of York* (HCY), ii, p. 240f.; for another dating of the letter see R. W. Southern, 'The Canterbury Forgeries', *EHR*, 72, 1958, p. 209.

[3] *Ibid.*, p. 233.

The strong words, pronounced however, from a position of weakness, for all the exaggerations, still contained a grain of truth and touched a weak spot in York's argument. This province, almost too large a diocese in itself, suffered from an obvious lack of suffragans. There was certainty only in the case of Durham; and there was a claim to jurisdiction over Scotland. As can be seen in a treatise by Gilbert of Limerick, a very concise statement of the Roman concept of Church organisation at the beginning of the century, the notion was that an archbishop should have at least three, at most twenty suffragans.[1] It is interesting to see how the question of the suffragans of York was kept alive in the following decades. Ralph's successor William of Corbeil offered Thurstan three of his suffragans, Bangor, St. Asaph, and Chester, on condition that Thurstan should accept the archbishop of Canterbury as primate by word of mouth only; his successors should promise verbally obedience and reverence due to a primate.[2] On the other hand, Pope Innocent II urged Thurstan to create new bishoprics in his province.[3]

The consecration of Thurstan by Calixtus II had been a severe set-back to Canterbury's claim. The archbishops now turned their mind to another means of subjecting York. Documents were 'copied' at Canterbury which proved beyond doubt that York in the past centuries had been subordinate to Canterbury. When Archbishop William of Corbeil, in 1123, went to Rome to collect his pallium, he took these documents with him and had them read to the papal court in the presence of Thurstan of York by Bishop Bernard of St. David's.[4] It was immediately found that they were not genuine, and the Canterbury claim was rejected. Successive popes strictly forbade the archbishops of York to make any profession of obedience to Canterbury. Henceforth, equality was established between the two metropolitans, even if at times only physical force maintained what had been legally well defined.[5]

Scotland in the twelfth century was subject to the attention of two English metropolitans who both desired her subjection. Church reform, from the Celtic monastic organisation to the Roman monastic organisation and finally to territorial bishoprics was first introduced there by St. Margaret, wife of King Malcolm III (reigned 1058–1093)[6] who

---

[1] 'De statu Ecclesie', *Migne, PL*, clix, col. 997–1004: 'Archiepiscopus ... ut plurimum viginti episcopos regit, ut minimum vero tres', *ibid.*, 998C.

[2] *Hugh the Chantor*, ed. Charles Johnson (NMT, 1961), p. 123; see also D. Nicholl, *Thurstan*, p. 95.

[3] *HCY*, iii, p. 57.

[4] Southern, *loc. cit.*, 223f.

[5] E.g. *Brut*, ed. Thomas Jones, s.a. 1176.

[6] G. W. S. Barrow, 'From Queen Margaret to David I: Benedictines and Tironians', *The Innes Review*, xi, 1960, pp. 22–38.

kept in close contact with Archbishop Lanfranc. Bishops, however, do not appear in Scotland prior to the twelfth century[1] when the archbishops of York were asserting their influence over individual sees in Scotland as opportunity presented itself, a solution which had been allowed by Lanfranc in 1072.[2] But since the sees were newly created, the kings of Scotland took care to avoid as far as possible a subjection by their bishops to York or Canterbury. The bishopric of Glasgow set an example. Of the four bishops there prior to 1192, three were consecrated by the Pope and one, Jocelin, by the archbishop of Lund at Clairvaux (1175). Scottish bishops set forth the claim to their own metropolitan province from 1123 onwards. The papacy was originally satisfied with the *status quo* that had been negotiated between the two English metropolitans. But Henry II wanted to go further. After the defeat of the Scottish king in 1174, the Treaty of Falaise stated that 'the Church of England shall also have the right in the Church of Scotland which it lawfully should, and that they (i.e. the bishops of St. Andrews and Dunkeld) will not oppose the right of the church of England'.[3] This had been granted under pressure, and the bishop of Glasgow quickly obtained the privilege from Pope Alexander III to have his see recognized as *filia specialis*, subject to the pope alone.[4] In the following year, the state of the Scottish Church as presented in the Treaty of Falaise was declared null and void, and the question of position of the Scottish Church was opened again.[5]

In 1192, Pope Celestine III granted the bull *Cum Universi* to King William I in which he declared that the Scottish Church (*Scotticana Ecclesia*) consisting of nine bishoprics was recognized as *filia specialis*.[6] It was to remain a province without a metropolitan, which dignity was conferred on St. Andrews only in 1472. Through *Cum Universi* the pope acknowledged not only the independence from York or Canterbury, but gave to the *regnum Scotie* a final shape, which one could call sovereignty. This is not suggesting that Celestine III granted the

---

[1] See, however, Gordon Donaldson, 'Scottish bishops' sees before the reign of David I', *Proc. of the Society of Antiquaries of Scotland*, lxxxvii, 1952–3, pp. 106–117.

[2] *Haddan & Stubbs, Councils and Ecclesiastical Documents relating to Great Britain and Ireland* (Oxford, 1869–78), 3 vols., ii, 1, p. 12.

[3] *Anglo-Scottish Relations, 1174–1328, Some selected Documents*, ed. E. L. G. Stones (NMT, 1965), p. 2.

[4] *Haddan & Stubbs*, ii, 1, 41–3.

[5] *Ibid.*, 245f.

[6] *Ibid.*, 273f., there incorrectly ascribed to 1188 and Pope Clement III. See also Dietmar Willoweit, 'Die Entstehung exemter Bistümer im deutschen Reichsverband unter rechtsvergleichender Berücksichtigung ausländischer Parallelen', *ZSRG, kan. Abt.*, lii, 1966, pp. 176–298, esp. 277 ff.

metropolitan province to Scotland because it was a kingdom of its own, but such an idea may have made the decision easier. There are some clear indications that the post-reform papacy tried to avoid, as far as possible, an archbishopric extending into neighbouring kingdoms. When, therefore, the Scottish bishops in 1123 claimed the metropolitan dignity in Rome, they supported their case by the statement that Scotland was not part of the realm of England.[1] Surely they would not have used such an argument if it would not have carried any weight at the curia. Indeed, Thurstan took pains to show to the pope that Scotland was part of the English realm, thus indirectly acknowledging the validity of the demand 'if kingdom, then archbishopric'. Similarly, the treatise of Gilbert of Limerick, for all its schematic form, makes it clear that ideally speaking a king should have a primate in his country.[2]

It may not be mere coincidence that *Cum Universi* was issued at a time when the archbishopric of York was weakened by the troubled accession of Geoffrey Plantagenet in 1191. The letter to King William, on the other hand, clearly indicated which institution was behind the Church reform in Scotland; a list of prominent persons would include, besides the names of bishops, those of St. Margaret, Alexander I (*c.* 1107–1124), David I (*c.* 1124–1153) and William I (1165–1214); to these the question of Church reform would not be a purely ecclesiastical problem.

Lanfranc and his successors would have liked to extend their influence to Ireland, too. A preliminary success they achieved only as far as the Norse settlements on the east coast which had had trade links with England[3] were concerned. Between 1070 and 1140, bishops of Dublin, Waterford, and Limerick were consecrated by archbishops of Canterbury and on that occasion professed canonical obedience as the English suffragans did.[4] Such a peripheral success, however, was far out-weighed by the transformation which took place in the rest of the Irish Church. Contact with Europe had never completely lapsed, but it increased in the tenth and eleventh centuries, and the need for a reform of the Church was felt in Ireland. A reform of the Celtic monastic Church came late, and was almost immediately superseded by more

---

[1] 'Sociam non esse de regno Anglie', *Hugh the Chantor*, p. 126.

[2] 'Coniungitur autem imperator papae, rex primati, dux archipontifici, comes episcopo, miles sacerdoti, quia istae personae pares illis in saecularibus iure decernuntur', *loc. cit.* (above, p. 25), col. 999A; for more detail (and presumably one of Gilbert's sources) see Walafrid Strabo, 'De ecclesiasticarum rerum exordiis et incrementis', *Migne, PL*, cxiv, cols. 919–966, esp. chapter xxxi, 'Comparatio ecclesiasticorum ordinum et saecularium', cols. 963–66; see also Alois Dempf, *Sacrum Imperium*, third edition (Darmstadt, 1962), p. 160.

[3] Kathleen Hughes, *The Church in Early Irish Society* (London, 1966), p. 255ff.

[4] *Canterbury Professions*, nos. 36, 42, 51, 54, 69, 81, and *ibid.*, pp. lxxxvi-xcv.

far-reaching innovations. Gilbert of Limerick is traditionally remembered as the first Roman legate to Ireland. He would appear to have been the leading figure in the synod of Ráith Bresail, which in 1111 transformed the monastic Irish Church into a diocesan one.[1] The parallel movement of two rival and simultaneous church reforms came to an end in 1152 when, at the synod of Kells, the papal legate Paparo brought four pallia to Ireland which were given to Armagh as primate, Cashel, Dublin, and Tuam as metropolitans. Thus Ireland had apparently escaped from the strong grip of Canterbury.[2]

The synod of Kells, however, was not the end of the Irish Church reform. With a new (English) pope, Adrian IV, the policy of his predecessor Eugenius III was reversed. In 1155 he granted the famous bull *Laudabiliter* in which he gave permission to the English king to invade Ireland, in order to reform its church, and to lead the Irish on the path to civilisation.[3] There are strong indications that Archbishop Theobald of Canterbury, who had failed to prevent the synod of Kells and its consequences, took pains to obtain this privilege, through his secretary John of Salisbury. Henry II was prevented in 1155 from taking action against Ireland, but when he finally in 1171 invaded the island, he did so with the full approval of the papacy.

The reform of the Church of England, begun by Lanfranc, continued throughout the century, which proved rich in great personalities like Anselm, Theobald, and Thomas Becket. At times they had the energetic support of the kings, even if only to further their own ends. The influence which the monarchy could exercise through the Church was considerable. But it is precisely here that the clue to the ensuing resistance and reaction lies. A strict hierarchical church laid bare a state of dependence by the suffragans which had not been so clear in the past. Thus the Church reform itself carried the seeds of particularism which became apparent in the cases of Scotland and Ireland. In practice in the 12th century dependence on an archbishop of Canterbury or York was not equally strongly felt at all times, but at least at the consecration of the bishop, in the profession of obedience, subjection would become real and important. It carried a similar weight in Wales, which now has to be analysed more closely.

---

[1] Hughes, *op. cit.*, 267f.

[2] Michael Richter, 'The First Century of Anglo-Irish Relations', *History*, 59, 1974, pp. 195–210.

[3] *Ibid.;* also J. F. O'Doherty, 'Rome and the Anglo-Norman Invasion of Ireland', *Irish Ecclesiastical Record*, Fifth Series 42, 1933, pp. 131–145.

The bishops in Wales prior to 1148.

With the military progress of the Normans in Wales went the attempt of Canterbury to include the newly established bishoprics in their province. Although the archbishops of Canterbury had claimed a leading position over all the churches in Britain from the 10th century onwards, this must not be seen as more than a declamation. Prior to the twelfth century, the occasional Welsh bishop may have been consecrated by an archbishop of Canterbury, but this situation had neither been the regular one nor was it insisted upon in England.

The Gregorian reform of the eleventh century meant throughout Europe a new emphasis on the hierarchical structure of the Church. In England, the office of the archbishop was filled with new meaning and found vigorous defenders in Lanfranc and Anselm. The episcopal elections were jealously supervised by them, and the consecration of the bishop-elect by his metropolitan showed the effect of such a reform. The consecration of a bishop carried with it a profession of canonical obedience to the archbishop. The surviving professions, from the time of Lanfranc to the middle of the twelfth century, give evidence of the period in which the Gregorian reform was fully established in England.

The Welsh Church had not been in line with Roman administrative concepts before the Normans changed this. The Celtic Church did not require a metropolitan for the consecration of a bishop. It would appear that there as in Scotland and Ireland, the bishops consecrated each other. The 'monastic bishop' of the Celtic Church was materially different from his namesake in the Roman Church. After the Norman conquest of England foreign ideas of the ecclesiastical office spread in Wales, and a slow transformation towards the Roman organisation has to be assumed. The title of bishop remained in the Church, but its content altered materially. The presence of the Normans in Wales was instrumental in giving this transformation its last organisational form. This occurred with the bishops of the twelfth century who were elected under the impact of the new reform movement. They were consecrated by the archbishops of Canterbury along the lines which had been established for the English suffragans. Canterbury went further. From the fact that they consecrated bishops in Wales they claimed that these bishops were their suffragans, that the Welsh bishoprics were part of their metropolitan province. The main evidence for this are the professions given to the acting metropolitan by the Welsh bishops. It is difficult to say how far the superiority of Canterbury, which was legally still undefined, extended to other matters. Records and chronicles report that Welsh and English bishops attended Church Councils, and the abler ones from both areas would be called to assist the archbishop in his administrative work.

A survey of the bishops introduced into Wales before 1148, a year which is a landmark in the development of the Welsh Church, will concentrate mainly on the aspect of the consecration and the profession. Wherever the Normans had effective power in Wales, they could press the choice and election of a suitable candidate. In the territory outside their control a subjection to Canterbury would be rather more voluntary.[1]

The first effective advance of the Normans into north Wales under Hugh of Avranches, Earl of Chester, brought a bishop to Bangor, the Breton Hervey who, in 1092, was consecrated bishop by the archbishop of York, since Canterbury was vacant at that time.[2] There is no indication that Hervey made a profession of obedience to Canterbury,[3] and the archbishop of York may not have pressed him to do so, if we think of the dispute with the southern archbishop over the primacy of York. Hervey's diocese was designed to cover the territory west of the Conway, coinciding roughly with Gwynedd, but the effective expulsion of the Normans from Gwynedd prevented this. Although Hervey, as a Breton, might perhaps have had fewer difficulties with the Welsh than would a Norman, he very soon submitted to the hostility he encountered from the native population and left the country.[4] He spent almost two decades in England in various capacities,[5] trying to obtain translation to another see. Despite papal approval of this Archbishop Anselm refused to agree, and so it was only after his death that Hervey was translated to Ely, a new diocese carved out of the bishopric of Lincoln in 1109.[6] The see of Bangor was not filled until 1120. It is not quite clear who performed the episcopal function in the area until then. While Dr. Conway Davies thinks that the bishops of St. David's may have temporarily gained some influence there,[7] the political events in Gwynedd under Gruffydd ap Cynan[8] would rather suggest a connection with Ireland.

---

[1] For other aspects of Welsh Church history see Lloyd, *Hist.* II, 377–92; 400–11, *Ep. Acts*, I, 77–101.

[2] *Haddan & Stubbs*, I, 299.

[3] In the course of the 13th century a form of profession to Canterbury 'sede vacante' was set up, e.g. *Canterbury Professions*, p. 110, no. 3.

[4] 'Unde quia episcopali timori nullam servabant reverentiam, gladium bis acutum ad eos domandos exeruit, nunc crebro anathemate, nunc propinquorum et aliorum hominum eos cohercens multitudine. Nec minor fuit eorum contra eum rebellio. Tanto periculo ei insistebant ut fratrem eius perimerent, simili eum modo punituri, si possent in eum manus inicere', *Liber Eliensis*, ed. E. O. Blake (Camden Third Series, XCII, London, 1962), p. 245.

[5] He was present, in 1100, when St. Peters Church, Gloucester was dedicated, cf. *Gregory of Caerwent*, B.M. Cotton MS Vespasian A v, f. 196v.

[6] Cf. *Liber Eliensis*, p. 246 ff.

[7] *Ep. Acts*, I, 98.

[8] *Hanes Gruffydd ap Cynan*, The History of Gruffydd ap Cynan, ed. A. Jones (Manchester, 1910), pp. 39 ff. et passim.

In 1120 the Welshman David was elected bishop of Bangor under the predominant influence of Gruffydd ap Cynan.[1] His election was free from Norman interference, as was the decision of Gruffydd to have David consecrated by the archbishop of Canterbury. In a letter preserved by Eadmer[2] Archbishop Ralph was reminded of the duty he owed to the church of Bangor, which was a daughter of Canterbury. Should he fail to consecrate David, Gruffydd threatened to have somebody sent over from Ireland or somewhere else to do it. The archbishop consecrated the bishop-elect on his return from a lengthy visit to the continent, on 4th April 1120, at Westminster. At his consecration, David promised canonical obedience to Canterbury in the same way as was done by the English suffragans.[3] He seems to have kept satisfactory loyalty both to the archbishop and to his temporal lord, Gruffydd ap Cynan. Under his guidance, Gruffydd 'made Gwynedd glitter then with lime-washed churches like the firmament with stars'.[4]

The next election to Bangor occurred at a time when the situation in Wales had changed in the political and ecclesiastical field. The power of the Normans was severely challenged after the death of Henry I when King Stephen proved unable to get a firm grip of England, let alone Wales. Owain Gwynedd and his brother Cadwaladr had succeeded their father Gruffydd; they were favourable to Bishop Bernard of St. David's and his attempt to obtain metropolitan power over the whole of Wales.[5] Thus it was doubly significant that Archbishop Theobald succeeded in maintaining Canterbury's superior position towards Wales when he consecrated Meurig, bishop-elect of Bangor, early in 1140[6] and obtained the usual profession of obedience.[7] Perhaps because of this, but more likely for the fact that Meurig had sworn fealty to King Stephen at Worcester in December 1139,[8] the princes of Gwynedd

---

[1] An. Wigorn., p. 377, *An. Mon.*, ed. H. R. Luard, iv (RS, 1869) 'quendam David nomine Walensem natione'; see also *Hanes*, p. 89f.; Florence of Worcester, ed. Thorpe, ii, 1849, p. 74. Other sources maintain that David was the famous David 'the Scot' who had strong links with the English royal family, William of Malmesbury, *Gesta Reg. Angl.*, ed. W. Stubbs (RS), ii, pp. 420, 498.

[2] *Hist. Nov. in Anglia*, ed. M. Rule (RS), p. 260.

[3] *Canterbury Professions*, no. 67, p. 38.

[4] *Hanes*, 155.

[5] The *Hanes* actually referred to St. David's as an archbishopric, p. 125, but this was not more than wishful thinking.

[6] For the exact date see A. Saltman, *Theobald, Archbishop of Canterbury* (London, 1956), 92f; Lloyd, II, 483; Shaw, 'Giraldus Cambrensis and the Primacy of Canterbury', *Church Quarterly Review*, 48, 1949, pp. 82–101, 52, p. 85; *Ep. Acts*, I, 193.

[7] *Canterbury Professions*, no. 83, p. 42.

[8] *John of Worcester*, 58.

took objection to the new bishop. If they disliked Meurig's oath to
Stephen, Bishop Bernard disliked his profession to Archbishop Theobald.
In a combined effort they could perhaps remove the bishop. This is
the tenor of a letter by Owain Gwynedd and his brother, in which they
promised in future to support Bernard's metropolitan aspirations.[1]
They suggested a meeting to discuss the current points of mutual interest
between representatives of Gwynedd and Bernard for 1st November
1140. There is no indication as to whether this meeting ever materialized.
When Bernard appears next in the records, he is found to be in alliance
with the Empress Matilda[2] and King David of Scotland;[3] thus it
would be rash to pass a harsh judgement on Bernard for the fact that
Meurig eventually stayed in his bishopric.[4] Meurig himself had
difficulties with his flock to the end of his life.[5]

   The diocese of Llandaff, in the form it adopted in the twelfth century,
was essentially the creation of its first 'Norman' bishop, Urban. It
covered a territory held as early as Urban's accession, if not by the crown
itself, by strong royal favourites.[6] The last pre-Norman bishop,
Herewald, died in 1104 at the age of 100 years. Three years later his
archdeacon, Urban (whose residence was at Llancarfan) was consecrated
bishop. About his election or his electors nothing is known.[7] If scholars
stress time and again that Urban's consecration followed exactly the
lines of that of Canterbury's English suffragans, by pointing to his
profession of canonical obedience, one should equally notice that in
Urban's profession, as in almost all earlier Welsh professions, the fact

---

[1] Gir. Cambr., *De Invectionibus*, ii, 9, 142f.

[2] R. H. C. Davis, *King Stephen* (London, 1967), p. 56.

[3] G. W. S. Barrow, 'King David I and the Honour of Lancaster', *EHR*, 70, 1955, pp. 85–89.

[4] Saltman, *op. cit.*, 'He (Bernard) thus failed the Welsh Church in its hour of need', p. 92.

[5] *Letters of John of Salisbury*, I, Ep. 135–6.

[6] *Ep. Acts*, II, p. 536.

[7] *Ep. Acts*, I, 125 J. C. Davies quotes a letter claiming to be sent by the 'clergy and people' of
     the church of Glamorgan as electors to Archbishop Anselm of Canterbury asking him to con-
     secrate Urban. The value of this piece of evidence is slight. This kind of letter was a formality,
     designed according to the 'Mainzer Pontificale' which had been introduced into England half
     a century earlier, cf. supra. This 'Decretum quod clerus et populus firmare debet de electo
     pontifico' was often given unwillingly in the required form, whether that would fit the events
     or not. In the present case not even a genuine letter is preserved but only the Canterbury draught
     of it, *Canterbury Professions*, p. 115, no. 7. In the case of Bishop Bernard of St. David's there
     are good reasons to believe that a similar letter was written years after his consecration, cf.
     Richter, 'Professions', *loc. cit.*, 200 ff. See now also Wendy Davies, 'The Consecration of Bishops
     of Llandaff in the Tenth and Eleventh Centuries', *BBCS*, xxvi, 1974, pp. 53–73.

that the respective bishop is residing *in Wales* is added to the usual formulary. Urban is called '. . . electus . . . Clamorgatensis ecclesie antistes que in Walis sita est'.[1]

When Urban died in 1133 after the long controversy over diocesan boundaries, it was seven years before a new bishop was elected. Among the reasons for this were the Welsh rising after the death of Henry I, and a prolonged vacancy in Canterbury before the election of Archbishop Theobald. Likewise, these years saw bishop Bernard of St. David's pressing his claim for metropolitan dignity over the whole of Wales. This had repercussions in Llandaff. The recent humiliating decision over the diocesan boundaries was enough to make St. David's an unbearable rival. In Llandaff the material concerning the ancient dignity of the church was presumably gathered then.[2] This work not only disproved St. David's claim over the disputed territory, but her metropolitan pretensions, too. The rivalry was also expressed in the Saints' Lives. Rhigyfarch's *Life of St. David* reported David's consecration as archbishop of Wales by Dyfrig (Dubricius)[3] who, after all, was one of the patrons of Llandaff. The position of a 'Rome in Wales' was claimed by the church of Llandaff.[4] The tradition according to which St. David translated the metropolitan see from Caerleon-on-Usk to Mynyv was never accepted by the Llandaff clergy, for they would thereby have admitted their own defeat.

After the see of Canterbury had been filled by the election of Theobald, Llandaff received a bishop again. The archdeacon Uctredus was consecrated, as was Meurig to Bangor, early in 1140. In Glamorgan, there was no protest, as was the case with Meurig, against this procedure. Uctredus gave the usual profession of obedience, styled there as 'Uctredus ad regimen ecclesie Landavensis electus'.[5]

Uctredus died early in 1148, and the election of his successor was straightforward. Nicholas, son of bishop Urban,[6] was consecrated by Archbishop Theobald on 14th April. His profession of obedience

---

[1] *Canterbury Professions*, no. 59, p. 36.

[2] C. N. L. Brooke, 'The Archbishops of St. David's, Llandaff, and Caerleon-on-Usk', *SEBC*, 204 n. 3; Wendy Davies, *EHR*, 88, 1973, pp. 335–51.

[3] For the content of the Life of St. David at this time see *infra*, p. 35.

[4] *LL*, p. 133; it is interesting to notice that in 1119 Abp. Ralph of Canterbury likewise had claimed for his see the title of 'Rome in Britain', HCY, II, 229.

[5] *Canterbury Professions*, no. 82, p. 42.

[6] *Ep. Acts*, II, 521.

is noteworthy in that here for the first time the original piece of vellum was used to enter on the reverse a short notice concerning the consecration, the date, and the personalities involved. One of the suffragans taking part in the consecration was Bishop Meurig of Bangor, entered as 'Mauricio Bangornensi de Walis'.[1] It is noteworthy that all the three bishops of Llandaff in the first half of the twelfth century came from the diocese itself. But although local people, they submitted to Canterbury willingly.

The material concerned with the Norman advance into the south-west of Wales is incomparably richer than in any other part of Wales. Llanbadarn Fawr and St. David's were the cultural centres of the late Celtic civilisation. Thus we are able to perceive more clearly the development of the Church prior to the Norman conquest. We may start with Bishop Sulien, the last bishop of St. David's to be completely outside the grip of Canterbury. He was bishop twice, for the first time between 1073 and 1078, in which year he resigned the position, to take it up again in 1080 after the death of bishop Abraham and to hold it until his final resignation in 1085. Most likely he appointed and consecrated his successor Wilfred according to the customs of the Welsh Church.

Sulien had been married and is known to have had four sons, Rhigyfarch, Arthen, Daniel and Ieuan.[2] The youngest son, Ieuan, wrote a *Vita* of his father in verse[3] and later became the first archdeacon of Cardigan, appointed by Bishop Bernard.[4] His brother Daniel became archdeacon of Powys under the same bishop: he died in 1127. But the most remarkable member of this distinguished family was Rhigyfarch. His *Lament* is a moving account of the anxiety felt by the Welsh in face of the Norman advance, condensed in the following lines:

'Gens inimica Deo tunc britanna?
Non audes humero ferre faretam.'[5]
[Are you, British people, at enmity with God?
You, (Wales), do not dare to carry the quivers of arrows
  on your shoulder.]

---

[1] *Canterbury Professions*, no. 90, p. 44.

[2] Lloyd, II, 459–61; *Ep. Acts*, II, 493–506.

[3] See Michael Lapidge, 'The Welsh-Latin Poetry of Sulien's Family', *Studia Celtica*, viii–ix, 1973–74, pp. 68–106, at p. 80–89.

[4] In 1137 the *Brut* records the death of Ieuan, 'archpriest' of Llanbadarn, ed. T. Jones (RBH), p. 117.

[5] 'The Lament of Ricemarch', ed. H. J. Lawlor, *The Psalter and Martyrology of Ricemarch*, Vol. I (London, 1914), p. 121–3; Lapidge, pp. 88–93.

Equally important is his *Life of St David* in which David is presented as archbishop of Wales, owing this position not to Rome but to an election by the people among whom he lived. This remarkable declaration of independence may well have been inspired by the first actions of Anselm, archbishop of Canterbury and representative of the Roman tradition, against a bishop of St. David's, in 1095.[1]

Wilfred's episcopate witnessed the change that came over Wales. The Normans established themselves firmly in Pembrokeshire, thus gaining control over St. David's. Archbishop Anselm suspended Bishop Wilfred, although the effectiveness of this act is doubtful. The structure of the church remained untouched till his death in 1115; it was to be completely remodelled according to Roman tradition by his successor, Bernard.

On 19th September, 1115, Bernard was consecrated bishop of St. David's by Archbishop Ralph of Canterbury. The former chaplain of Queen Matilda and at one time custodian of the see of Hereford[2] had been elected bishop a few days before by command of King Henry I 'against the will and in despite of all the clergy of the Britons'.[3] Before his consecration he made the usual profession of obedience to the archbishop of Canterbury in which he is called 'ecclesie sancti Andree et sancti Dauid que in Gualis est electus'.[4]

The exact circumstances of his election remain obscure. The fact that a letter of the chapter of St. David's to Canterbury survives, asking for Bernard's consecration, in its present form of a much later date,[5] gives support to the assumption that originally a Welshman, probably Daniel ap Sulien, had been demanded as the next bishop.[6] The issue is rendered even more obscure by the various accounts given later of Bernard's election.

The last of the Welsh medieval bishoprics, St. Asaph, is, in the first years of its history, difficult to trace. A reference to a bishopric (unnamed) situated between Bangor and Chester occurs in 1125 in connection

---

[1] *Rhigyfarch's Life of St. David*, ed. J. W. James. Of all the preserved versions, the one written by Giraldus Cambrensis seems to come nearest to Rhigyfarch's original, cf. Michael Richter, 'Canterbury's Primacy ...'. As to the date of the first composition by Rhigyfarch, Mrs. N. K. Chadwick would favour an early one (c. 1081), cf. *SEBC*, p. 174f.; J. W. James a later one (after 1095), cf. *op. cit.*, p. xi. In view of strong suggestions that the *Life of David* was written as a reply to Lifris' *Life of Cadoc*, cf. Emanuel, *loc. cit.*, the later date seems more likely.

[2] H. Round, *Calendar of Documents preserved in France ...* (London, 1899), I, p. 408, no. 1138.

[3] *Brut*, ed. T. Jones, p. 83.

[4] *Canterbury Professions*, no. 64, p. 37f.

[5] *Ibid.*, p. 117, no. 11.

[6] Lloyd, II, 453, and n. 216; *Ep. Acts*, I, 134, II, 503.

with the Canterbury – York dispute; then William of Corbeil, archbishop of Canterbury, offered the transfer of these three bishoprics
to the province of York in return for a profession of canonical obedience
by Thurstan of York.[1] St. Asaph was first filled in the forties of the
century. We shall attempt to fix the date as precisely as possible, since
the hitherto accepted date (1143) seems doubtful in view of new evidence.
The first post-conquest bishop in St. Asaph, Gilbert, is named only on
three occasions.

Among the correspondence concerning the metropolitan claim of
St. David's raised by Bishop Bernard, a letter from the chapter to Pope
Eugenius III (1145–53) points out that Bernard's (alleged) metropolitan
dignity in Wales had recently been violated on two occasions: with
the consecration of Meurig of Bangor and Uctredus of Llandaff by
Theobald (1140) and with the consecration of the bishop of St. Asaph:
'... Ricardus vero in Laneluensi ecclesia electus a ministris ecclesie
ceteroque clero cum literis regis et comitis terre metropolitano nostro
B. ad consecrandum est destinatus. Sed eius nimirum consecrationis
termino per captionem regis Stephani necessario dilato, Cantuariensis
eum ... presumptuose promouit'.[2] Here it is unambiguously stated
that Gilbert[3] was consecrated during the captivity of King Stephen.

The second reference to bishop Gilbert occurs in a Canterbury source:
'Anno ab incarnatione domini nostri Ihesu Christi MXLIII° Teobaldus
cantuariensis archiepiscopus et totius britannie primas sacrauit gilebertum
laneluensis ecclesie de Wales electum in episcopum apud Lamhetham,
accepta ab eo pro more scripta de subiectione et obedientia sibi exhibenda
professione presentibus et cooperantibus Roberto lundoniensi episcopo
et Atselino rofensi antiste suffraganeis ecclesie christi cum ...' (deest).[4]

While the Canterbury document claims that Gilbert was consecrated
in 1143, the letter by the St. David's chapter places the consecration
within the nine months' captivity of King Stephen in 1141.[5] The
St. David's letter is closer to the events recorded than the Canterbury
note. It makes the interesting point that King Stephen at one time
consented to Bishop Bernard's metropolitan ambitions. Is that credible
at all? One month after Stephen's captivity we find Bishop Bernard
attending the Empress Matilda at Winchester, where Bernard was given
special attention by the papal legate Henry of Blois, the bishop of

---

[1] See *supra*, p. 25.

[2] *De Invect.*, ii, 6, 139–41.

[3] This seems to be his real name, see *Ep. Acts*, I, 89 n. 516. Gilbert, bishop of St. Asaph,
witnesses a charter in 1146, see *Hist. MSS. Comm., 4th Report*, Appendix, p. 364.

[4] *Canterbury Professions*, no. 93 (endorsement), p. 46.

[5] Stephen was captured 2 February, 1141, and released 1 Nov., see Davis, *op. cit.*, pp. 53, 65.

Winchester.[1] Later in the same year he acted for King David I of Scotland;[2] no more evidence of Bernard's support of Stephen's rivals has survived, but with regard to this it is not unlikely that Stephen may have offered to consent to Bernard's claim in exchange for a promise to support him against the Empress, but that Bernard changed sides as soon as the king was captured. For Archbishop Theobald the consecration of Gilbert was a double triumph, against Bernard and against Henry of Blois, his great rival.

The Canterbury document, on the other hand, which appears to draw from a source which has not survived, assigns the consecration of Gilbert to 1143.[3] For Theobald it was decisive that he was able to consecrate Gilbert to St. Asaph in 1141, and thus secure his position as *de facto* archbishop over the Welsh dioceses. It is noteworthy that no professions of obedience given by Gilbert is known to exist.[4] There is, however, little doubt that Theobald insisted on the profession, but by some mistake the Canterbury monks who kept the registers of the professions failed to include Gilbert of St. Asaph.

Between 1092 and 1141 the archbishops of Canterbury had succeeded, by the act of consecrating the bishops-elect of the Welsh dioceses, in enlarging their province, which now comprised seventeen suffragans. Their success was limited in two ways: it lacked sanction from outside and acceptance in Wales. We shall see presently that the four bishops of the Welsh dioceses were in a special position towards Canterbury, a position which, although escaping legal definition, was generally noted. It becomes apparent even in the professions of the Welsh bishops themselves. Additional notes that the elects would be bishops 'in Wales' ('in uualis', 'in gualia') show that even the rather inflexible legal terminology did not manage to include the Welsh dioceses harmoniously into the province of Canterbury. Similarly, contemporary historians refer to the Welsh bishops in that way, thus drawing a clear line between them and the English suffragans.[5]

As regards Rome, on the other hand, the archbishops of Canterbury were anxious to include Wales – tacitly – in their province and in the 'regnum Anglie'. This becomes apparent in the documents which

---

[1] *Ibid.*, p. 56.

[2] H. A. Cronne, 'The Honour of Lancaster in Stephen's reign', *EHR*, 50, 1935, pp. 670–80, esp. 672; G. W. S. Barrow, 'King David I and the Honour of Lancaster', *EHR*, 70, 1955, pp. 85–9.

[3] Saltman, *op. cit.*, p. 94, quotes Gervasius of Canterbury who, in turn, quotes the Canterbury document.

[4] None of the registers, which at this time are generally complete, quotes a profession.

[5] Eadmer, *Hist. Nov.*, pp. 187, 235, 293, 295; 'Benedict', I, pp. 84, 125, 144, 159, 160; ii, 79; Howden, *Chron.*, iii, p. 15.

conferred on the archbishop of Canterbury the position of papal legate. Whereas throughout the century this position was to embrace 'Anglia et Scotia,[1] Wales was included but not mentioned. This was not because the popes recognized Canterbury's position in Wales, but because they knew no better. If the archbishops asked for legateship over 'Anglia et Scotia', these would be the terms used in the papal chancery, too, because they were regarded as sufficient. Canterbury was glad to avoid discussion of the position of the Welsh church as long as the *status quo* was maintained which in fact amounted to jurisdiction over Wales. That such an interpretation is not too far-fetched becomes clear when we look at the way in which Bishop Bernard reacted towards the Canterbury policy.

Bishop Bernard's metropolitan claim and Canterbury's reaction.

When in 1920 a new edition of Giraldus' *De Invectionibus* was published, valuable additional material for the later stage of the St. David's controversy was made available. This, however, was little compared to the information about Bishop Bernard of St. David's, who here emerged as the major figure of Welsh Church history in the first half of the twelfth century. Not that he had been unknown before. A long episcopate was bound to leave traces in official records, and the contemporary historians have something to say about Bernard, too. But only through the documents preserved by Giraldus can we fully appreciate the importance of Bernard. Once this line had been established, there developed a growing interest in the intellectual background of the first metropolitan claim of St. David's. Here, recent investigations into Welsh hagiography have proved fruitful.

The metropolitan claim has a fascination in itself, if only for the fact that it was urged by the first *Norman* bishop in St. David's. It gains in importance, if it is accepted, as we can do now quite confidently, that it was brought forward at a time when Bernard was on good terms with King Henry I and William of Corbeil, archbishop of Canterbury. Thus it preceded the political 'national revival' in Wales which followed the accession of King Stephen. Bernard, while dependent on the support of Canterbury in his controversy with Urban of Llandaff over the diocesan boundaries, tried to assert his independence from Canterbury; the path he followed was narrow, the situation delicate, but success in both fields was conceivable. As far as the evidence goes, the Llandaff–St. David's and the St. David's–Canterbury controversies, although

---

[1] E.g. the one given to William of Corbeil, 25 January, 1126, B.M. Cotton MS, Cleopatra E i f. 31b–32a.

negotiated simultaneously before the papacy, were treated quite separately. This is very remarkable because in both controversies all three parties were involved.

If we had to name one single reason for Bernard's first move towards metropolitan dignity, this would be the defeat of Canterbury's claim of primacy over York. Bernard had witnessed as an onlooker the emergence of Thurstan of York at the Council of Rheims in 1119, and had been actively involved in the humiliating experience of 1123 in Rome where the Canterbury forgeries, which tried to establish the same supremacy over York, were ridiculed. An approach by Bernard to Thurstan could be useful, and, indeed, we are informed that in 1125 he apologized to Thurstan for the way he had acted two years earlier as a supporter of the Canterbury case.[1] Frequent meetings with Thurstan could not have been without an influence upon his attitude.[2] It is possible that Bernard likewise profited from Thurstan's trouble with the Scottish bishops who tried to establish their independence from York. Certainly the case of the bishop of Glasgow was well-enough known to encourage Bernard in his own plans.

But we would hardly do justice to the Welsh cause by stopping here. Bernard claimed for himself the position of a Welsh archbishop. In the twelfth century the notion of an archbishop would appear to have been more loose than modern scholarship sometimes allows. We have studied the arguments of Archbishop Ralph of Canterbury against the see of York as an archbishopric: lack of suffragans, no creation of new bishoprics, nor consecration of bishops, and earlier dependence on Canterbury. Still, the pope had confirmed Thurstan as archbishop, and thus it could appear to Bernard that one might be archbishop even if one had only few suffragans, if they were consecrated by him, and if one could manage to escape from subjection to Canterbury.

This line of thought perhaps carried Bernard to the second source which supported his claim: the Welsh tradition of an ecclesiastical independence from Canterbury. This had recently found its way into literature. The *Life of St. David* by Rhigyfarch maintained, after all, that David had been archbishop of Wales. Bernard employed in his diocese two of Rhigyfarch's brothers, Ieuan and Daniel, and these were men who could bring to his notice the *Life of St. David*, if, indeed, the bishop had not known of it earlier. William of Malmesbury tells

---

[1] Hugh the Chantor, *The History of the Church of York* 1066–1127, ed. Charles Johnson (NMT, Edinburgh, 1967), pp. 121f. For a fuller discussion see Michael Richter, 'Canterbury's Primacy . . .', *JEH*, xxii, 1971, pp. 177–189.

[2] Both appear frequently together in witness lists, see J. H. Round, *Documents preserved in France . . .*, no. 284, 288, 378, 1052, 1386.

that Bernard sought the body of David but could not find it.[1] Perhaps we witness here an initiative inspired by events in Llandaff where in 1120 the body of St. Dyfrig was translated into the cathedral church which was then under construction.[2]

The first move towards establishing an archbishopric of St. David's was made in an undated letter[3] to Pope Honorius II (1124–30). This is a most skilful piece of craftsmanship, and we have to analyse it closely. It falls clearly into different parts, which will be treated separately, namely:

(i) The portion relating to St. David's starts with the introduction of Christianity into Britain. In AD 140,[4] when Eleutherius was pope in Rome, he sent two preachers, Faganus and Duvianus, to Britain where King Lucius reigned. The missionaries instituted 27 bishoprics according to the number of previously existing cities, and three arch-bishoprics, one in Wales. After some time David, a man of great sanctity, was elected in Western Britain by a synod of clerics and laymen, and then, it is said ('*legitur*'), he was made archbishop by his predecessor Dubricius and by a synod, as was customary in that church. His successors held this position until recent times.

It is noteworthy that of all (presumptive) archbishops of Wales only David is named. The actual reference to a book where his consecration was recorded is too obvious to be overlooked. That the book in question was the *Life of St. David* there can be no doubt. It remains only to be established whether we have any version of the *Life* in which the story of David is told in these lines. The recently established earliest version[5] gives an account which is quite different: it tells how David succeeded in demolishing the Pelagian heresy and was, by agreement of all the people who attended the synod, made archbishop and his city was made the metropolitan see of the whole country (Wales). The important difference from the account given in the letter to Honorius is that in this *Life of St. David* the saint was made the first archbishop of Wales, whereas in the letter there had been archbishops since the time of conversion to Christianity. This Honorius-account, however, agrees with the version of the *Life of St. David* written by Giraldus Cambrensis

---

[1] *De Gestis Regum*, ed. William Stubbs, 2 vols. (RS), i, 28.

[2] *LL*, 84–6.

[3] *De Invect.*, ii, 10, 143–6. Its genuiness has been doubted by *Haddan & Stubbs*, i, 317, but accepted by Christopher Brooke, 'The Archbishops ...', *loc. cit.*, 208–233, and idem in Dom A. Morey and C. N. L. Brooke, *Gilbert Foliot and his Letters* (Cambridge 1965), p. 156.

[4] Cf. Bede, *HE*, ed. Charles Plummer (Oxford, 1896), lib. I, c. 4, p. 16, for the year 156.

[5] J. W. James, *op. cit.*, 'Nero Version'.

c. 1192–94,[1] but based, as shown by J. W. James, on a version different from and prior to that of *c.* 1150. Giraldus tells how David was consecrated bishop by the patriarch of Jerusalem before being made archbishop at Brefi.[2] Thus one source of the letter to Honorious can be established: it is Rhigyfarch's *Life of St. David* as it then was, and this is a version of the *Life* similar to, if not identical with, the one which was the source of Giraldus' text.

(ii) The letter establishes further the independence of the Welsh archbishopric from the exclesiastical organisation which was created by St. Augustine. No subjection of Wales to Canterbury followed. For it is maintained that Pope Gregory (I) confirmed the independence of the Welsh Church as created by his predecessors. There follows an appeal to a tradition cherished by the papacy to renew privileges which had been issued by their predecessors[3] which the clergy of St. David's wanted to see applied to their case too. Augustine's conversion of the Saxons did not affect the situation in Wales which had remained a Christian country.[4]

The reference to Bede's *Historia Ecclesiastica* is obvious. To establish a direct source of inspiration for including a 'Bede' section in the letter would be rash under ordinary circumstances, taking the popularity of Bede into account. But it should be noted that Archbishop Ralph in his letter to Calixtus II in 1119, the content of which was certainly known to Bernard, drew heavily from Bede, even if to Ralph Bede had to prove something else!

(iii) It is stated that archbishop Ralph had consecrated Bishop Bernard, but that this had been done 'saving the dignity of our church'. For all archbishops of Wales before Bernard had been consecrated by their predecessors and by a church synod, according to local customs.

---

[1] Michael Richter, 'The Life of St David by Giraldus Cambrensis', *WHR*, iv, 1968–69, pp. 381–6.

[2] In the Nero Version (*op. cit.*), the events at Jerusalem were carelessly emendated, cf. c. 46, the arrival of three men is mentioned to the patriarch, all of them he is to consecrate bishops, but later: the patriarch consecrates only one *arch*-bishop. c. 49 Paulinus recalls a man recently been made bishop by the patriarch. The Giraldus version tells a straight development of David, *Op.* iii, 375–404.

[3] 'In Romana quippe ecclesia apostolicorum decreta precedentium ... assertione omnimoda succedentium irrefagabiliter sanctiuntur tenenda', *op. cit.*, 144; similarly in Ralph's letter to Calixtus II: 'Solent enim Romani pontifices de observandis indeclinabiliter decretis antecessorum ante consecrationem suam profiteri', *HCY*, ii, 248.

[4] *Loc. cit.*, see esp. the distinction made by Ralph between the regulations made for London and Canterbury, p. 231 and our letter's distinction between Trinovantia and Cantuaria, p. 144.

(iv) Bernard's predecessors had been archbishops, even if their pallium had at one time been taken by Samson to Dol (Brittany), never to return to St. David's. The letter relates in great detail of what the archiepiscopal functions consisted: not only the advice given to inferiors (suffragans), but the consecration of bishops who were sent out as missionaries to Ireland and other parts of the world. The most famous churchman to come from Wales was St. Patrick who preached in Ireland.

To sum up: Wales has been an archbishopric from the earliest Christian ages. It had been left untouched by the mission of Augustine. It had spread Christianity beyond its borders, although it had been without a pallium part of the time. Down to the twelfth century Wales had been independent from Canterbury, and thus the consecration of Bernard was an exception without much impact. It is consistent with the tone of the letter that the chapter of St. David's requested the pope to have the ancient privilege of an archbishopric renewed for Bernard to the benefit of his flock (*natio*).

The inspiration, if not the authorship, of this letter, which owed much to contemporary and older sources, came from Bishop Bernard himself. His quick identification with the Welsh past is astonishing. At a time when Canterbury was in a position of weakness with an archbishop of little standing, Bernard tried to claim for himself what had been granted to York and was claimed by the Scottish bishops: papal approval of an archbishopric for Wales. How far Pope Honorius considered Bernard's application, we do no know.[1]

If Bernard's first application for the pallium had been based on a wide historical justification, the second move known to us, set out in a letter to Pope Innocent II (1130–43), speaks only of Bernard's own time. It is difficult to determine when this letter was sent. It was possibly inspired by the national revival in Wales after the death of King Henry I in 1135. Canterbury was vacant between November 1136 and January 1138, and this space of time appears the most likely for Bernard's renewed application.[2]

In this letter Bishop Bernard had to account for his late application for the pallium. Normally this had to be collected in the first six months after the consecration of an archbishop, not two decades later. Bernard had a twofold excuse:

---

[1] The anonymous author of 'De successione episcoporum et gestis eorum, videlicet Bernardi et David secundi', ed. Michael Richter, *BBCS*, xxii, 1967, p. 247f., refers to Honorius, Lucius and Innocent, 'quorum scripta adhuc in Menevensi continentur ecclesia'.

[2] *De Invect.*, ii, 7, 141–2. It should be noted that in 1139 Bishop Malachy of Armagh applied for a pallium as well, see J. A. Watt, *The Church and the Two Nations in Medieval Ireland* (Cambridge, 1970), p. 27f.

(i) the fact that he himself had personally and through intermediaries applied for the pallium earlier, a statement which possibly refers to the letter to Honorius II,[1] whom, as we know, Bernard had met over his dispute with Urban of Llandaff in 1129.

(ii) the poverty of his see prevented him from applying effectively at an earlier date. As Bernard said, he could maintain his position in St. David's only through the generosity of the king.

The applicant did not try to hide the fact that he had been consecrated by the archbishop of Canterbury, but he had two interesting remarks to make concerning his consecration. It had been claimed that he should be consecrated archbishop of the first and greatest province of the island, and that he was the first bishop of St. David's to have been consecrated at Westminster, which had been done in spite of his protest. With ingenious obscurity Bernard employed here a vague expression, for it remains uncertain against what he had protested: to have been consecrated bishop, but not archbishop; to have been consecrated at Westminster; to have been consecrated at all?

Different from the previous argument, but arriving at the same result, is the closing phrase of the letter. Here it is stated that Wales is very far from Canterbury and that the Welsh are different from the other people: 'populos nostre provincie natione, lingua, legibus et moribus, iudiciis et consuetudinibus discrepare'.[2] Thus Wales as a 'nation' would have a right to an archbishopric. It has to be remembered that a decade earlier the Scottish bishops had claimed their independence because their country was a 'regnum'. This could not be said about Wales, but the argument that Wales was a 'nation' could hardly be disproved. It has to be granted that the positive proof was difficult to establish, yet the importance of this passage is that here for the first time a comprehensive catalogue of the criteria of the medieval Welsh 'nation' is given, which, even if not formulated earlier, can be expected to have been held by contemporaries. This stands quite apart from the question as to how far it enabled Bernard to push his argument further.

Again we know nothing of a papal response to Bernard's claim. What can be made of Henry of Huntingdon's tantalisingly short remark that Bernard had received a pallium from Innocent II and lost it

---

[1] *Ibid.*, 141: 'pulsavi personaliter et per submissas personas'.

[2] *Ibid.*, 142. For an interesting parallel see a letter by Innocent III to Ottokar I of Bohemia dated 1204, April 21, 'supplicasti . . . ut in Bohemia metropolim construere dignaremur, cum spaciosa et populosa sit terra, et ab ecclesia Maguntina, cui est metropolitico iure subiecta, tam locorum distantia quam linguarum diversitate divisa . . .', Migne *PL*, ccxv, 337.

immediately?[1] If nothing else it proves that Bernard's ambitions were well enough known in England before 1141[2] to attract the attention of the contemporary historian.

In Wales after 1136 the political situation had changed to the disadvantage of the Normans. Gruffydd ap Cynan established a powerful centre of Welsh resistance in Gwynedd, favoured by his ecclesiastical dignitaries.[3] In this situation it is not surprising to find that Gruffydd's sons, Owain (Gwynedd) and Cadwaladr, should have joined forces with Bernard over the institution of the bishop of Bangor in 1140; one rather wonders why such a joining of forces had not taken place earlier. What Bernard tried to achieve in the ecclesiastical field, the lords of Gwynedd attempted in the secular field: the exclusion of the Normans from Wales. From 1140 to his death in 1148, Bernard drew support from Gwynedd, and he found a capable and influential friend in the archdeacon of Bangor, Simeon.

It is likely that Pope Innocent II was favourable to Bernard's claim. How else should we explain the fact that at his death Bernard immediately hurried to Rome to put his case to the next pope, Lucius II?[4] Lucius, in a letter dated 14 May, 1144, not only spoke favourably of Bernard's claim, but referred to other letters written to the same end.[5] The pope's open-mindedness may have been due to Bernard's personal appearance in Rome, although it did not extend beyond the promise of a commission to enquire into the case. The early death of Lucius prevented even this commission from starting its work.

In the pontificate of Eugenius III (1145–53), Bernard's campaign reached its climax. It was seriously considered by Eugenius as it had been by Lucius II. Again Bernard seems to have hurried personally to Rome; he took with him a letter of his chapter in which the request

---

[1] *Hist. Angl.*, ed. Th. Arnold (RS, 1879), p. 10 'Tempore autem nostro recepit episcopus S. David pallium a papa, quod scilicet fuerat olim apud Kairlegion, sed statim tamen amisit'.

[2] Henry only knows of three bishoprics in Wales, *ibid.*

[3] According to *Hanes*, Bishop David of Bangor and his archdeacon Simeon were at Gruffydd's deathbed, *op. cit.*, 157.

[4] Bernard's presence at Rome 14 May 1144 (date of letter by Lucius to Bernard) is attested by a papal letter sent to the church of St. Andrews in Scotland in which Lucius confirmed the establishment of Augustinian Canons in the priory of St. Andrews at the intercession of Bernard, bishop of St. David's, see *Ep. Acts*, II, 562; Alan Orr Anderson, *Early Sources of Scottish History AD 500–1286* (Edinburgh, 1922), 2 vols, ii 205–6. It is interesting to note that Archbishop Theobald was in Rome at the same time, and that he was disappointed by Pope Lucius' unfavourable attitude towards his claim to legatine position, cf. Saltman, *op. cit.*, p. 20f.

[5] Could they come from North Wales? *Ep. Acts*, p. 260, D 123 obscures the issue by an incorrect translation, speaking of a plurality of letters by Bernard.

for a pallium was stated.[1] This letter was presumably written in 1145, for Eugenius's election (15 February) was spoken of as a recent encouragement of the Welsh cause. Bernard had obvious reasons to press his claim.

In this letter is is stated categorically: St. David's is the metropolitan see of Wales, the greatest province of Britain; the bishops in Wales are suffragans of St. David's. They used to give a canonical profession of obedience to their archbishop when they were consecrated. A few examples are given here extending back into the eleventh century of such consecrations to the bishoprics of Bangor, St. Asaph and Llandaff. This had been the situation since the synod of Brefi.

The account of what had happened in Brefi differs materially from that given in the earlier letter to Honorius and in the earlier version of the *Life of St. David:* David, on account of his merits in extinguishing the Pelagian heresy, was made the first archbishop in Wales. Rome approved of this act and sent the pallium, confirming David as archbishop with his suffragans, Teilo and Padarn. The same story of the main events at Brefi is found (with no reference to Rome) in the *Life of St. David* in a version not prior to this stage of Bernard's metropolitan attempt and most likely interpolated into the standard version during these years.[2]

What follows in the letter to Eugenius is a logical continuation of the formerly established 'fact': all of David's successors had effectively been archbishops of Wales, consecrating their suffragans even if after Archbishop Samson without a pallium. Only the very recent political upheaval with the arrival of the Normans in Wales had brought some confusion into the otherwise undisturbed scene: yet, it is stated that Bernard was elected and consecrated *arch*bishop. His authority had been infringed only lately when Archbishop Theobald of Canterbury had consecrated the bishops of Llandaff, Bangor, and St. Asaph (i.e., between 1140 and 1141). It is against this that the chapter of St. David's protests, with the request that the church be confirmed in its ancient dignity.

If we are to judge by the extant sources, it is only at this stage that the archbishop of Canterbury felt his position seriously threatened. For the first time we know about Theobald's reaction, which was quick and energetic. He was anxious to secure support in this from his

---

[1] Letter: *De Invect.*, ii, 6, 139–41. To Bernard's possible appearance, cf. the last sentence 'plures autem aut nos omnes . . . venissemus'. Doubts on the genuiness of the letter by Lloyd, ii, 485; *Ep. Acts*, i, 89; Saltman, *op. cit.*, 94–5; unconvincing.

[2] 'Nero version'; cf. James, *op. cit.*, c. 53, p. 24. Richter, 'Canterbury's Primacy . . .' Appendix.

suffragans. Six letters to Pope Eugenius are preserved, written by the bishops of Winchester, Hereford, Ely, Bath, Exeter, and the former bishop of Norwich.[1] The choice of the suffragans may not have been accidental: Henry of Blois, bishop of Winchester, was a dangerous rival to Archbishop Theobald. When his position as papal legate expired with the death of Pope Innocent II, he himself made tentative moves, which he may have coordinated with Bernard, to secure a pallium for Winchester.[2] Both these bishops, together with those of Lincoln, Ely, Hereford, Bath and Chichester, supported the Empress Matilda in 1141[3] against the authority of Theobald and King Stephen. It was a late triumph of Canterbury to have these bishops now compelled to support Theobald against St. David's. On the other hand, the support of Canterbury by the three Welsh bishops would have strengthened Theobald's case considerably, but there is no evidence of such a support; if it was demanded and given, no record has survived.

Henry of Blois, in his letter to the pope, spoke against Bernard only in vague and general terms.[4] One cannot help feeling that this was the utmost support Theobald could obtain from him. More to the point were the identical letters of the bishops of Hereford, Ely, Bath, and Exeter.[5] Not only did they report that Bishop Bernard had been consecrated by the archbishop of Canterbury and on that occasion, by virtue of his profession of obedience, shown himself a genuine suffragan, but they maintained that similar professions had been given by Bernard's predecessors, a statement which, to our knowledge, was not correct. Most detrimental, however, was the testimony of Everard, the former bishop of Norwich. In addition to what the other bishops said, he called Bernard's intention by its proper name: 'episcoporum de Wallia consecracionem et subiectionem ei praeripere et sibi uendicare impudenti praesumptione

---

[1] Everard of Norwich resigned his see or was deprived in 1145, became a monk at Fontenay and died there 1146 (*First Register of Norwich Cathedral Priory*, ed. H. W. Saunders, Norfolk Record Society, xi, 1939, p. 70); cf. *Chron. Jo. Oxenedes*, ed. H. Ellis (RS 13, 1889), p. 53. His obituary was commemorated on 12 October (*The Customary of the Cathedral Priory Church of Norwich*, ed. J. B. L. Tolhurst, Henry Bradshaw Soc. lxxxii, 1948 p. 10; Norwich, D. & C, Sacrist's Book, p. 6v; B.M. Harley MS. 3950, f. 74); he may therefore have died *c.* 12 October 1146. The information on Everard was kindly supplied by Dr. Diana Greenway. It seems unlikely that the letters came to the notice of the pope only in 1147; so, however, Saltman, p. 113, n. 1.

[2] Diceto, i, 255, *Ann. Wint.*, 53 report that Henry actually received a pallium from Pope Lucius, cf. H. Böhmer, *Kirche und Staat*, 348–9; Saltman, 21f.

[3] R. H. C. Davis, *King Stephen* (London, 1967), p. 56.

[4] The letter is printed Lena Voss, *Heinrich von Blois*, pp. 176f. and Richter, 'Professions', *loc. cit.*, 203–4.

[5] Infra, Appendix I, p. 131.

contendit.' He recalled how in the preceding half century the Welsh bishops had been consecrated at Canterbury, how Bernard himself had behaved like an ordinary suffragan, and finally about his contest with Urban of Llandaff: 'sicut compares et coepiscopi coram Willielmo Cantuariensi archiepiscopo sicut *metropolitano suo* causam agebant'.

The intention of Theobald, as can be seen in these letters, was to push one point as far as possible: the fact that Bernard himself had been consecrated by Canterbury, had admitted his subjection to that see by the canonical profession of obedience, and had behaved during the past years like any other suffragan. The subjection of Bernard's predecessors was introduced only as an additional proof of an otherwise sufficiently established case. A fair evaluation of the argument would prove, however, that Theobald's points were not altogether sound. The consecration of Welsh bishops at Canterbury since the time of St. Augustine was certainly an invention. Although Canterbury, as early as the tenth century, had claimed primacy in Britain, there is no evidence that such a claim ever carried any effective weight. Probably Bernard felt that the story recorded by Bede, and used by Ralph of Canterbury, would strengthen his position, since the Augustinian scheme of English Church organisation was not concerned with Wales. Finally, what about his own consecration and profession? They did not imply *ipso facto* Bernard's and his successors' subordination to Canterbury. The case of the Irish bishops proves the point. It would however, be seriously damaging to Bernard's claim if Canterbury continued to consecrate the Welsh bishops. Thus Theobald's institution of three bishops between 1140 and 1141 was an important step towards establishing the actual subjection of the Welsh sees, but not because Wales was legally subordinate to Canterbury. This must be stated in all clarity before we approach the final stage of Bernard's contest and an evaluation of its significance.

Theobald's energetic measures against St. David's may have induced Bernard to put his case again personally before Pope Eugenius. So in the spring of 1147 he crossed over to France,[1] thereby hoping to establish an advantage over Theobald. But the archbishop arrived at the papal court shortly afterwards,[2] in the company of several witnesses who

---

[1] It would have been either on his way to France or on his return that Bernard visited the tomb of Wulfstan in Worcester, cf. R. R. Darlington, ed., *Life of Wulfstan* (London, 1928, Camden Third Series, xl), p. 106.

[2] His presence at the papal court in company of Gilbert Foliot, abbot of Gloucester, is established by A. Saltman, *op. cit.*, 23f, 108; see also Davis, *Stephen*, p. 104.

were to testify against Bernard.[1] Nothing but the result of the contest between the two strong-minded churchmen is known.

In a letter, dated 29 June 1147 at Meaux, Pope Eugenius pronounced a decision. The letter is addressed to Theobald; Giraldus half a century later found a copy of it in the papal registers in Rome, and an identical original papal letter to the clergy of St. David's in the cathedral there.[2] It is striking to see how the contending parties stressed opposite points to prove their case. Bernard insisted on the pallium by reason of the fact that St. David's had been a metropolitan see in the past, while Theobald tried to get as much as possible out of Bernard's profession of canonical obedience. Theobald insisted that Bernard was irrevocably subject to Canterbury because of the form of his consecration, and because he had acted as a suffragan. Bernard denied his profession, against which Theobald introduced two witnesses.

What importance the pope attached to the canonical profession in this case is unknown. His decision, interpreted as closely as possible, yields the following result: (a) Bernard should be subject to Canterbury as his metropolitan see; (b) question of the dignity of the respective churches and persons would be finally settled in the following year. The first item must be seen together with the second, for it then becomes clear that Eugenius' decision in 1147 was but a temporary one. For the time being Bernard was subjected to Canterbury as his metropolitan see.[3] This did not mean that the validity of his cause had been disproved. The issue has been obscured by the fact that, owing to the death of Bernard, a new hearing of the case never came about, only because Theobald forced the succeeding bishop David fitz Gerald not to raise it again. This is the last document in the struggle before the pope.

---

[1] 'De Successione . . .', loc. cit., p. 248; 'quorum unus erat monachus falsus, alter uero laicus'. Should the monk mentioned be Gilbert Foliot? Brooke comments on Gilbert: 'his experience of the churches of the March may have made him a useful adviser in dealing with the Welsh bishops', Foliot, p. 92, cf. the same, The Letters and Charters of Gilbert Foliot, p. 505 and n. 1, and letters no. 69, 70. If Gilbert was present at the proceedings between Bernard and Theobald, this would provide an interesting clue to his obstinate refusal to renew his profession to Thomas Becket when he himself conceived of the idea of a metropolitan province of London, cf. D. Knowles, The Episcopal Colleagues of Archbishop Thomas Becket (Cambridge, 1951), p. 47; Morey and Brooke, Foliot, 149–51.

[2] Eugenius to Theobald, De Invect., ii, 2, 135–6; cf. Op. iii, 187 'tandem literas easdem super statu bullatas bulla Eugenii papae, variato tantum principio, quia clero et populo Menevensi directas, . . . fere obsoletas et obesas diuque deperditas . . .'

[3] Richter, 'Professions' p. 205f. This is stressed by the fact that no arrangement concerning Bernard's successors was made which e.g. had been the case in the decision by Honorius II in favour of Bishop Urban of Llandaff in 1129, LL, 52f, which, incidentally, was later reversed

A summary of the impact this dispute was to have for the future establishes that here, for the first time, the Welsh Church had been presented to Rome as a complete entity, unlike the situation in the dispute between Bernard and Urban, where St. David's and Llandaff had appeared as suffragans of Canterbury. What was the result of Bernard's claim in Rome?

When Giraldus put the same problem before the papal court in 1200, he was encouraged by Eugenius' letter of 1147 which had been incorporated into the registers. This was not his only evidence. He mentions another source, namely a 'registrum ... ubi de universo fidelium orbe singulorum regnorum tam metropoles per ordinem quam earum quoque suffraganeae numerantur ecclesiae pontificales'.[1] This *provinciale* of Innocent III has not been preserved, but Giraldus' description is sufficient to attempt a reconstruction of it:[2] the papacy then tried, as far as possible, to have 'regna' and (a plurality of) 'metropoles' coinciding, and used a separate rubric for each metropolitan province. The *provinciale* did not list the four Welsh dioceses as suffragans of Canterbury but in a separate rubric. We read there: 'In Wallia vero sunt iiii^or, Menevensis ecclesia, Landavensis, Bangorensis, et de Sancto Asaph'.[3] According to that list, Wales was not subordinate to Canterbury, as Giraldus pointed out to Innocent. Apparently we are dealing with the papal recognition of a special status concerning the Welsh church.[4]

It is not known when this papal list of episcopal sees, as it was extant in 1200, was composed. The papal tax-book of the Chamberlain Cencius composed in 1192, yields the same evidence on Canterbury and Wales,[5] but was not the source of our *provinciale*.[6] The fact that St. Asaph is mentioned in the list points to a date after 1141. The version given by Giraldus mirrors the situation as it stood in 1147. In the *provinciale* the issue of the Welsh church was undecided. It may thus have been composed under Eugenius III or one of his immediate successors;[7] the exact rendering of the British ecclesiastical

---

[1] *Op.*, iii, 165.

[2] Heinrich Börsting, *Das Provinciale Romanum* (Dissertation, Münster, 1936), 1, 13ff.

[3] *De Invect.*, iv, 2, 166, slightly different *Op. iii*, 165.

[4] Michael Tangl, *Die päpstlichen Kanzeiordnungen von 1200–1500* (Innsbruck, 1894), p. xvii.

[5] *Le Liber Censuum*, ed. Fabre-Duchesne, p. 223f. (henceforth quoted as *LC*).

[6] Börsting, *op. cit.*, p. 14.

[7] *Ibid.*, 34, et passim; Fabre-Duchesne, *LC*, 43. Not longer tenable now M. Spaethen: 'In der Tat hat das Provinciale durch die hier vorliegende, nur an dieser Stelle bezeugte, in den späteren Texten absichtlich vermiedene Fassung der früheren, im Verschwinden begriffenen kirchlichen und politischen Sonderstellung von Wales in dehnbarer (?) und deutlicher (??) Form Rechnung getragen', 'Giraldus Cambrensis und Thomas von Evesham über die von ihnen an der Kurie geführten Prozesse', *Neues Archiv für ältere deutsche Geschichte*, xxxi, 1906, p. 609.

situation even suggests that the list was drawn by someone who was closely acquainted with the country.[1]

We should add here that the negative result of Giraldus' metropolitan claim found its way into the revised *provinciale* under Innocent III. This was done *c.* 1210[2] and is possibly the source for Gervase of Tilbury's list of episcopal sees in his *Otia Imperialia*. This new version is unambiguous about the Welsh Church: 'In Wallia hos habet Cantuariensis suffrageneos: Meneuensem uel S. David, Bangorniensem, Landavensem, de S. Asaph'.[3]

It would be impossible to recapture the implications felt by Welsh churchmen towards Canterbury if we had only the matter-of-fact letters of procedure to judge from. Legal language defies and denies emotions. That they were strong, indeed, becomes apparent from the last letter of Bernard. It was written, presumably early in 1148, shortly before he died (22 April).[4] A final decision in the contest between Bernard and Theobald had been fixed for 18 October, 1148 ('beati Luce festivitate');[5] but Theobald would appear to have intended pressing his claim at the Council at Rheims in spring. This is indicated by Bernard's letter to Simeon, archdeacon of Bangor.[6] Simeon was an influential personality in Gwynedd, cherished by Gruffydd ap Cynan[7] and Bishop David; he had tried to dissuade Bishop Meurig in 1139 from swearing fealty to King Stephen.[8] He was the man to share Bernard's anxiety about the advance of the Norman control over the Welsh Church. Bernard asked Simeon to go to Rheims to testify there for the true dignity of the church of St. David's. 'For', the letter finishes, 'it will be shameful and highly lamentable if the eminent position (*sublimitas*) of the kingdom of the Britons, held in honour for such a long time, should in our present time be enslaved, and if your mother, bereft of the acknowledged freedom (*titulo libertatis*) should be imprisoned and given free forever to the lubricity and lust of Canterbury'.[9]

---

1 Cardinal Boso, Chamberlain under Adrian IV and Alexander III, is suggested as a possible author by R. L. Poole, *Lectures on the History of the Papal Chancery* (Cambridge, 1915), pp. 193ff.

2 Börsting, *op. cit.*, 35ff: 'Provinciale der Klasse B'.

3 *Scriptt. Rer. Brunsvicensium*, ed. G. W. Leipnitz (Hannover 1707), p. 917.

4 Brooke, 'The Archbishops', *loc. cit.*, 218, n. 2.

5 Not for the council at Rheims, as stated Brooke, *Foliot* p. 156.

6 Simeon died in 1152, cf. *Brut*, 131; 'a man who was ripe in years and wisdom', *Hanes*, p. 157.

7 *Hanes*, 157.

8 *John of Worcester*, p. 58.

9 *De Invect.*, ii, 11, p. 146.

Here Bernard joined skilfully the recollection of the glorious British past with the problem of ecclesiastical liberty in his time. If the process of loss continued, as it appeared to do, then the British glory would be *in toto* a thing of the past. Bernard exposed thereby his own ambition to the support of secular politics. He addressed Simeon in a way which would find open ears in Gwynedd and thus proved once again his skill as a tactician.

With Bernard died the most competent defender of Welsh ecclesiastical liberty. This becomes apparent in the contemporary sources. The Welsh chronicle, which had spoken against Bernard in 1115, hardly found words enough in his praise in 1148: 'In that year Bernard, bishop of Menevia, died in the thirty-third year of his episcopate, a man wondrous for his renown and godly in his sanctity, after immense labours on land and sea to obtain for the church of Menevia its ancient liberty.'[1]

Was Bishop Bernard, the Norman, the defender of the Welsh autonomy, 'a Welsh patriot'?[2] His career was too complex to admit such simple labelling. He had been imposed upon a Welsh see by the Normans in an area where their position was strong. He kept in close touch with England, court and church. When he reorganized his bishopric according to the tradition in which he had been brought up, it was necessary to modify, if not to suppress altogether, customs cherished by the Welsh Church. He did this with astonishing smoothness, mainly, it appears, by employing Welsh ecclesiastics in the new administration. Bernard had been introduced to help the Normans with the conquest of Wales. How far he fulfilled these expectations it is difficult to say. In his cause against Urban of Llandaff he depended on the good-will of the English hierarchy as much as on the co-operation of his own churchmen, while at the same time he entered into his metropolitan claim which ran completely opposite to Canterbury's intentions. Both suits, however, would tie him to his bishopric and make him acceptable to the Welsh clergy.

It has been rightly said that Bishop Bernard 'was one of the greatest bishops whom St. David's, a bishopric which has been prolific in great bishops, has ever had'.[3] Greatness, however, must have resources to draw from. In this case it seems to have been an initial unfaltering support by the Norman monarchy, and then, when Bernard had established himself firmly, a period of comparatively little interference from England. Thus Bernard could push his claim so far. It is difficult

[1] *Brut*, p. 127.

[2] W. S. Davies, 'Materials', *loc. cit.*, 320.

[3] *Ep. Acts*, II, 562.

to imagine that Henry I would have allowed this; but Stephen was working hard to establish himself in England, and, of necessity, had to leave Wales to itself more than he would have liked to.

If Stephen lacked the opportunity to deal with Wales, archbishop Theobald who was a political key-figure during the civil war, did his best to keep his province together, against such a formidable personality as Henry of Blois, bishop of Winchester, and against Bernard. This does not in the least diminish the latter's astonishing achievements. In the course of time Bernard became a rallying point of national resistance in Wales, and possibly even, in the early stages of his metropolitan claim, one of the intellectual initiators of it. With the exception of St. David's archenemy, Llandaff, he gathered the whole of Wales behind him.[1]

Bernard's achievements were not without their limitations. The most obvious one is that he did not succeed with his metropolitan claim. One reason for this failure was the legacy he inherited from the Celtic Church: there had been no acknowledged head of the Welsh Church prior to the Norman invasion. Canterbury stepped into a vacant position. Bernard's introduction into St. David's, like that of the other bishops, underlined this point. Equally limiting was the political face of Wales: unlike Scotland, this part of Britain in the 12th century failed to produce one singe figurehead. The piecemeal conquest by the Normans resulted in the situation described by Giraldus: 'Wallia ... portio est regni Anglicani, et non per se regnum'.[2] In Wales there was not a single kingdom which could be 'recognized' by the papacy by granting a metropolitan province, as was later to happen in Scotland. Bernard's case was weakened by factors on which he had no influence. He had done as much as could be done by anyone, be he Welshman or Norman, to stimulate the Welsh on the way towards unity.

The first half of the twelfth century had seen a steady advance of Canterbury's control over the Welsh Church. All her bishops had been elected and consecrated according to the plans in England. But the system was not yet complete: Canterbury's domination was legally still undefined, and Bishop Bernard's case had proved that this could be a dangerous situation; Bernard had also shown that a Norman bishop would not *ipso facto* support the Norman cause. Thus Theobald conceived of the idea of binding the next bishops of St. David's – the only potential Welsh metropolitan champion – closer to him than other suffragans. The future bishops-elect had to promise, prior to their consecration, not to take up the St. David's claim again. The form

---

[1] The letters dealing with his metropolitan claim are calendared *infra*, Appendix I.

[2] *Op.* iii, 166; and cf. above, p. 26f.

of this oath, uncanonical as it was,[1] is unknown, since it was to our knowledge given orally only. A fair picture of how such an obligation looked may be gathered from a charter given by Giraldus in 1203 in which he abrogated all future metropolitan ambitions.[2]

There was another weakness in the Canterbury preference for the legally undefined *status quo* as opposed to a full discussion and final settlement of the Welsh ambitions: it guaranteed success fairly certainly only if the archbishop was unhampered in his office in England. Thomas Becket's long exile on the continent shows this. What became apparent then was a situation highly favourable to the Welsh Church, and just as unfavourable to Canterbury. That such a situation could arise demonstrates what Wales could achieve, and how Canterbury was powerless in the face of it, despite strong support from the papacy: for sixteen years, after 1161, the see of Bangor remained vacant due to different conceptions of Becket's idea of a bishop and the idea held in Gwynedd.

The sources for the tough struggle between Owain Gwynedd and the chapter of Bangor on the one hand and Archbishop Thomas and Pope Alexander III on the other are the dozen letters covering a few months in 1165 and 1166. Archbishop and pope demanded that Bangor elect a personality suitable to them. This was disobeyed by Bangor; Owain Gwynedd claimed to be subject to Canterbury not by law, but by his free choice.[3] This was impossible for Thomas to accept, and he maintained in strong and unambiguous terms that Bangor was subject to Canterbury; in this he had the firm papal support.[4] But the clergy did more than just disobey Thomas. A long vacancy in the bishopric would raise the problem of who should perform the necessary episcopal functions. We hear that the Bangor clergy in this case re-established old links with Ireland for the purpose, in the words of Thomas 'as if recently an archbishopric had been established for you in Ireland'.[5] It was in vain, however, that Thomas absolved the chapter of Bangor from the oath, demanded by Owain Gwynedd, to elect somebody suitable to him,[6] and that the archbishop asked them to accept the person he himself would appoint. As never before we are able to follow

---

[1] See 'De hiis que fiunt a maiore parte capituli', *Liber Extra*, 3, 11, 1 from the Third Lateran Council, quoted in Giraldus *De Invect.*, v, 20, p. 201.

[2] Discussed and printed infra, p. 126, 134–5.

[3] 'non ius aliquod nos cogit vobis subjici, sed voluntas', *Materials for the History of Thomas Becket*, ed. J. C. Robertson, J. B. Sheppard, 7 vols. (RS), v, 229, no. cxxii.

[4] *Ibid.*, no. cxx,

[5] *Ibid.*, no. cxxv, cxxix.

[6] *Ibid.*, no. cxxiv.

the difficulties involved for Canterbury in enforcing a decision on a distant diocese. Similar frictions could occur in England, too, but there the archbishop could more easily enforce his will if supported by the king. The Bangor case shows also how anxious Becket was not to allow a single occasion where a bishop in Wales would be installed by anybody except Canterbury.

Compared to Bangor, the two elections following the death of Bernard to the see of St. David's were uncomplicated. In the first case a vacancy of eight months preceded the installation of a new bishop, but the reason for this was not a dispute between St. David's and Canterbury but a controversy between Theobald and King Stephen. Theobald had attended the Council of Rheims, together with some suffragans, against the strict command of the king. Therefore he was exiled from England for six months.[1] Only in October was he back to perform his spiritual functions, among them the filling of number of English sees.

The chapter of St. David's was split over the election, and it would seem that the division was between Welsh and English canons. The Welsh demanded strongly the elections of a native Welshman,[2] presumably because they expected that such a personality would be more sympathetic to their metropolitan demands. An election to a bishopric was rarely as free from outside interference in the 12th century as canon law would demand.[3] Mostly a chapter would only have the right to suggest a candidate to the archbishop and the king, and then hope for the best. So it was in this case. Some canons went to Theobald and elected there, under pressure, as one source suggests,[4] the arch-deacon of Cardigan, David fitz Gerald 'of mixed Norman-Welsh descent'.[5] He was a mediocrity, of no strong will, but this in itself seems to have recommended him to Theobald.

A contemporary Canterbury account of David fitz Gerald's election does not mention complications in the procedure. It reports David's election on 14 December 1148, in the presence of Theobald and other bishops, and his ordination to the priesthood on 18 December, together with Robert de Chesney, bishop-elect of Lincoln. Both were consecrated bishops the following day; both had to give a profession of canonical obedience. These professions differ greatly from the usual form. With

---

[1] For a contemporary account from Canterbury see Richter, 'Professions', *loc. cit.*, 206f., which is the source of Gervase, *Op.* i, 134–6; see also Saltman, p. 25–30.

[2] Giraldus, *Op.* iii, 154.

[3] For a recent discussion R. L. Benson, *The Bishop-Elect* (Princeton, N.J., 1968).

[4] 'De successione . . .', p. 248.

[5] 'ingenuis de gente utraque natalibus ortum', Gir., *Op.* iii, 154.

clear reference to Bishop Bernard's metropolitan claim David gave a profession 'in which the duty of canonical obedience was especially elaborated ... Yet his profession did not imply a stricter duty of obedience'.[1]

As has been elaborated elsewhere, it was only due to the oral oath extracted from David fitz Gerald, not to the specially adapted profession, that Theobald secured David's abandoning of the metropolitan claim. Yet, Canterbury was in so far successful that the person most suitable to raise this claim was thus forced into inaction. This was shown when the canons of St. David's attempted to have their problem discussed in 1176 at the Westminster synod. Giraldus says that they first sounded Henry II's opinion on their attempt. The king is said to have answered 'quod nunquam id tempore suo rex permitteret, nec caput Walliae dando Walensibus archiepiscopum contra Angliam erigeret'.[2] Hard to believe as it is that this happened, it neatly sums up a potential opinion (if from a Welsh point of view) as to what a metropolitan province in Wales could amount to: a focus of Welsh separatism against England. The same obligation which was demanded from David was required from the following bishop of St. David's, Peter de Leia, prior of Wenloc. When he attended the Third Lateran Council in 1179,[3] he did not join his canons who once again demanded a metropolitan province for Wales.[4]

Peter's election had been performed in the same way as that of his predecessor. The candidates of the chapter, the four archdeacons, were refused by the king. Giraldus, one of them, quotes the warning of Henry II to the archbishop of Canterbury against Giraldus' election, for 'nec regi nec archiepiscopo opus est aut expediens nimis probum aut strenuum, ne vel Angliae corona vel Cantiae cathedra detrimentum sentiat, in ecclesia Sancti David episcopum esse'.[5] Although one would hesitate to assign this statement to 1176, it expresses the issue involved, although Giraldus commented on it possibly with his own defeat in 1203 in mind.

---

[1] '... in dem die Pflicht des kanonischen Gehorsams besonders begründet war ... Eine Verschärfung der Gehorsamspflicht bedeutete diese 'Profess' nicht', Theodor Gottlob, *Der kirchliche Amtseid der Bischöfe* (Bonn, 1936), 146ff; cf. King Henry II's opinion on an abbatial profession: 'Professio ... non est contra dignitates ecclesiarum. Non enim qui professionem faciunt, nisi quod debent, promittunt', D. Wilkins, *Concilia*, i, 430. The account is on the dorse of Robert de Chesney's profession, *Canterbury Professions*, no. 92, p. 45f.

[2] *Op.* i, 40.

[3] Mansi, *Sacr. Conc.*, xxii, 217: Provinciae Angliae: Petrus Menevensis.

[4] Gir., *Op.* i, 48–9.

[5] *Ibid.*, 43. According to *De Invect.*, v, 7, 188, Roger, bishop of Worcester, informed Giraldus about this.

Peter de Leia was elected 'more Anglicanae tyrannidis' in the king's presence at Winchester. Giraldus' attempt to warn the new bishop against the secret oath to Canterbury was to no avail. The archbishop, Richard of Dover, was not in England at the time, so Peter was consecrated by his representative, Gilbert Foliot, bishop of London, 7 November 1176.[1] Due to this arrangement, Peter's profession of obedience took a different form from the one usually demanded.[2] He had to give a second profession to the archbishop personally when he was back in England,[3] an unusual precaution, but explicable because of the St. David's claim. This was done 16 March 1177, and is recorded by 'Benedict'. It is interesting to notice that this contemporary work by Roger of Howden[4] does not yet mention the special oath. This comes up two decades later during Giraldus' fight for the bishopric of St. David's, where Roger reports that both preceding bishops, David and Peter, had to give that oath.[5]

Thus the archbishops of Canterbury continued successfully to have Wales included *de facto* into their province. But still it was felt that Wales was a separate unit in itself; this becomes apparent in an entry of the Annals of Worcester, connected with Hubert Walter's appointment as papal legate by Celestine III 18 March 1195. Whereas the letter of the pope speaks only of England,[6] the Worcester Annals recorded that 'in that year Hubert Walter received on 30 April the legateship over England, Wales, and Scotland'.[7] – If not ecclesiastically, so at least politically Wales appeared as a separate entity, apart from the 'regnum Angliae'. In Worcester, on the Welsh border, the distinction was felt possibly more clearly than in other parts of England.

---

[1] Diceto, *Opera Historica*, ed. William Stubbs, 2 vols. (RS), i, 145.

[2] *Canterbury Professions*, no. 112a, p. 52.

[3] *Ibid.*, no. 112b; cf. Gottlob, *Amtseid*, 146, n.34ff.

[4] D. M. Stenton, *EHR*, lxviii, 1953, 574–82, cf. *Gesta Regis Henrici* (RS), i, 154–5.

[5] *Chron.*, iv, 104–06.

[6] 'Ideoque nos ad honerem Dei, et Cantuariensis Ecclesiae salutem, et pacem per totum regnum Angliae, non obstante exceptione vel privilegio venerabili fratri nostro Gaufrido Eboracensi archiepiscopo, aut ecclesiae suae vel alii facto, officium tibi legationis concedimus', Jaffé, *Reg. Pont.*, ii, no. 17 202, Migne, *PL*, 206, col. 1074–5.

[7] *Ann. Mon.*, iv, 388.

II. THE NOTION OF THE WELSH NATION

This chapter will be concerned with Giraldus' view of the Welsh, our assumption being that he perceived them as a nation. Our enquiry seems to be hampered, from the outset, by the difficulty that medieval society did not have one single term equivalent to the modern term *nation*. Yet it has to be accepted that, although there may not have existed one term corresponding to the modern concept of *nation*, the perception itself may have existed. It has been said that 'thought and language, which reflect reality in a way different from that of perception, are the key to the nature of human consciousness. Words play a central part not only in the development of thought, but in the historical growth of consciousness as a whole'.[1] Even when the meaning of words may be distorted deliberately and not be purely objective description, they still reflect the beginnings of definite attitudes and concepts. Relevant to our argument is the underlying idea that there could be a perception of the Welsh as a nation although the term itself was not actually used in the way in which it is employed today. If we thus analyse in the following pages a number of terms which, all taken together, are contained in the modern term *nation*, we will have shown that the perception and notion of this phenomenon existed although it was as yet expressed in a variety of ways.

By way of illustration we want to recall a phrase preserved in a letter by Bishop Bernard of St. David's. He said that the Welsh as a people were different from their Eastern neighbours 'natione, lingua, legibus et moribus, iudiciis et consuetudinibus'.[2] This supports the argument that there was the perception of the phenomenon of the nation without as yet sufficient clarity in the terminology; but the phrase is more valuable to our central argument in that it lists the *natio* itself, which, however, at that time and in this context had a meaning more narrow and technical than the modern *nation*. These two terms, the medieval *natio* and the modern *nation*, show aptly that 'word meanings are dynamic rather than static formations';[3] they may have been so dynamic as to make it impossible to group them with any precision, yet it is highly important to see that the ideas associated with the medieval *natio* remained so central to the modern concept of *nation* that the word was retained but its meaning broadened. If our assumption is accepted, then Bishop Bernard's phrase takes a new importance: it not only illustrates that

---

[1] Lev Semenovich Vygotsky, *Thought and Language*, translated by E. Hanfmann and G. Vakar (Cambridge, Mass., 1962), p. 153.

[2] *De Invectionibus*, ii, 7, p. 142.

[3] Vygotsky, *op. cit.*, p. 124.

there existed at that time the notion of the nation, but he also gives the relevant terms which demand closer attention. In other words, what Giraldus, our main source, has to say about *natio*, *lingua*, *leges*, *mores*, *consuetudines* and *iudicia* of the Welsh can be equated with a notion of the Welsh nation. Yet it is imperative not to concentrate on these terms alone, so. e.g. *patria* has to be taken into account also. Likewise, other aspects will have to be considered which are not summed up in a single word but which are also peculiar to the situation of the Welsh and which form part of both their tradition and political reality. Under this category fall the prophetic poetry and certain propaganda tales.

Our study is therefore less a semantic analysis of various terms than the attempt to re-create Giraldus' perception or notion of the Welsh nation which was expressed in his descriptive accounts of Wales and the Welsh. It is subdivided into three groups: a discussion of the origin of the Welsh works against the background of the author's career; a description of Giraldus' concept of the Welsh; and finally a comparison of his concept with other contemporary attitudes towards the Welsh. We begin, however, with the descriptive discussion of some terms as they occur in other contexts and works in order to show the width of the field and to be able to profit from other investigations which are in their result of some importance to our enquiry. The method which we employ is conditioned by the sources at our disposal; it offers results which might encourage scholars to enquire into the notion of other nations, although in these cases other methods may be more rewarding.

The term *patria* is a legacy to the Middle Ages from Roman times. From classical Rome, the best-known and widely quoted statement is perhaps a line from Horace: 'Dulce et decorum est pro patria mori'.[1] The *patria*, of course, is Rome in the sense in which it expanded, covering first only the city with its immediate surroundings, while it was gradually applied to the whole of the Italian peninsula and later to more distant parts of the Empire.[2] *Patria* was to a Roman the territory inhabited by people who would call themselves *civis Romanus*. The word conveys the sense of sharing something with others, literally something which comes down from father to son. It is indicative of a bond. The common factor in Roman as well as in medieval times was the application of the word to a territory. There can be no *patria* without territory. Yet the word itself remained a loose term throughout the Middle Ages; it was

---

[1] Odes, III, 2, 13. Roman law rules: 'Roma communis nostra patria est'. *Dig.* 50. 1. 33.

[2] In AD 212, the edict of Caracalla (*Dig.* 1.5.17) extended Roman citizenship over the whole empire: 'in orbe Romano qui sunt ex constitutione Antonini cives Romani effecti sunt', cf. Gino Segré, 'L'editto di Caracalla sulla concessione della cittadinanza Romana e il Papiro Giessen 40. 1', *Studi in onore di Silvio Perozzi* (Palermo, 1925), pp. 139–219.

occasionally used in a technical sense, but as such it would be meaningful only to a limited number of people. Let us illustrate this. In legal records, the term is said to signify the district in which one court of law is responsible. The strictest and most accurate application can be found in England and Scotland, where *patria* is identical with the sheriffdom.[1] Similar also in Norway: although there the territorial boundaries did not exist with the same precision as in England, it has been shown that the equivalent term for *patria* is the Norwegian *lǫg* i.e. law, and again it carried 'a strictly administrative sense, as defining sharply circumscribed districts'.[2] A slightly wider sense is attached to the word in twelfth century Spain where it is used to define the territory under the rule of one count.[3] Here we see that half the way is covered already between the narrow legal term and a wider political one. To people writing on religious topics, the word was flavoured by a meaning deriving from their outlook on life. To them *patria* was a small territory, perhaps the possessions or sphere of influence of a monastery or a parish church.[4] Again it is used to describe the extension of an ecclesiastical province.[5] More specifically, the theologian would refer to Jerusalem as *patria celestis*,[6] whereas it was a common convention to refer to heaven as the proper *patria* of the Christian in general and the saint in particular.[7] Here then *patria* has an emotional dimension.

In addition to this, the recent research of E. H. Kantorowicz and Gaines Post[8] into the growth of canon law in the twelfth century has drawn attention to a concept of *patria* in a political sense, which followed

---

[1] W. C. Dickinson, 'Patria or Sheriffdom', *Scottish Historical Review*, 24, 1927, pp. 240–43; cf. *Glanvill*, ed. G. D. G. Hall, NMT (London, 1965) c. xiv, 3, p. 175: 'et hoc per iuratam patrie fuerit in curia legitime testatum'. *Patria* was also used in the sense of 'jury', meaning county or local population.

[2] H. Koht, *A*(rchivum) *L*(atinitatis) *M*(edii) *A*(evi), ii, 1925, p. 95.

[3] Lluis Nicolau D'Olwer, *ALMA*, iii, 1926–27, p. 147.

[4] 'Teliaus episcopus ... ad se familiam suam, hoc est plebem sue patrie (vocavit)', *LL*, p. 113; cf. *ibid.*, p. 109.

[5] Gervase of Canterbury writes on the election of Archbishop Becket 'ut circumvenirent sibi archiepiscopum totiusque patrie primatem electuri', quoted D. Wilkins, *Concilia*, I., p. 430.

[6] H. McKinnon, 'William de Montibus: A Medieval Teacher', *Essays ... Presented to Bertie Wilkinson* (Toronto, 1969), p. 38.

[7] E.g. Giraldus, *Op.* i, p. 404; *LL*, p. 81, 101; G. Dupont-Ferrier, *Revue Historique*, 188, 1940, p. 92; P. J. A. Juffermanns, *ALMA*, v, 1929–30, p. 63.

[8] Ernst H. Kantorowicz, *The King's Two Bodies* (Princeton, N.J., 1957); Gaines Post, *Studies in Medieval Legal Thought* (Princeton, N.J., 1964). On the term *defensio regni* and its development in 13th century France cf. J.R. Strayer, 'Defence of the Realm and Royal Power in France', *Studi in onore di Gino Luzzatto* (Milano, 1949), pp. 289–96. The usage of *gens* and *natio* in early Christian literature has been analysed by Karl Bierbach, *Kurie und nationale Staaten*, pp. 10–22.

the transformation of the Church into a mystical *body* and the empire into a *holy* empire, a concept which is aptly summarized in the phrases *pro patria pugnare* and *pro patria mori*. In this context the *patria* would embrace a kingdom or the empire, and it can be regarded as the emotional equivalent of the more technical *regnum*. Yet it remains uncertain to what extent these implications won the acceptance of the total articulate population or whether they were employed by the canon lawyers merely for the lack of any less ambiguous term. Eventually, *patria* would be commonly accepted as meaning kingdom, but it is impossible to say when this happened. Yet sufficient references have been given to show that in the framework of the twelfth century, *patria* was a concept discussed and disputed in law, theology, ethics and politics.

Different from *patria*, *gens* and *natio* are not territorial in their connotations, but are applied to people. *Gens* is the more common term. Bede in his *Historia Ecclesiastica Gentis Anglorum* expressed his concept even in the title of his work. In a similar way, Henry of Huntingdon mentions the acceptance of the Empress Matilda 'ab omni gente Anglorum, . . ., exceptis Kentensibus'.[1] It is significant that Henry adds the qualifying *omnis* to *gens*, and the rest of the sentence shows that a *gens* could be subdivided; yet the people of Kent clearly were part of it. The term is widely used in historical and hagiographical writings;[2] it also occurs, with the same connotations, in charters.[3] But the ethnical adjective with *natio* and *gens*, although it is the most common, is not the only feature. When attempting to establish what made the English, French, Bretons or Welsh into *gentes*, the most ready badge, applied repeatedly, was that of the common language. Again Bede may set the example. Britain was subdivided into 'quinque gentium (linguas) . . . Anglorum videlicet, Britonum, Scotorum, Pictorum et Latinorum'.[4] It was a common-place in high medieval hagiography[5] and also used in the same context by Giraldus.[6]

---

[1] *H.A.*, p. 275.

[2] For the latter cf. 'ad armoricas terras Britannice gentis transire . . . *LL*, p. 18: 'totius gentis Armorice', *LL*, p. 112; 'tota gens Britannica', *LL*, p. 81.

[3] One of many examples 'Omnibus ecclesie filiis Francis et Anglis atque Gualensibus et cuiuscumque sint nationis hominibus', *LL*, p. 87.

[4] *H.E.* i, 1., and the same iii, 6: 'Denique omnes nationes et provincias Britannie, que in quattuor linguas, id est Britonum, Pictorum, Scottorum, et Anglorum divisae sunt'.

[5] 'Ipse Guidnerth et Brittones et archiepiscopus illius terre essent unius lingue et unius nationis, *LL*, p. 181.

[6] *Life of St. David*, Op. iii, p. 397 'Cum autem diversas nationum linguas audirent . . .'.

Once the elements of *gens, natio* and *lingua* are combined, it does not take very long to ascribe habits to such a group as being characteristic of them alone, and then it is a short way from describing habits to describing only the unfavourable habits. The Picts are called in the *Life of Teilo* 'quidam populi de Scithia, qui sive a pictis vestibus, sive propter oculorum stigmata, picti dicebantur', and a little later 'nam picta gens erat subdola, et multis conflictionibus terra et mari exercitata'.[1] – What we wanted to show by way of introduction was that all three terms were used throughout the Middle Ages with a variety of meanings. Yet apart from different shades, it seems to be possible to single out a territorial element as particularly common to *patria*, and an ethnical one, however vague, to *gens* and *natio*.

The Welsh works: motivation and intention

By 1194 Giraldus had finished the first version of his *Descriptio Kambriae;* it was the fourth and last work in a series dealing with various topographical, political and cultural aspects of Ireland and Wales. Giraldus had intended to write more books of this kind, treating in a similar way with Scotland or England,[2] but he never completed his series. It appears that his change of interest was connected with events in his career. For by then he had left the English royal court after working there for about ten years as a clerk; he then withdrew into private life, taking up once again the study of theology. A few years later he was called to the see of St. David's. The prolonged dispute over the validity of his election, together with his preoccupation with theological topics in a wider sense, provided material for the second major group of his works. It begins with a *Life of St. David* which he wrote at the same time as the *Descriptio Kambriae*, but which, for the first time, betrays a generally sympathetic approach to Wales and its past history. Thereafter, still before his election to St. David's, he wrote the *Gemma Ecclesiastica*, a handbook on liturgical topics and basic aspects of canon law, written for use in his archdeaconry of Brecon, and more generally for the Welsh clergy. This was followed, after the dispute and defeat in his election to the bishopric, by a threefold account of these events, a worthy and dramatic climax of his literary activities, in the *De Rebus a se Gestis*, the *De Invectionibus*, and the *De Iure et Statu Menevensis Ecclesie.*

---

[1] *LL*, p. 99f.

[2] 'Cum de utriusque terrae, Walliae scilicet et Scotiae situ et properietate ... tractabimus', *Op.* v, p. 59; similarly *ibid.*, p. 403; *Op.* vi, p. 158.

The *Descriptio Kambriae* marks an epoch in the life of Giraldus in another sense also. It shows the great progress which he had made as a writer, a progress which comes out strongly when one compares this book with the first of its kind, the *Topographia Hibernica*. Not only was Giraldus more familiar with the Welsh and could therefore produce a more valuable book, but he also had improved his style. The approach in the later work was more thorough, the presentation better controlled, and due to such qualities the treatise on Wales cannot be rivalled easily. A work of such standing naturally attracted attention and received praise from the contemporaries. Giraldus perhaps took this for granted and recorded it only rarely. He showed himself much more sensitive to criticism, especially if it came from former friends and associates. Such criticism had been expressed by a friend like William de Montibus, chancellor of Lincoln.[1] The way in which he defended his works betrays an intellectual superiority over the petty and narrow-minded outlook of his opponents. It shows Giraldus fully aware of the value of his topographical writings; he was convinced that they would withstand criticism and retain their value. On this occasion Giraldus was forced into a harsh judgement of other people's works, especially those of theologians or would-be theologians. As he said, books by such people may appear new and original at first sight, but an intelligent reader would not be misled by appearance. Theologians and philosophers often claimed new results derived from independent thought, but in fact they presented in most cases a mere concoction of a number of previously existing writings and often had nothing original in them apart from the title.[2]

Modern scholarship, on the few occasions where it refers in an original way to his Welsh works, has been generally favourable to Giraldus the topographer. Despite the shortcomings of his Welsh works, which are perhaps inevitable in the approach of a totally new subject, Professor Thomas Jones has summed up his analysis with the words: 'Anyone who would study and understand the Welsh way of life, Welsh history and literature, cannot do better than by taking Gerald's *Description of Wales* as his first textbook'.[3] Giraldus remained, throughout the Middle Ages, the only competent author who wrote about the Welsh. He did not have any predecessors worth mentioning, although

---

[1] Giraldus' reply is preserved in a letter contained in the *Speculum Duorum*, pp. 168–75. The letter has been edited previously by R. B. C. Huygens, 'Une lettre de Giraud le Cambrien à propos de ses ouvrages historiques', *Latomus*, 26, 1965, pp. 90–100.

[2] *Ibid.*, p. 172, lines 61–68.

[3] *Loc. cit.* (*NLWJ*, vi, 1949–50), p. 249.

he himself claimed to follow the example of Gildas.[1] Yet other sources are more easily perceptible, although each contributed only small sections: Bede, Geoffrey of Monmouth, and Nennius. Giraldus certainly also drew from contemporary literary and oral information. In most cases these sources cannot be made out any longer with the exception of two: Rhigyfarch's *Life of St. David*[2] and the *History of Llanthony Priory*.[3] Yet even if more direct sources of his Welsh works should be discovered, this would in no respect diminish the quality of his book nor his singular and original presentation.

Over the praise which Giraldus has received for his Welsh works it should not be overlooked that they represent, when speaking about the Welsh, the personal opinion of the author. His description of the Welsh, which at times is so generalized that it comes close to a concept of the Welsh, voices views which may have been shared by his contemporaries. Should it be possible to show this, then the book would gain a further dimension apart from providing valuable factual information. It would be rash to claim that it is either typically medieval in outlook or that it presents the general attitude towards the Welsh as held by Englishmen in the twelfth and thirteenth centuries. Singularity and high quality are above such simple classifications and must be appreciated on their own terms. Yet a work like the *Descriptio Kambriae* is a product of the twelfth century; it may perhaps not be accepted as a fair and truthful account of Wales and her people, but it has to be taken as one possible point of view. This is not all: intellectual attitudes, as the one under discussion here, are always at least in part the product of more general current opinion and may become in turn material for the formation of later attitudes. We shall see that his books on Wales, for all their outstanding singularity, owe a great deal to information and opinions by other people. They also voice an attitude which is similar to, although perhaps not directly responsible for, many later attitudes towards the Welsh.

In the preface to the two Welsh works, addressed to representatives of the English episcopate, Giraldus complained bitterly that his previous service for the English crown had been left unrewarded. Neither King Henry II nor his son Richard had shown any appreciation of a man

---

[1] 'Gildam itaque Giraldus sequitur', *Op.* vi, p. 158. It would be typical of Giraldus to include the line mainly to show off with the alliteration.

[2] M. Richter, *WHR*, iv, 1968–69, pp. 381–86.

[3] Cf. *Op.* vi, pp. 37–47, and the *History* [British Museum, Cotton MS Julius D x, ff. 31ʳ–53ᵛ, printed in parts in] W. Dugdale, *Monasticon Anglicanum*, vi (London, 1849), pp. 128–34. The indebtedness of Giraldus to the *History* is particularly obvious in the description of the site of the monastery and the philological derivation of its name, compare *Op.* vi, p. 37, and *History*, f. 33ʳ/ᵛ, Dugdale, p. 129A. See also *Speculum Duorum*, p. lvi.

who had been their loyal follower and had dedicated his two books on Ireland to them. Would the English bishops be equally unappreciative? Giraldus did not feel quite sure, but he gave them a chance to prove themselves worthy patrons of literature. To the English bishops he offered his two new works. The *Itinerarium* deals with Archbishop Baldwin preaching the crusade in Wales in the spring of 1188, on a tour where Giraldus had been a welcome companion in the archbishop's entourage. The narrative about the itinerary is, however, only one aspect of the book. Much of its value it owes to the pages where the author did not keep strictly to his subject, but told stories inspired by the recollection of the places which the party visited or passed by. Formally, the treatise suffers from some unbalance. But much valuable information about the life in Wales in the twelfth century is offered in passing.

The second book, the *Descriptio*,[1] is of a different class. No spectacular events like the archbishop of Canterbury's first circuit of Wales lie behind it. It is the product of a curious man who looked around, compared and evalued what he saw. Giraldus had travelled a good deal in the preceding period, spending some years in France, Ireland and England. Thus differences between peoples may have become more evident to him, and when he toured Wales in 1188, he may have felt stronger than ever before that the Welsh were a people different from all other peoples.[2] This feeling, together with the desire to be remembered by posterity as a great writer of the contemporary scene, formed him into the author of the 'last corners of the earth': Ireland and Wales. If the *Itinerarium* lacked at times in disciplined writing, scholastic formalism is the dominant feature of the *Descriptio*. The author divided it into two parts, but it has been shown[3] that more appropriately a division would have to be made into four parts: (a) a geographical and topographical description of the country (book i, cc. i–vii), (b) the praiseworthy (book i, cc. vii–xviii) and (c) the unpraiseworthy (book ii, cc. i–vii) characteristics of the Welsh, and (d) reflections on some problems of the conquest of Wales (book ii, cc. vii–x). It has to be noted that in the *Descriptio* Giraldus presented a purely Welsh Wales. Apart from the concluding chapters, which deal with the conquest of the country, there is no mention of the precarious political situation of Wales, a country already by that time to a considerable extent colonized by Normans, English, and Flemings, and which was in some districts losing

---

[1] Both works have been translated several times, but even the latest edition (Everyman's) does not satisfy any longer.

[2] *Op.* vi, p. 155: 'aliis alienam nationibus et valde diversam'. Also once again Bishop Bernard's remark in his letter to Pope Innocent II, *De Invect.*, p. 142.

[3] Thomas Jones, *loc. cit.*, passim.

its Welsh characteristics altogether. How different from the *Itinerarium!* Some pages of that book vividly portray the life of people of different origin and language. Clearly, any valuable findings on life in Wales in the time of Giraldus can only reached by considering the *Itinerarium* as complementary to the *Descriptio*.

Giraldus' dedication of the Welsh works to English bishops appears to be indicative of his approach to the subject. He wrote for a potential English audience, for listeners who were in contact with the Welsh or would at least know about them. Their knowledge of the country was more incomplete than his. To such an audience the Welsh works would appeal in the first place.[1] Giraldus tried to give an account more sober than enthusiastic, providing patterns of thought easily understandable rather than trying to explain phenomena which in many cases would defy an easy explanation. It is a distinctive feature of the treatise on the Welsh that Giraldus gives clues, theories, and rumours about virtually anything connected with the Welsh: their descent, language, laws and customs. While keeping thus his eye on the Welsh, or what he imagined the Welsh were, he delineated them for an audience and placed them apart. This underlines the place which his Welsh books have in his career. For up to that time he had been a loyal supporter of English royal politics, especially when they had been directed against Wales. Only at a comparatively late stage did Giraldus see that he had been mistaken in supporting the English. His subsequent involvement in the affairs of the Welsh Church, his struggle for Welsh ecclesiastical autonomy, which for a short time modified his approach to the Welsh, came only after he had completed his books about Wales. A description of the country based on these recent experiences would perhaps have taken a different form and produced results more favourable to the Welsh. Unfortunately Giraldus never wrote this book. At the end of his life he had been disappointed by English and Welsh alike, and then admired the French more than any other people. His late detachment from the Welsh made him leave his earlier description of them almost completely unaltered in their later recensions.

We contend that Giraldus approached his subject in a quite conventional way, as is also shown in the prefaces to the two Welsh works, concerned as they are foremost with the author's keen interest in the immortality of his fame.[2] Giraldus quite frankly admitted this. He pointed out that only the choice of the topic was original. It would be difficult to

---

[1] In this respect the interest in the *Descriptio* has changed radically. Twelfth-century Welshmen would have found it uninteresting, twentieth-century Englishmen hardly study it.

[2] In this Giraldus was a follower of classical ideals, cf. Wilhelm Berges, *Die Fürstenspiegel des hohen und späten Mittelalters*, Schriften der MGH 2 (Stuttgart, 1952), p. 147.

find a genuine patriotic motivation in his writing.[1] The Welsh works
do not fit into such a category, a branch of literature which began to
flourish on the continent at that time. There, the merciless struggle
between the papacy and the empire had given a new incentive to the
rise of national states, and the literature hailed and glorified these states.
The spirit of that struggle and its intellectual background produced
men like Alexander of Roes in Germany and Vincentius Hispanus in
Spain. It would be a misjudgement to put Giraldus Cambrensis on
the same level with them, at least as long as one refers to his Welsh
works. That he was not completely untouched by the intellectual
controversies of his age becomes apparent in the last chapter of the
Descriptio where he showed sympathy for the Welsh fight *pro patria*.
Yet this passage is the most controversial one in the entire book, and
by no means representative of his general outlook.

Wales and the Welsh as seen by Giraldus

Wales in the twelfth century was a clearly defined concept,
geographically as well as politically. *Kambria*, the name of the country,
had comprised traditionally the territory west of the Severn, and the
course of that river had formed in the past the boundary with
England.[2] In the twelfth century, however, the land was considerably
smaller; the political expansion of England had pushed the frontier
westwards as far as the river Wye. Wales was a country of high mountains,
deep valleys, dense forests, waters and bogs. These physical features
had prevented the neighbours in the East from penetrating deeper into
the country; this became clear when the fate of the Welsh was compared
to that of the people of Cornwall: they were Britons like the Welsh,
but had been defeated quickly and decisively because their country lay
open to the invader.[3] In Wales, the physical features of the country
accounted for the distinctive military methods. The Welsh were keen
on defending their independence and given completely to the use of
arms.[4] Fighting was their main concern from youth to old age. One
rarely fought on horse-back, since the country was not suitable for this.
In the South, the bow was the principal weapon, in the North the

---

[1] It would be wrong, I think, to take Giraldus too literally when he said he wrote 'ob patriae
favorem et posteritatis', *Op*. vi, p. 157.

[2] *Op*. vi, p. 171.

[3] *Ibid*., p. 165: 'adeo rebelles esse non valuerunt'; cf. also J. K. Wright, *The Geographical Lore
of the Time of the Crusades* (New York, 1965, reprint of 1925 ed.), p. 233.

[4] *Op*. vi, p. 179, 182: 'gens igitur haec gens levis et agilis, gens aspera magis quam robusta, gens
armis dedita tota'.

lance.[1] Giraldus' knowledge of warfare in Wales was based on acute observation. Not only was he in the position to devise a plan whereby the Welsh should be conquered, but his strategy was actually used by Edward I at the close of the thirteenth century, and it brought final and lasting success to the English.

Wallia was the name most commonly used. It was a name which had originated not among the Welsh, but was imposed from outside. The Saxons traditionally called everything foreign 'Welsh' and gave, after they had settled in England, this name to their Western neighbours.[2] 'Welsh' thus was a pejorative term,[3] indicating the contempt of the Saxons. Giraldus acknowledged this proper origin of the term, ridiculing attempts made by Geoffrey of Monmouth to derive the name from a fictitious duke Walo or a queen Wendolena. He tried in this respect to evade the traps of mystification and aimed at a sober account; that he did not always succeed in this is a different matter. Yet he followed Geoffrey in other points and readily accepted the tradition of the descent of the Welsh and the reason why they called themselves Kambri:[4] the Britons derived their name from Brutus, descendant of Aeneas, and thereby linked with the people of Troy.[5] Brutus divided the island among his sons, the second of whom, Kambrus, received the portion west of the Severn and gave it his name, Kambria.[6] If it appeared that the Welsh on the whole were more witty, clever and acute than other people of Western Europe, Giraldus regarded this as the last reminder of their origin in the East.[7] Coming from a warmer region, as did the Romans and the Franks, they would be naturally more easy-going, self-confident and bold than the English, who, like the Germans and Saxons, were heavier and slower, due to the climate in which their ancestors had lived and which had formed their national characteristics.[8] The Welsh preserved the recollection of their descent from the people of Troy, which could be seen in the names they traditionally gave their children.[9] Giraldus even saw a striking similarity between the Greek and the Welsh language, but he had his doubts about the theory that

---

[1] *Op.* vi, p. 123.

[2] *Ibid.*, p. 179. For Welsh=foreign see also Gaston Paris, 'Romani, Romania, lingua Romana, Romanicum', *Romania* 1, 1872, pp. 1–22, esp. p. 5f.

[3] Cf. Franks=the free people; Slavs = the slaves.

[4] *Cymry*, originally 'co-proprietors', does not appear before *c.* the tenth century; earlier the people were known as Britons, cf. Lloyd, i, p. 194 f.

[5] *Op.* vi, p. 193; cf. Arno Borst, *Der Turmbau von Babel* (Stuttgart, 1959), II, 2, p. 694, ff.

[6] *Op.* vi, p. 178: 'Hinc igitur proprie et vere patria Kambria, hinc patriotae Kambri dicuntur'.

[7] *Op.* vi, p. 186: 'totaque communiter haec natio, prae gentibus aliis occiduo climate degentibus, arguta nimis est et astuta'.

[8] *Op.* vi, p. 193.

[9] *Ibid.*, p. 194.

the name for the language, *Kembraec*, stood for *Kam Graeco*, meaning distorted Greek.[1] The Welsh language was closely related to those spoken in Cornwall and Brittany;[2] linguistically, these areas had retained a strong cultural link marking a clear distinctness from the English. Giraldus commented on the varying quality of the Welsh language and of the various dialects: that in North Wales appeared to be purer than that in the South because the area in the past had seen only few foreign invasions and settlements. In a similar way he also accounted for the relative purity of the English language in the South-West of England, especially in Devon.[3]

Whereas in his *Description* Giraldus presented the country as virtually monolingual, a feature which may have been dictated by his theory about the Welsh, a look at the *Itinerary* shows the greater complexity of the situation. The crusade was preached both by Archbishop Baldwin and Giraldus either in Latin or in French[4] and had to be translated into Welsh to the greater part of the audience. Alexander, archdeacon of Bangor, acted as an interpreter.[5] Giraldus claimed that his audience was deeply moved by his own preaching, although they were not conversant in Latin.[6] He went even so far as to say that once his sermons were translated into Welsh, people reconsidered their determination to take the cross.[7] French and Latin were at that time in England and Wales the languages of the educated class, while the common people would speak English and Welsh respectively.[8] Whereas not very much is known about the situation in Wales at that time, it can be assumed that the linguistic pattern was more complex than Giraldus presented in his account. In the areas settled by the Marcher Lords, French[9]

---

[1] *Op.* vi, p. 194, 178; cf. C. C. Coulter and F. P. Magoun, 'Giraldus Cambrensis on Indo-Germanic Philology', *Speculum*, 1, 1926, pp. 104–109; attempts in the field of Welsh philology are not uncommon at that time and even earlier, e.g. *History of Llanthony* (Dugdale, *Mon. Angl.*, vi. p. 129A) and *Vita Sancti Gildae* (English Historical Society, 3, 1838), p. xli.

[2] *Op.* vi, p. 177.

[3] Wright, *op. cit.*, p. 340f. on linguistic geography.

[4] *Op.* vi, p. 83.

[5] *Ibid.*, p. 14, 55.

[6] *Ibid.*, p. 83.

[7] *Ibid.*, p. 77.

[8] It must be regarded as exceptional when some leading churchmen or politicians could speak the common language. Gilbert Foliot apparently was conversant in English, but Henry II's linguistic abilities were certainly unique: '(Henry) had a knowledge of all the tongues used from the French sea to the Jordan, but spoke only Latin and French', Walter Map, *De Nugis Curialium*, ed. E. S. Hartland (Cymmrodorion Record Series, ix, 1923), p. 261; cf. Giraldus, *Op.* vi, p. 64f.; Henry understands English without speaking it. For more general information cf. D. M. Legge, 'Anglo-Norman and the Historian', *History*, 26, 1941, pp. 163–175, and R. M. Wilson, 'English and French in England', *History*, 28, 1943, pp. 37–60.

[9] The Marcher Lords are commonly referred to in the Welsh Chronicles as 'the French'.

would have been widespread, while the Englishmen in their entourage would presumably speak English. Even *pura Wallia*, the north, could hardly have been monolingual at that time due to the penetration of the Church which had introduced Latin into Wales. Giraldus recorded that at Llandaff the audience listened to the preaching while being segregated according to the language which they spoke.[1]

Our point about the complexity of the linguistic situation of Wales would appear to be proved even more strongly by looking at Giraldus himself who was born in Wales and had strong affinities with the country through his family connections. In his work he gave a number of quotations in Welsh,[2] but there is no positive evidence that he himself was fluent in the language. Nor is this surprising: his mother tongue was French, and this he betrayed occasionally,[3] while his professional language, both as a clerk and as a writer, was Latin. In these two media he was completely at ease, and these were also the media of conversation in England. Not only was he apparently unable to preach in Welsh but he did not regard a knowledge of that language as desirable for a man of his standing. Some years later he rebuked his nephew Giraldus fitzPhilip for not showing enough effort to overcome his exclusive knowledge of the primitive tongue (Welsh), and learn decent languages instead, like French or Latin.[4]

Thus the criterion of language did not establish, in Wales, membership in the community. This, on the other hand, is true as far as the legal position is concerned. The Welsh term *alltud* (foreign) signified the want of attachment to the soil[5] but did not have any relation with the language a person spoke. The *alltud* status, thus, did not apply to the Marcher Lords, since they possessed lands in Wales, and were subject to a special law. It would appear that language was not yet a sign of nationality but rather of rank, that it cut across national or ethnical distinctions. On the other hand, it is perhaps true that a generalizing observer like Giraldus would identify as Welsh those who spoke Welsh, and thereby introduce a widely accepted, although not strictly accurate criterion which would embrace the majority of Welshmen, i.e. all people who lived in the geographical region called Wales.

---

[1] *Op.* vi, p. 67: 'astantibus hinc Anglis, inde Gualensibus, ex utroque populo plurimis ad crucem allectis'.

[2] *Op.* vi, p. 177, 127, 188 et passim, cf. M. Hammerström-Justinen, 'Glossae Cambricae apud Giraldum Cambrensem . . .', *Societas Scientiarum Fennica, Commentationes Humanarum Litterarum*, viii, 2, 1935, pp. 1–17.

[3] *Op.* i, p. 223: 'Quid aliud huic garrulo palponi nisi *vulgare* illud suo idiomate respondeam? Ki si veit si feit'.

[4] *Speculum Duorum*, pp. 12, 32, 50–52, 74.

[5] Lloyd, i, p. 293.

In constitutional terms, on the other hand, the question as to which law was applied in a certain area was much more a sign of nationhood. Law is decreed by somebody who does not recognize a superior and who is for this reason 'emperor in his own realm',[1] to borrow a phrase which began to be popular on the continent in the twelfth century. Welsh law remained throughout the thirteenth century the only law current in Welsh Wales and gave the country a remarkable sign of unity and distinctness from England.[2] Giraldus himself mentioned the Welsh laws only in passing, not attaching any special significance to them.

We have to note now some peculiarities which Giraldus found predominant in Wales. They could be summarized under the heading of customs (*mores et consuetudines*). The Welsh liked the stylistic form of alliteration, as did the English.[3] Giraldus gave examples of alliteration in Welsh, English and Latin, noting with amazement that the French did not show the same liking for that form. At first sight this seemed to contradict his belief that both French and Welsh descended from the people of Troy and thereby would share peculiarities in language. Did it not indicate, rather, a relationship between the Welsh and the English? Giraldus regarded the similarity as accidental, he did not think 'that the English and the Welsh, so different and adverse to each other, could designedly have agreed in the usage of this figure'.[4] It would appear that his preconceived idea about the Welsh dictated such a conclusion that he preferred myth to evidence.

There were other features in the Welsh way of life which pointed in a different direction. Decidedly the Welsh way of singing was peculiar to this people. Giraldus did not know anything quite like it, although the music produced by the people in Yorkshire was slightly similar. Giraldus was no musician himself[5] so the terms in which he described their way of singing remain imprecise.[6] Yet it is more important that

---

[1] Cf. the Especulo of Alfonso of Castile, i, 13: the king makes the law because 'por la merced de Dios non habemos mayor sobre nos en el temporal', quoted by Gaines Post, *Studies in Medieval Legal Thought* (Princeton, 1964), p. 483, n. 166.

[2] Equally important for the centralisation of England was the introduction of common law from the time of Henry II onwards. In the March of Wales the law of the March applied.

[3] *Op.* vi, 187: 'verborum ornatu duae nationes, Anglici scilicet et Kambri, in omni sermone exquisito utuntur'.

[4] *Op.* vi, p. 189: 'nec . . . crediderim, quod priores populi duo, tam diversi ab invicem et adversi, in hoc verborum ornatu ex arte conveniant sed potius ex usu longo'.

[5] That Giraldus disliked Welsh music, especially when his nephew spent hours playing the Welsh harp instead of working and studying, he made clear in the *Speculum Duorum*, p. 138.

[6] *Op.* vi, p. 189; cf. Lloyd Hibberd, 'Giraldus Cambrensis and English 'Organ Music', *Journal of the American Musicological Society*, viii, 1955, pp. 208–212; *idem*, 'Giraldus Cambrensis on Welsh Popular Singing', *Essays on Music in Honour of A. T. Davison* (Cambridge, Mass., 1957), pp. 17–23.

he saw the difference from what the English people produced. A certain cultural affinity among the people of Wales, Ireland, and Scotland he detected in the instruments they used.[1] Other features common to the Welsh were their way of dressing,[2] of cutting their hair and of cleaning their teeth.[3]

Giraldus did not go into any details about the economic conditions in Wales. A rural economy was dictated both by the physical character and the political structure of the country. There was little agriculture, but more emphasis on the raising of livestock instead. Welsh society still showed traces of a nomadic civilisation, not living in towns but in primitive huts in the wilderness.[4]

Giraldus was certainly correct in seeing an essential difference between the Welsh and their neighbours. Sometimes his observations led him to this conclusion, while at other times his preconceived ideas were supported by his observations. It is remarkable how he gave explanations for certain phenomena. They were mostly historical and to a large extent incorrect, but at least he thought historically when he was confronted with strange features of the homogeneous Welsh society, albeit his results were occasionally crude.

Up to this point we have followed him giving 'objective information' about the Welsh. There are, however, passages in his work which go further and seem to show how the Welsh regarded themselves in their precarious political situation. The steadily increasing presence of the Normans was a question of concern to Normans and Welsh. To the monarchy in England the Norman domination was not complete nor stable enough and had to be pressed further, while to the Welsh it was a question of self-preservation to reverse the situation. Both sides used a primitive form of propaganda to boost the morale of their fellow-countrymen. In the Norman camp, their presence in Wales had to be justified as being both necessary and desirable, while the Welsh regarded

---

[1] *Op.* v, p. 154–5; J. L. Davies, 'The Contribution of Welshmen to Music', *Cym. Trans.* 1929–30, pp. 38–113, at p. 45–54.

[2] *Op.* vi, p. 184; one could apparently tell from the dress who was a Welshman, cf. *Speculum Duorum*, p. 8, describing a Pembrokeshireman, *ibid.*, pp. 36–8, and an Englishman, *Op.* iii, p. 240: 'per habitus ipsorum et vestes Anglicos esse perpendens'.

[3] *Op.* vi, p. 185.

[4] *Ibid.*, p. 200; in similar remarks about the Irish, Giraldus has been pointed out as a representative of people who believed in the evolution of society which has to go through all the stages of civilisation successively. According to such categories, the Irish (and the Welsh) were certainly more primitive than the Anglo-Normans, cf. Amos Funkenstein *Heilsplan und natürliche Entwicklung* (München, 1965), p. 54.

the Normans in their country as the cause of all evil. The stories with prophetic or propaganda elements from the Welsh works of Giraldus have to be understood in these terms,[1] and for this reason we shall have to deal with them at some length. Prophetic and propaganda tales did perhaps originate spontaneously, but their preservation was due to deliberate acts, fostered by the party which would profit from a spread of them. The tales from Giraldus' works can be classified as either pro-Norman or pro-Welsh and will be grouped separately.

Pro-Norman tales:

When in 1163 Henry II waged war against Rhys ap Gruffydd, on his way through Wales he had to cross a small stream called Nant Pencarn. A prophecy of Merlin Silvester about a ford in this stream said: 'Whenever you shall see a mighty prince with a freckled face make a hostile irruption into the southern part of Britain, should he cross the ford of Pencarn, then you must know that the force of Cambria shall be brought low'. This prophecy was fulfilled on that day, Henry II, strong and freckled, passed the said ford without any difficulties. Welsh onlookers, naturally aware of the implications of this event, 'returned to their homes, alarmed and dismayed at the destruction which seemed to await them'.[2]

A similar story, based on the same motive of folklore, was associated with Henry II's visit to St. David's in 1172 on his return from Ireland. The off-putting manner in which the king had disregarded a petition from a local woman provoked her to call on *lechlavar*, a miraculous stone, to revenge her on the king. For it was commonly believed that Merlin had predicted about this stone which lay as a bridge over a small brook in front of the cathedral of St David's 'that a king from England and conqueror of Ireland should be wounded in that country by a man with a red hand and die upon lechlavar on his return through Menevia'. This curse, spelled out by the woman, the king ordered to be translated. He then approached the stone, hesitated a moment and then crossed it without any harm. He then turned round and spoke the words: 'who will hereafter give credit to the lying Merlin?' At this point the story originally had ended, and in this form Giraldus had included it in his *Conquest of Ireland*, but in the *Itinerary through*

---

[1] The field of prophetic propaganda is naturally much wider than the incidents reported by Giraldus, cf. Griffiths, *Vaticination*, and for a summary review Thomas Parry, *A History of Welsh Literature*, translated by H. I. Bell (Oxford, 1955), pp. 26–33. For French and German parallels the latest review is Dietrich Kurze, 'Nationale Regungen in der spätmittelalterlichen Prophetie', *Historische Zeitschrift*, 202, 1966, pp. 1–23.

[2] *Op*. vi, p. 62f.

Wales he added one further piece. For when the king had spoken, someone is reported to have said: 'you are not the king by whom Ireland is to be conquered or of whom Merlin prophecied'.[1] In this later from the story loses its strong pro-Norman effect.

These two tales favoured the Norman cause in two different ways: in one an alleged prophecy against the Welsh was fulfilled, in the other case a prophecy in favour of the Welsh appeared to be wrong. Apart from the prophetic content, the second tale is worth reading in the original since it shows Giraldus at the height of his qualities as a writer. The two pages are the most brilliant piece of prose in the *Itinerary* or in any other of his topographical works for that matter. It begins with an account of the story to the point where the woman invokes the curse of Merlin: at that crucial moment, when the reader is anxious to learn whether the curse would be fulfilled, Giraldus interrupts to tell the story connected with the stone. It is then beautifully completed with Henry II's proof that Merlin could not be trusted.

Pro-Welsh tales:

In the reign of King Henry I, Gruffydd ap Rhys returned to Wales from the royal court in the company of Miles of Hereford and Payn fitzJohn. When they approached Llangorse Lake, near Brecon, the two Normans, remembering a proverb which said that the birds living around the lake would proclaim the true and rightful Lord of the area, asked Gruffydd to show the truth of this traditional belief. Gruffydd wanted to make sure that he would win, and therefore asked the two Normans to try their luck first; naturally the birds did not react: the Norman lords were marked thereby as usurpers in Wales. Gruffydd, on the other hand, seriously prepared his task, fervently praying to God that he should be proclaimed as the rightful Welsh ruler (*naturalis Walliae princeps*). God granted the request, and the birds acclaimed Gruffydd. When these events were reported to the king, his reaction was: '... it is no matter of such wonder, for although by our strong force we commit acts of violence and wrong against these people, yet they are known to be the rightful heirs of this land'.[2] This story portrays perhaps best the mood of the Welsh at that time. They would regard the predominance of the Normans in their country as against God's law. There is also an impressive difference between the lighthearted and irresponsible behaviour of the two Norman lords and the trust in God by the Welsh prince, a contrast which is, of course, a necessary feature

---

[1] *Ibid.*, pp. 108f.

[2] *Ibid.*, p. 34f.

of such propaganda tale. The Welsh may have felt that the present
age was hard on them, but they were convinced that God was on their
side, and that for this reason justice would be done to them one day.

The other story in favour of the Welsh cause is of a different calibre.
Its propaganda value is betrayed in that it shows how the Normans,
for all their military stength, could be outwitted by the Welsh, as
Goliath was overcome by David. When in his campaign of 1163 Henry II
had captured Rhys ap Gruffydd and taken him to England,[1] he wanted
to obtain information about the strategic position of Dinefwr castle. So he
sent one of his knights to Wales. This man took for his guide the local
dean Guidan and asked him to be shown the easiest and shortest way to
Dinefwr. The rest of the story is best told by Giraldus himself. The
dean purposely chose ' . . . the most difficult and inaccessible paths, and
whenever they passed through woods, the priest, to the general surprise
of all present, fed upon grass, asserting that, in times of need, the inhabitants of that country were accustomed to live upon herbs and roots.
The knights, returning to the king and relating what had happened,
affirmed that the country was uninhabitable, vile and inaccessible, and
only affording food to a beastly nation living like wild animals.'[2] This
story, amusing as it is, testifies the skill of Welsh propaganda. In the
eyes of many contemporary Englishmen Wales was just as the knight
described it, uninhabitable for ordinary people, and thoroughly inaccessible.[3] It would be neither very rewarding nor easy to conquer
this country, and it would be, moreover, completely futile.

Giraldus closed his *Description of Wales* with the oft-quoted prophecy
of the old man of Pencadarn concerning the Welsh destiny. The man said
to Henry II: 'this nation . . . can never be totally subdued through the
wrath of man, unless the wrath of God shall occur. Nor do I think that
any other nation than this of Wales, or any other language, whatever
may hereafter come to pass, shall on the day of severe examination before
the Supreme Judge, answer for this corner of the earth'.[4]

It is at all times difficult to recapture the emotions, hopes or despair
of an entire people, and historical research normally shrinks from the
effort to do so. Yet the stories told by Giraldus, whatever their historical
setting may have been, bring the reader closer to the national emotions
of the time. It is important to know that such stories were told and
preserved, giving evidence of the concern in England and Wales about

---

[1] *Brut*, p. 143–5.

[2] *Op.* vi, p. 81f.

[3] Cf. *infra*, p. 77, 79.

[4] *Op.* vi, p. 227; W. R. Roberts, 'Gerald of Wales on the Survival of Welsh', *Cym. Trans.*, 1923–4,
pp. 46–60.

the prospects of a conquest. They stand as proof of such concern and are as valuable as similar emotions expressed in poetry or in other forms of literature.

Giraldus has been taken as an expert on Wales in the twelfth century, and, indeed, our knowledge of Welsh cultural traditions would be much poorer without his general outlines. This is true also, though to a more limited extent, of the eschatological and prophetic tradition of Wales in the Middle Ages. Prophecies are a common feature in the history of mankind, yet each country has its specific needs and hopes which are expressed in them; their content changes according to the fluctuating political scene. With regard to the Welsh traditions, one theme was predominant for the millennium between the Anglo-Saxon invasion of England and Tudor times: the hope for a saviour who would lead the Welsh from the state of oppression by their neighbours to the powerful position which they once had held in Britain.[1] The hopes of the Welsh focussed on names with the magic sound of military and political strength like Arthur or Cadwaladr; they clung to the prophecies associated with the figure of Merlin. These hopes were expressed in the bardic poetry which claimed to come from the age of Taliesin in the sixth century.

In the eleventh and twelfth centuries, the prophetic literature shows the impact of the fights between the Normans and the Welsh. Poems which had been lyrical in their original form were then enriched with political prophetic stanzas, expressing 'the cruelty and oppression which the Welsh must have suffered' and revealing 'the hopes and desires of the people'.[2] A new element came into the foreground with Geoffrey of Monmouth's *History of the Kings of Britain* (c. 1139). Whereas Arthur had been a hero of Welsh tradition for a long time, Geoffrey's version about him appealed to the Welsh hope for a better future by casting his history into a cyclic pattern, whereby a period of political decline would not foreshadow complete disaster for the people concerned, but would be followed instead by a revival and a regaining of earlier powerful positions.[3]

Giraldus was familiar with some of these traditions. He made reference to Merlin[4] and Arthur, yet on the whole he did so in the manner of an antiquarian, including such material to present a complete picture of a

---

[1] Glanmor Williams, 'Prophecy, Poetry and Politics', and see Proinsias Mac Cana, 'Conservation and Innovation in early Celtic Literature', *Etudes Celtiques*, 13, 1972, p. 73f.

[2] Griffiths, *Vaticination*, p. 87.

[3] R. W. Hanning, *The Vision of History from Gildas to Geoffrey of Monmouth* (New York 1966), p. 140f.

[4] A. O. H. Jarman, *The Legend of Merlin*, An Inaugural Lecture (Cardiff, 1960); also R. Taylor, *The Political Prophecy in England* (New York, 1911), p. 20ff.

strange society. In 1188 he encountered a book which contained prophecies of Merlin written in Welsh. He planned to translate them with the assistance of linguistic experts into Latin,[1] but it seems that he never accomplished this.[2] The prophetic sayings of Merlin in favour of a glorious future for Wales remained unrecorded by him. He also failed fully to recapture the hopes which the Welsh attached to the name of Arthur. Their belief that he would return was to Giraldus nothing but a fable.[3] On the contrary, he recorded with interest how in 1170 the body of Arthur was found at Glastonbury, the body of the hero whose immortality was essential to the Welsh hopes.[4] Giraldus drew a definite line between what he regarded as fables and prophecies. To him the Bible proved that prophecies existed as part of God's work.[5] By restricting himself to this orthodox Christian position, he was unable to record with sympathetic understanding the Welsh secular prophecies of his age.

Giraldus was extremely cautious not to commit himself in his *Description* to express a clear-cut opinion about the Welsh. Not that statements are lacking; it is rather that he praised and condemned them for the same characteristics in different parts of his books,[6] which obscures his own opinion. That he indirectly expressed a view by selecting certain information and suppressing other is obvious, and perhaps it is not insignificant that he should have listed the unpraise-worthy characteristics of the Welsh after the positive ones. Yet the intention of the book did not require such judgement at all.

It is remarkable, to say the least, to find in a book describing a country reflections about the way that country could best be conquered and ruled. These remarks betray an attitude towards the Welsh not unlike the one which Giraldus held towards the Irish,[7] with the significant difference, however, that Giraldus ended the *Descriptio* with a chapter encouraging the Welsh to resist the English conquest.

---

[1] *Op.* v, p. 401f.

[2] Strangely enough, he referred almost invariably to his *Expugnatio Hibernica* as a *vaticinalis historia*, although what he wrote was largely a historical work: 'Vaticinali historiae vaticinorum librum non incompetenter annectens, barbarae linguae tenebras Latini luce sermonis illustravi', *Op.* v, p. 403. It may, however, be suggested that Giraldus presented the conquest of Ireland as an act of God's providence, which in turn may explain why he dedicated the work to Richard, King Henry's son.

[3] *Op.* vi, p. 49: 'fabulosi Britones et eorum cantores fingere solebant'. Of course, Giraldus owed much to Geoffrey of Monmouth in his ideas about the Welsh past.

[4] *Op.* iv, p. 47ff.

[5] *Op.* vi, p. 197.

[6] A comparison of these statements has been made by Thomas Jones, *loc. cit.*, pp. 211–15.

[7] The parallels between the Irish and the Welsh works, as far as this section is concened, have also been pointed out by Thomas Jones, *loc. cit.*, p. 222, n. 84; the fundamental difference, however, is that the Irish work as a whole was devoted to the subject of war.

The advice to the Normans[1] was practical and factual: Wales could be conquered in a year. The enemy should be weakened by sowing discord among the Welsh princes, by a complete blockade from land and sea, followed by frequent and small expeditions which would inflict loss on the Welsh that could not be amended quickly. Giraldus' advice was to imitate the tactics developed by the Marcher Lords who had had experience in fighting the Welsh. He laid bare the greatest problem concerning the conquest of Wales when suggesting that the Marcher Lords be bound by a special oath to the crown. All too often in the past the Marchers had fought purely in their private interest. The advice how to govern the Welsh was nothing but an utopian play: yet when suggesting a mild government at first Giraldus did so because of a prejudice which he held about the Welsh and which sums up one facet of the views he held: 'This people, like all uncivilized peoples, desires to be treated honourably above all things, although they are strangers to the principle of honour; and approve and respect in others that truth which they themselves do not profess'.[2] If a mild government would not work, Giraldus advised to drive all the people out of the country, to settle them somewhere else, and to transform Wales into a colony: 'For there are some who hold the opinion that it would be much better and safer for a good ruler to leave exposed to the wild animals and as a forest a country so wild, so impenetrable . . .'.[3]

After this brutal plan how the Welsh should be treated, the final chapter of the book strikes a different note: it deals with the way how the Welsh should resist the Normans. Giraldus included the chapter in order to underline once again his impartial attitude.[4] He did not make any practicable suggestion to them and bewailed instead what made them weak vis-à-vis the Normans: all their military efforts would be to no avail as long as they were not united among themselves. One prince of high standing for whom all would fight would make them insuperable

---

[1] Book ii, chapters viii–ix.

[2] *Op.* vi, p. 233: 'Gens haec enim, sicut et gens barbara quaevis, quanquam honorem nesciant, honorari tamen super omnia quaerunt; et veritatem, quam in se non habent, in aliis approbant et venerantur'.

[3] This is how the chapter ends in the first version (cf. *Op.* vi, Introd., p. xxxix and printed p. 225, n. 4). The text is not clear as it stands. A slightly better version is found in Corpus Christi College, Cambridge, MS 400 (no foliation here): 'Porro terram [iam, *recte*] tam hispidam et tam inviam tamque colonos domabiles habere nesciam quasi desertam penitus bestiis relinquere atque forestam inde facere, provido principi longe tutius et consultius fore nonulli sunt qui arbitrentur'.

[4] *Op.* vi, p. 226: 'sicut autem ex utraque gente originem duximus, sic aeque pro utraque disputandum ratio dictat'.

as well as inseparable. This strong emotional and ethical statement amounting to the moral superiority of the Welsh over the English and Normans, put into an optimistic framework, follows: 'The English fight for material advantage, the Welsh for freedom, the English mercenaries for money, the Welsh for their country (*pro patria*)'.[1] The memory of their noble ancestry should give them strength to do such things.

The *Descriptio Kambriae* is a book which in its inconsistencies betrays best the author's ambiguous attitude towards Wales. It should be taken in the first place as a source of information about Wales, stemming both from Welsh and English oral traditions and concepts. That it is not clear-cut in its commitment, neither completely pro-English nor entirely pro-Welsh shows that Giraldus had not yet come down on one side or the other. He stood between two nations at a turning point in his life, and he did not know where he belonged. Giraldus never solved this deep emotional conflict.[2] The only *nation* which he ever belonged to was the class of scholars, the *natio* in the medieval academic sense.

Other opinions about the Welsh

In works other than his *Description of Wales*, Giraldus had little to say about the Welsh that was flattering. This was certainly due to his personal experiences in Wales. Master David of Oxford complained that the Welsh were notorious for not keeping their oaths,[3] a statement readily supported by Giraldus. This characteristic, moreover, was not confined to the laity of Wales, but it was also adopted by the priests who lived among them.[4] Not only the Welsh, but all people living in Wales, were inclined to disregard the sanctity of ecclesiastical buildings, and plundered and burned them 'like pagans'.[5] They behaved in fact as barbarous and perverse people would behave. The Irish were just as bad as the Welsh. Giraldus recalled a monk at Strata Florida who proved this point, having inherited from his Irish father and his Welsh mother the worst possible characteristics.[6] The Irish were a 'gens

---

[1] *Ibid.*, cf. E. H. Kantorowicz, *The Kings' Two Bodies* (Princeton, 1957), p. 223 ff.: *pro patria mori*.

[2] The phrase is taken from Wilhelm Berges, *Die Fürstenspiegel des hohen und späten Mittelalters*, p. 150: 'den nie gelösten seelischen Konflikt des Verfassers'.

[3] *Speculum Duorum*, p. 110–112.

[4] *Ibid.*, p. 100: 'per testes falsissimos ac periurios, et tamen presbiteros, quia qualis ibi populus talis et sacerdos'.

[5] *Ibid.*, p. 278: 'more paganico'.

[6] *Op.* iv, p. 161.

spurcissima, gens vitiis involuntissima, gens omnium gentium in fidei rudimentis incultissima',[1] a statement in which Giraldus gave a 'striking example of Norman propaganda'.[2]

That Giraldus' opinion did not differ essentially from views expressed in England will be shown by the following examples. Already in the mid-twelfth century, the anonymous author of the *History of the Priory of Llanthony* had said about the Welsh: 'Gens vicina fera, verbo dei inculta, vaga, inconstans, rapina vivere gaudens, certarum sedium ignara quousque eam rapit tempestas hospitia fertur'.[3] Significantly it would seem that Giraldus knew this work.[4] King Henry II, in a letter to the emperor of Constantinople, had expressed a similar view: 'in a certain part of this island there is a people, called Welsh, so bold and ferocious that, when unarmed, they do not fear to encounter an armed force; ... the beasts of the field over the whole face of the island became gentle, but these desperate men could not be tamed'.[5] In the same style, John of Salisbury wrote about the Welsh to Pope Alexander III: 'Gens enim rudis et idomita, bestiali more vivens, aspernantur verbum vitae, et Christum nominetenus profitentes vita et moribus diffitentur'.[6] The examples could be multiplied while the general tenor would remain the same.[7] We shall however, conclude our survey with two examples of a slightly different nature. Both come from the late thirteenth century.

I take my first example from an exchange of letters in the year 1282, the last year of Welsh political independence, between the Welsh and Archbishop John Pecham of Canterbury.[8] Pecham had offered his services as mediator between the Welsh and King Edward I, in the

---

[1] *Op.* i, p. 68.

[2] F. X. Martin, 'Gerald of Wales, 1146–1223, Norman Reporter on Ireland', *Studies*, 58, 1969, pp. 279–92, at 286.

[3] British Museum, Cotton MS Julius D. x, f. 33ʳ.

[4] Cf. above, p. 63.

[5] *Op.* vi, p. 181f. Henry II's letter has not been preserved, cf. F. Dölger, *Regesten der Kaiserurkunden des Oströmischen Reiches*, 5 vols. (München, Berlin, 1924 ff.), ii, p. 86. nos. 1524, 1548; also A. Vasiliev, 'Manuel Comnenus and Henry Plantagenet', *Byzantinische Zeitschrift*, xxix, 1929–30, p. 233 ff.

[6] *The Letters of John of Salisbury*, ed. W. J. Millor, H. E. Butler, C. N. L. Brooke, I (NMT, 1955), p. 135; cf. John of Salisbury's *Policraticus*, ed. Webb (Oxford, 1909), vol. ii, p. 59f.: 'Hanc tamen uterque et institutae et instituendae praescripsit formulam, ut *vita civilis naturam imitetur* quam optimam vivendi ducem saepissime nominavimus. Alioquin non modo incivilis sed potius *bestialis et bruta rite* vocabitur'.

[7] E.g. Bishop Giles of Hereford writes to Archbishop Stephen Langton: '... inter barbaram Walensium nationem', *Hist. MSS. Com.* Report, Various Collections, I, 1901, p. 251.

[8] For a general account see Decima L. Douie, *Archbishop Pecham* (Oxford, 1952), pp. 235–71. The sources quoted here are taken from *Registrum Epistolarum Fratris Johannis Peckham*, ed. C. T. Martin (RS, London, 1894), ii.

weeks after the Welsh rising. Since the archbishop could hardly be expected to remain impartial in any Anglo-Welsh war, his choice as arbiter was certainly unfortunate to the Welsh cause. The correspondence, however, is of special importance in that here for the first time Welsh national consciousness is expressed on a wide range, in the letters from princes and people alike, and that all of them eventually can be summed up in very basic statements: the Welsh are a nation different from the English, and the difference becomes apparent in the fundamental points of language, laws and customs; the Welsh have a right to defend these essentials and by doing so defend only their inalienable heritage, laws and freedom.[1] It will be noticed that the terms of identification are the same as those employed by Giraldus,[2] but that they are used here, unlike in his descriptive account, as arguments to justify political and military action. Finally, on this occasion we also for the first time are able to see that the lesser nobles felt like their princes and expressed their identity in national terms: 'Also the people of Snowdon say that even if the prince would intend to hand them over to the king, that they had no intention to do homage to a foreigner (*alicui extaneo*) whose language, laws, and customs are completely unknown to them.'[3]

Let us finally look at a short contemporary account of the Welsh wars of 1282 written by an anonymous Englishman.[4] This chronicler began by listing the familiar 'facts' about the Welsh, their belief in the Trojan descent, the diabolical advice which brought them into the country, and a number of vices.[5] That the author was not concerned with merely listing these vices becomes apparent in a question which he put: 'Perhaps it could be asked: what has the English nation done in the past, why have they not annihilated all traces of that repulsive people from the face of the earth?'[6] He answered the question himself: Christ commanded

---

[1] 'lingua, mores, leges ac consuetudines' and 'propria hereditas, jura, libertates', see *Reg. Peckham*, ii, pp. 470, 471.

[2] Pecham writes, *loc. cit.*, p. 475-76. 'Et nos querimus ex cuius vel quorum istud sit iudicio declaratum, nisi per vos, qui in causa propria iudicium usurpatis, et per singulas lustrales periodos pacem infringitis, innocentes jugulatis, incendia faciatis, munitiones regias pro viribus vastatis, ac Howelda, qui talia iniurarum remedia in lege sua, quam vidimus, instituit acutoritate quam ei diabolus delegavit.' It is important to see that Pecham recognized the difference of Welsh law as an essential part of Welsh tradition, even though he referred to it in the most unfavourable terms.

[3] *Ibid.*, p. 471.

[4] Printed *Hist. MSS. Com. Report*, Various Collections, I, 1901, pp. 246–50.

[5] *Ibid.*, p. 248: 'Et breviter bonum facere non credebat nisi dum vacabat ebrietatibus, carnis luxui, homicidiis, incendiis, vel rapinis'.

[6] *Ibid.*, p. 248: 'Set forte queri posset quid fecit natio Anglicana temporibus retroactis, quare gentis istius, quam totiens invenerat repugnantem memoriam non abstulit de hoc mundo?'

that sins should be forgiven seventy times seven times (*Matth.* xviii, 22). Thereby the English king became the executor of divine wrath with the Welsh when he finally defeated them, a theme which had been hinted at in the correspondence of Archbishop Pecham already before the conquest.[1] This English account shows possible implications of the national awareness. Social groups not conforming to the common standard were labelled with a number of characteristics which were generally unfavourable. When King Edward I conquered Wales in 1282, some people felt obliged to find a moral justification for this act. They took the current national prejudices which circulated about the Welsh and, interpreting the Scriptures in a way which would suit their purpose, established a justification which showed them to be executors of the divine will.[2]

Conclusion.

By showing how Giraldus stood towards the Welsh when writing his Welsh books, we have been able to determine more precisely their significance: he wrote them in the first place for an English audience, with the expectation to be rewarded for them in England. While the topic was new, the approach was conventional. Giraldus spoke about the Welsh in terms comparable to those used by other English contemporaries. Yet since he was the only author during the Middle Ages to tackle this subject, he may be held responsible to some extent, if not for the creation, at least for the perpetuation of much prejudice towards Wales. In literature he is the only historian worth speaking of to put current myths about the Welsh on a firmer ground rather than shattering them. That the way in which he regarded the people in whose midst he was born and among whom he spent some years of his life was influenced by personal disappointment which he encountered from the Welsh explains part of such attitude. Likewise, he saw himself as a cosmopolitan figure, feeling at home more in Paris and London than in Brecon, and speaking the language of the educated international

---

[1] *Op. cit.*, p. 477: 'sic certe aliter flagellat Dominus filios quos recipit, et aliter quos decernit ut arbores steriles extirpare'.

[2] This is expressed clearly in the opening section of the Statute of Wales of 1284, trsl. J. Bowen (London, 1908), p. 2, but also elsewhere, see e.g. Welbeck Cartulary, BM MS Harley 3640, f. 18ᵛ: 'Qualiter autore domino terra nostra Wall' nobis ac progenitoribus nostris Anglie regibus a tempore non modico feodali iure subiecta nunc non tantum virtute potencie sed via iusticie tanquam capiti membrum ad dominium nostrum et heredum nostrorum unita est ...', a charter of Edward I of 1285.

community better than Welsh. His education and career give other indications why he was eventually unable to write about the Welsh with a sympathetic understanding approach.

But Giraldus also testifies through his books that there existed at that time a notion of the Welsh nation. The concept of the modern term *nation* is conveyed when he speaks about Wales (*patria*), the descent (*natio*) of the people, their languages, laws and customs. The Welsh thus were perceived, and understood themselves, at the close of the twelfth century at the latest, as a social group which, living in a clearly defined area, claimed a particularly noble descent, were proud of it, and tried to preserve their identity against encroachment from England. Further justification for their efforts was not necessary, the consciousness of their distinctness demanded in itself a predetermined political behaviour. The realisation that they were different from others, that they shared essential things demanded that they should maintain this identity.

The Welsh lost their political independence in the last quarter of the thirteenth century. The conquest of 1282 put the final seal under a policy which had been pursued by the English monarchy for the past two centuries. Wales was gradually conquered. Some parts, like the far South West, fell quickly and permanently under English control; other parts, especially Central and North East Wales, were battle-fields for a century and changed hands more than once; while the fate of the North West, the principality of Gwynedd, was decided in the battle which had Llywelyn ap Gruffydd, Prince of Wales, among its victims. It is possible that the gradual conquest of Wales heightened the national consciousness of the Welsh exceptionally early. Perhaps they were made to realise earlier than other people that they belonged together, and that they would lose something essential if they fell under the rule of foreigners. But it is also possible that the notion of the nation in the Middle Ages can be grasped easier in Wales than elsewhere due to the full information in the works of Giraldus.

Whether the case of Wales offers exceptionally early evidence for the notion of the nation will have to be decided by future comparable studies. Certainly it offers a wealth of material and points out a number of terms which will repay future attention.

III. THE FIGHT FOR A WELSH ARCHBISHOPRIC.

In his two books about Wales, which Giraldus completed by 1194, he appears as a man who knew the Welsh but did not feel part of their tradition. Five years later, a fundamental change had taken place. In 1199 he was elected to the bishopric of St. David's, against the strict commands of the king and the archbishop of Canterbury. The archbishop would not accept as a candidate for the most prominent bishopric in Wales a man who openly declared his intention of making Wales an archiepiscopal province in its own right, independent of Canterbury, a plan which, had it been achieved, would have been a great encouragement to those people in Wales who wanted to gain greater political autonomy. For Giraldus' election two conditions had to be fulfilled: his personal acceptance of the bishopric and the support of the electing body in the cathedral. Both aspects will be analysed.

One has to assume that Giraldus changed his attitude towards Wales and the Welsh profoundly within a few years, although even then he did not achieve a lasting attachment, for after suffering the complete defeat of his ambitions in Wales he modified his attitude once again and was, in the last years of his life, critical of the Welsh and of the English people alike. The sharp turn in the life of Giraldus before his election has not, in the past, been emphasised, for two reasons: firstly, it was not realised how critical Giraldus had been of the Welsh in the earlier part of his life, and secondly, Giraldus himself mentions hardly anything about the motives behind his change of attitude. These years were a time of contemplation for him, apparently fully dedicated to study and learning. This is the impression which he wanted to convey when he later wrote about his career. Not more than two pages in his autobiography are devoted to the five years before his election to St. David's,[1] and these pages do not give the slightest indication of his inner development. As is often the case with autobiographies and memoirs: crucial and controversial aspects were glossed over; but while direct evidence is lacking, we can find some indirect support of our assessment. It comes from the correspondence which Giraldus later assembled in his *Symbolum Electorum,* and to some extent from his literary works, including the *Life of St. David,*[2] and more clearly the *Life of Geoffrey, Archbishop of York.*

---

[1] *Op.* i, pp. 89, 93–94.

[2] Cf. M. Richter, *Welsh History Review,* iv, 1968–69, pp. 381–386.

Giraldus' development into a 'Cambrensis'.

Giraldus continued in his position of a royal clerk after the death of Henry II, which he witnessed personally.[1] As often happened, the death of an English king was the signal for rebellion and revolt in Wales:[2] on that occasion, Giraldus was sent there as a royal emissary at the instigation of Archbishop Baldwin. These missions were on the whole not successful. For whereas Henry II had come to terms with the Lord Rhys,[3] the leader of the Welsh rulers, his son Richard who showed little interest in Welsh affairs[4] risked an open affront with the Welsh prince. He was more concerned about the crusade on which he left in 1190: Giraldus, who had taken the cross at the beginning of the tour of Wales in 1188 in order to give an example to others to do the same, obtained a dispensation and never went to the Holy Land.[5]

When sending Giraldus to Wales,[6] the crown perhaps calculated that he might be useful because he was related to the Lord Rhys. If this was the calculation it proved to be wrong. One of Giraldus' later companions on such embassies, a Cistercian monk of Biddlesden (Bucks.), William Wibert,[7] denounced him later by spreading the rumour that Giraldus was a traitor of the English monarchy and had in fact encouraged the Welsh rebellion.[8] It must have been easy for Wibert to bring Giraldus into discredit because the missions were not successful: success is generally the best proof of loyalty.

The information which Giraldus has preserved about his dispute with Wibert is perhaps typical of those petty feuds which must have been frequent at the court among the clerks whose office implied the possibilities of either a substantial advancement in the administration

---

[1] *Op.* i, p. 80 ff., *Op.* viii, p. 304ff.

[2] Lloyd, ii, p. 573.

[3] Lloyd, *The Story of Ceredigion* (Cardiff, 1937), pp. 52–79.

[4] As late as 1197, Giraldus said of King Richard: 'dominus rex qui situm Walliae et statum non novit . . .', *Op.* i, p. 321.

[5] *Op.* vi, p. 14 and *Op.* i, pp. 84–85.

[6] Evidence for his missions is found in the Pipe Rolls, cf. *The Great Roll of the Pipe for the fifth year of the Reign of King Richard the First*, ed. D. M. Stenton (London, 1927), p. xiii–xiv.

[7] Wibert had appeared at the royal court *c.* 1192/93 ('anno quo dominus rex in Alemannia detentus fuerat', *Op.* i, p. 295).

[8] *Symbol. Elect.*, Ep. i, *Op.* i, pp. 203–13, esp. pp. 204–5. Giraldus wrote this letter presumably after he had left the royal service (*c.* 1194). In 1196, he was reconciled to Wibert who then became abbot of Biddlesden; their hostilities broke out again, and in 1198 Wibert was deposed because of immorality, cf. *Op.* i, Ep. xxviii, p. 294, written in autumn of 1198. On Wibert cf. Humphreys, *Some Types . . .*, p. 14ff, and D. Knowles, 'Some Enemies of Gerald of Wales', *Studia Monastica*, i, 1959, pp. 137–141.

or a complete fall into disgrace.[1] Giraldus later complained bitterly about Wibert's accusations: 'At the height of his malice he finally charged me with the crime of high treason. ... For he maintained that when the Welsh besieged that castle (? Swansea [2]) they did so at my instigation; and whatever evil had taken place in the March, this was allegedly done on my advice'.[3] Giraldus admitted indirectly that such an impression could have been conveyed to somebody who was not familiar with the language and customs of the country,[4] but he abhorred the idea of such accusations. Indeed, there is no reason to doubt his loyalty towards England at that time. Giraldus later revenged himself on Wibert by making known a scheme which Wibert and Bishop Peter had elaborated but which could not be executed because he himself intervened: that Bishop Peter should obtain his own translation to the see of Worcester, and Wibert should succeed him as bishop of St. David's.[5]

As far as direct evidence goes, it was only the slander spread by Wibert which brought Giraldus into discredit at the court, for although it is difficult to believe that Giraldus was ever popular there with everyone,[6] he then enjoyed the confidence and trust of Prince John, the Lord of Glamorgan, who offered him the see of Llandaff. Giraldus refused this, as he had earlier refused to become bishop of Bangor.[7] But there are some indications at least for the assumption that Wibert's intriguing was not the only reason for Giraldus' retirement. For Giraldus was inconsistent in at first following the royal court almost to the point of self-denial[8] and shortly afterwards retiring into private life and finding great words for the career of a scholar as being the only true path to salvation, while at the same time scorning and despising people who followed worldly fame at the court. Behind such changes lie unfulfilled ambitions and disappointment, due perhaps to unwise behaviour.

---

[1] On the subject of the royal clerks there is the excellent article by R. W. Southern, 'The Place of Henry I in English History', *Proc. Brit. Acad.*, 48, 1962, pp. 127–169.

[2] Lloyd, ii, p. 576.

[3] *Op.* i, p. 296.

[4] 'Tantum etenim mutus et elinguis a latere religionem habitu praeferens stabat, nec linguae notitiam habens, nec patriae vel gentis mores agnoscens', *ibid.*, on Wibert also *Op.* iv, pp. 156–61.

[5] *Op.* i. p. 300. Worcester was vacant in the latter half of 1193, cf. F. M. Powicke and E. B. Fryde, edd., *Handbook of British Chronology*. Second edition (London, 1961), p. 260.

[6] He claimed that 'mea tunc potestas in curia non minima (fuit)', *Op.* i, p. 204.

[7] *Op.* i, pp. 85, 87, 139.

[8] Cf. *Op.* i, pp. 245–47, where Giraldus prostrates himself before King Richard; typical phrases are: 'vir inclite, vir insignis, vir virorum perpaucorum . . .', 'non desunt artes, set artium honores . . .'.

Not very long after Giraldus had left the royal service, he completed a treatise different from anything which he had previously written, the *Life of Geoffrey, Archbishop of York*.[1] In this book, Giraldus wrote for the first time on contemporary political events in England. He praised in a rather unqualified and enthusiastic manner the deeds and character of Geoffrey Plantagenet, while this man was still living. This approach could not have endeared him to the royal court, where the eldest living though illegitimate son of Henry II was regarded with considerable suspicion. To take Geoffrey of York as the hero of a treatise amounted to the condemnation of those people who opposed him vigorously, and most of them were the trusted servants of King Richard. In praising Geoffrey, Giraldus condemned others in a very outspoken manner, in particular two men: the justiciar William of Longchamp and the bishop of Salisbury and future archbishop of Canterbury, Hubert Walter. It is true that William of Longchamp was forced to hand over the justiciarship as a consequence of the constitutional crisis of 1191, but he was able to regain the confidence of the king later. The other person under attack by Giraldus, Hubert Walter, was able to retain Richard's confidence all the time, and with his election to the archbishopric of Canterbury he rose to a position in England second only to that of the king. Thus whatever the justification for Giraldus' attack of these two men may have been, by his *Life of Geoffrey* and the opinions expressed therein Giraldus had drawn a clear line between himself and the royal administration. Perhaps it was unjust to write in such a way, but it was certainly unwise. Giraldus made enemies of two of the most important men in the kingdom while any support or sympathy from Geoffrey Plantagenet would be of little advantage.[2]

The Prologue to the *Life of Geoffrey* starts with reflections on the precarious condition of man and the lack of rewards for those who deserve them most.[3] Such statements are commonplace, but in this context they reflect accurately Giraldus' own frame of mind. He had retired

---

[1] As in most other cases, there is no precise indication as to when Giraldus wrote the treatise. In the *Introitus secundus* he writes: 'Vitae igitur anteactae, et quasi lustra per octo ab aetatis humanae perfectionis iam dimidiatae ...', *Op*. iv, p. 361f, i.e. forty years had passed, and this would bring the date to *c*. 1186 which is far too early. There is, in addition, an indication that Giraldus stayed at the royal court after Hubert Walter had become justiciar, i.e. between *c*. 1193 and 1195 (*Op*. i, p. 295). The *Life of Geoffrey* would hardly have been written before 1195. In his *Symbolum Electorum*, compiled *c*. 1198, Giraldus referred to this work as apocryphal, *Op*. i, p. 394, nos. xv–xvii.

[2] D. L. Douie, *Archbishop Geoffrey Plantagenet and the Chapter of York*, St. Anthony's Hall Publications No. 18 (York, 1960).

[3] *Op*. iv, p. 357.

from court perhaps in disgrace, certainly disappointed by lack of advancement. But what had he expected?

At a much later stage in his life he admitted his expectation: he had kindled the hope for promotion to a bishopric in England.[1] His subsequent election to the bishopric of St. David's and the ensuing great dispute in Rome about his election were perhaps the reason why he remained so quiet about his original ambitions. This reticence is not surprising, for here we touch the turning point of his life, a change which he tried to conceal. As long as he was a royal clerk, he cherished the hope for promotion to an English bishopric, a hope which was not unreasonable in view of the fact that the king in most cases filled the bishoprics with his trusted servants. Giraldus at that time rejected the idea of becoming bishop in Wales both because the Welsh sees were poor and because he disliked the barbarous nature of the Welsh people.[2] Similar reasons probably induced him to refuse several bishoprics in Wales and Ireland at that time[3] if indeed the offers had been serious. On the other hand, we do not know whether Giraldus was ever offered a bishopric in England. Thus, while it is impossible to fathom completely Giraldus' intellectual development at that time, it seems safe to say that initially he had hoped to make his career in England, rising from the position of a royal clerk to that of a bishop in England; that for some very strong reasons, the details of which can no longer be understood, he fell into complete disgrace in England so that his earlier ambitions seemed to have become unrealistic, whereupon he decided instead to become a bishop in Wales.

Little is known about the activities of Giraldus immediately after his retirement from court.[4] In 1196 he was reconciled to William

---

[1] '... iuxta numerum sedium cathedralium Anglie, ubi spes eius tota tunc fuerat', 'tam ipse quam amici eius, quibus hoc revelaverat, a spe promocionis eius in Anglia decidentes ... parum inde gavisi, quinimmo grandiora sibi speraverant, contristati se converterunt'. *De Invect.* (ed. Davies), vi, 11, p. 213.

[2] *Ibid.*, 'tam propter terre paupertatem quam eciam gentis enormitatem'. Although Giraldus told his former plans only in form of a vision, there is no reason to doubt its truth. *De Invect.* has 30 visions all of which give a good insight into the mind of Giraldus, in a similar way as do the 33 *laudabilia* told in *De Invect.*, v. On the topic in general see J. C. Holdsworth, 'Visions and Visionaries in the Middle Ages', *History*, 48, 1963, pp. 141–153, and E. R. Curtius, *Europäische Literatur und Lateinisches Mittelalter* (Bern, München, 1967), Sixth edition.

[3] *De Invect.*, v, 15, p. 195: 'omnes enim tam Wallie quam Hybernie oblatos honores ... recusavit, ... tum quia pauperes erant et inter barbaros ... Alio autem et ultimo presertim oblatos, quia numquam ab Hibernicis vel etiam Walensicis alienigena quivis, quantumlibet bonus et ydoneus, nisi per publice potestatis violentiam eligeretur'.

[4] He was apparently in West Wales when King Richard returned from the Third Crusade, cf. *Op.* i, p. 242: 'Adventus vestri fama in extremis iam Walliarum finibus audita ...'.

Wibert[1] and then settled at Lincoln to continue his studies, since the Anglo-French war prevented him from going to Paris to resume his studies there.[2] Perhaps he had spent two years before at Hereford where he was a canon and prebendary.[3] Some of the letters preserved in the *Symbolum Electorum* give evidence of his friendship with its bishop, William de Vere, and some of the canons, notably Ralph Foliot,[4] William Foliot, the precentor, Hugh the dean and a Master Albinus. Other letters point to the same geographical area, the counties bordering on Wales; Giraldus kept contact with Adam, abbot of Evesham, and the prior of Malvern (Worcs.).[5] Of a more lasting nature was his friendship with the archdeacon of Oxford, Walter Map.[6]

More problematical was his relationship at that time with the personnel of his home diocese, St. David's. This aspect must be treated at some length, because it is imperative to assess as far as possible the influence he had there before he was elected to the bishopric in 1199. The assessment must be limited to the available material, those letters which Giraldus collected after his final defeat in 1203 in the *Symbolum Electorum*. It would be a mistake, I think, to take this correspondence as being fully representative of the relationship. What we see there is, in fact, one factor only which would naturally produce letters: the controversies between Giraldus on the one hand, and the chapter of St. David's and the bishop on the other. For if these letters of bitterness and resentment were representative of the relationship generally, it would be inconceivable that Giraldus could ever have been freely elected in 1199. Granted

---

[1] *Op.* i, p. 294 'postquam enim apud Oxoniam in curia vestra transacto biennio ... Cantuarie concordati fuimus', Giraldus later wrote to Archbishop Hubert Walter.

[2] *Op.* i, p. 93f.

[3] On Giraldus and Hereford cf. Humphreys, *op. cit.*, p. 139–166. In 1202 Giraldus wrote: 'Destitutus sum redditibus meis, praebenda scilicet Herefordiae, et ecclesia de Chestretune', *Op.* iii, p. 237. See also *Op.* i, p. 270: 'post discessum meum' and 'capitulo nostro Herefordensi'.

[4] Ralph Foliot died in 1198, cf. the letter of condolence which Giraldus wrote to his brother William, precentor of Hereford, *Op.* i, pp. 268–271, and *ibid.*, pp. 334–335. This canon must not be confused with Ralph Folet who occurred at Hereford *c.* 1208, together with William Foliot, *Speculum Duorum*, pp. 160–67.

[5] *Op.* i, pp. 229–238. Letter x apparently dates from 1197–8: 'undique nos arma circumsonant, undique curae temporales exigant, et tamen solus in patria inter tot tam temporis quam patriae contumelias Minervam colo', *ibid.*, p. 235.

[6] Giraldus asked Walter Map to abandon childish preoccupations and to turn to more mature studies, notably that of theology, *Op.* i, 271–89. He never succeeded in getting a light touch in his writings the way Map did, and his dignity often rings of pomposity: 'Locum ergo statue, tempus praefige quo vel sero seriis intendere et sobrie consenescere satagamus, quo sacris apicibus et salutiferae scientiae saltem dies extremos applicemus', p. 289. Map's reply Giraldus unfortunately did not transcribe.

that his election was preceded by substantial negotiations, there must still have been a stock of trust between him and part of the chapter.[1] Giraldus, after all, in his function as archdeacon, was a canon and prebendary of St. David's. Although he did not work constantly in his archdeaconry, he still showed a considerable sense of responsibility in appointing people who would do the work for him. In addition, for a few years after 1179, he had run the administration of the whole diocese for the absent bishop, an activity which may not perhaps have made him popular there, but at least would have left an imprint on the administrative staff. And finally Giraldus' family, represented by his brother Philip, the lord of Manorbier, was one of the prominent families of the area which influenced the political scene to some extent. So when Giraldus abandoned his position as a royal clerk and turned to another occupation, he would find the ground not completely unprepared should he wish to return to Wales and try to obtain the bishopric of St. Davids'. When this precisely happened is impossible to say. It must suffice to have established that in the mid-nineties he had to abandon his long-cherished hopes for an English bishopric and that he then turned to Wales.

Giraldus' relationship with the bishop of St. David's, Peter de Leia, seems to have been permanently strained. This is not surprising, since Peter had been the successful rival of Giraldus in the election of 1176. Yet both parties tried repeatedly to come to a working solution which was feasible since the bishop was satisfied with his dignity alone; he showed no special interest in his Welsh diocese and seems to have spent considerable time outside his bishopric. Coming from Wenloc Priory, he always preferred to live in England, and he probably died at Tewkesbury, where he resided for some years.[2] He seems to have spent the greater time of his episcopate outside his diocese, but this, although Giraldus repeatedly complained about it, was not unusual for any bishop of Wales at that time.[3] While it would be going too far to suggest that the English king 'endeavoured to keep them (i.e. the Welsh bishops) in England as much as possible',[4] it is nevertheless true that the Welsh bishops at that time were chosen for their lack of interest in particularly Welsh problems of their diocese rather than for their spiritual qualifications. As such they were an easy target for anybody who wanted to criticise them. Such criticism, which would have some justification in principle,

---

[1] In a letter to Bishop Peter he refers to his relationship with the canons; *Op.* i, p. 228: 'Sed tantum sociorum et capituli iniurias quasi proprias reputans, ab illis quibus fraterna societate iunctus fueram me necessitatis tempore non seiunxi . . .'.

[2] *Op.* i, p. 322. *The Annals of Tewkesbury* are the only source to give the exact date of his death, 10 July, 1198, *Ann. Mon.* i, p. 56.

[3] *Op.* iii, p. 145, 161, 351.

[4] Humphreys, *op. cit.*, p. 254f.

may have served as a growing bond of common interest between Giraldus and the more involved dignitaries in the cathedral chapter of St. David's.

Yet Giraldus did not complain about the bishop's absence from the diocese as long as he himself was in charge of the administration, i.e., in the years 1179–83. A bishop would appoint in his absence one or several people to act on his behalf, and at that time it was not unusual that an archdeacon was chosen. Only later it became apparent that such regulations often tempted the archdeacons to overstep the limits of their authority. As long as Giraldus combined in himself the two functions of the archdeacon and the bishop's representative, everything was satisfactory to him. But in 1183 he was replaced as the representative of the bishop by three other people, apparently Englishmen, and in the following years the disputes between Giraldus and the men of the bishop became more frequent. That all parties were aware of the implications which this new arrangement involved is attested by a sentence which Giraldus quotes as a word of one of the bishop's representatives, the former monk Galterius: 'Sire, ne creez vus unques un sul de cel pais ne clerc ne lai. Ne ne suffrez vus unques danger del arcediakene Girold. Sujurnez en Engletere tant cum vus plerra. Entre mei e Joceaume le Deen guvernerum leuesche haltement e bien'.[1] It appears that in this particular case Giraldus had some basic justification for his malcontent, for he was able later to depose one the representatives, the rural dean Joscelin, at a meeting of the rural chapter at Keri.[2] This was perhaps only the outward appearance of the dispute. What Giraldus challenged in fact was the hierarchical tradition of the ecclesiastical administration wherever it worked against him which is indicated when he quotes to the bishop's representatives the following words: 'Si ergo ignorant quam proportionale quam connexum, immo ut expressius dicam, quam reciprocum sit inter fideles vinculum et fidelitatis debitum, legant epistolam Phileberti episcopi . . .[3]

Giraldus appears to have taken his discontent with the bishop's actions a stage beyond confining himself to a personal dispute with the bishop. He wrote a long letter of complaint to the bishop of Hereford,[4] a letter which unfortunately has not survived. Bishop Peter of St. David's later complained to Giraldus about this letter, and Giraldus' reply to that

---

[1] *Op.* i, p. 223f.

[2] *Op.* i, p. 228 in a letter to Bishop Peter: 'Jocelinus enim tunc decanus vester', and p. 325 in a letter to the chapter of St. David's: 'Unde . . . quid Jocelino decano, immo Diaboli filio, quem ibi in perpetuum deposuimus, in capitulo apud Karreu actum est, satis auditum fuit'.

[3] *Op.* i, p. 219.

[4] *Op.* i, p. 307: 'Iniurias mihi a domino Menevensi episcopo praeter merita nuper irrogatas, per magistrum Robertum in scedula conscriptas, destinando vestrae discretioni significare curavi'.

letter had been preserved.[1] Giraldus expressed his willingness to withdraw any statements which could be proved to be untenable, but what the bishop regarded as a libel may have been an enumeration of the duties which the episcopal office involved but which he failed to meet, and it might have been easy to detect behind such a theoretical account the man who was thereby accused.[2]

It is possible in one instance to follow a little closer a dispute between the bishop of St. David's, the cathedral chapter, and Giraldus. In April 1197, Bishop Peter had tried to arrange a peaceful settlement between the Lord Rhys and the Crown, in which he failed. At night Peter was captured by the sons of the Lord Rhys and was freed only on the following day by the men of William of Braose. Thereupon Peter called a synod where the Lord Rhys and his sons were excommunicated, and the whole area was put under the Interdict.[3] Rhys died shortly afterwards, on 28 April[4] while still excommunicated. Giraldus had been present at the synod. As it turned out later, the bishop spread the rumour that it was Giraldus who had given the advice to excommunicate the prince, whereupon his sons took their revenge on him by plundering his archidiaconal prebend, the church of Mathry. Giraldus summed up the charges against the bishop in the following way: 'Thus he persecuted me doubly, while at the same time feigning friendship in his appearance and words. To the French he denounced me as a Welshman and as an enemy of the realm, to the Welsh as a Frenchman and therefore hostile to them on principle'.[5] But Peter went further. Having excommunicated Rhys, he went over to France in order to report to the king. On his return he withdrew part of Giraldus' income, keeping some for his own use, while other parts he conferred upon Osbert, the new archdeacon of Carmarthen who had been appointed in the spring of 1197. Giraldus reacted with an appeal to Rome, accusing the bishop of abuse of his competence.[6] Once again his prejudice against Wales

---

[1] *Op.* i, pp. 227–28.

[2] The 'libel' may have been of a similar kind as the letter which Giraldus was to write more than ten years later to the next bishop of St. David's, Geoffrey de Henlaw, *Speculum Duorum*, pp. 208–41, which repeats, over long passages, charges laid against Peter de Leia, in the letter preserved in *Op.* i, pp. 218–26.

[3] *Annals of Winchester*, s.a. 1197, *Ann. Mon.*, ii, p. 66.

[4] Cronica de Wallia, p. 5: 'iiij Kalendas Maij Resus Griffini filius Suthwallie princeps, verum totius Walliae capud insuperabile, fato occubuit inportuno'.

[5] *Op.* i, p. 332.

[6] There was apparently no change of the situation by the time Giraldus wrote Letter xxxi: 'sed cessante iam excommunicationis et interdicti sententia quandiu terra penes ipsum manebit satis videbitis', *Op.* i, p. 321. This letter was apparently written after the death of Pope Celestine III (8 Jan. 1198), for it reads: 'non solum iudices sed dominum papam contemptui ducens. Unde forte si vixerit rumores adhuc audire poterit', p. 311.

and the Welsh comes out in this letter: 'contra Menevensem, episcopum scilicet vere barbarum, barbare regionis antistem, et barbaris moribus more solito utentem . . .'.[1] His appeal was answered favourably, but it seems that the bishop did not immediately take notice of this decision. It is, of course, impossible to say in how far this case was representative of the relationship between the bishop and Giraldus, but it can be seen that Giraldus voiced some basic resentment, and a more conscientious pastor might perhaps have tried to avoid such points of conflict with his subordinates.

The chapter of St. David's appears to have sided with Giraldus in 1197. In the spring of that year he reminded the canons in a letter[2] of an oath they had given pledging to support a just cause. But a year later he had to realise that the majority of them now supported the bishop. So he wrote again to St. David's, pointing out that it was not so much his personal losses which grieved him but rather the fact that the bishop's behaviour would adversely affect all Welsh people.[3] Yet one has the impression that his appeal to Welsh solidarity against the foreigner was unsuccessful. Giraldus stayed at Lincoln, and Peter acted through his representatives in the diocese, and thus there was little point in reminding the canons that a concerted action in the preceding year had forced the bishop to give way.[4] The letter was Giraldus' last attempt to draw the chapter of St. David's over to his side. It started by listing the church property which the bishop had alienated,[5] continued by pointing to several instances in which the bishop had proved himself untrustworthy, and in this way demonstrated that Peter was unworthy to hold the office.[6] There is a further letter to the chapter which, however, does

---

[1] *Op.* i, p. 308. The letter of complaint to Rome has not survived, but perhaps we have the accompanying letter in Letter No. xxx, p. 308f. There Giraldus mentions that three years earlier he had sent the *Topography of Ireland* and the *Description of Wales* to Rome.

[2] Cf. 'Petro de Leche, archidiacono Wigorniensi, nuper defuncto'. This was in 1197, for Letter No. xxiii reads 'Petro anno preterito Wigorniensi, nunc vero vir praeclarus, . . . Radulfus Foliot, Herefordensis archilevita decessit', *Op.* i, p. 271. On Ralph Foliot also Morey & Brooke, *Gilbert Foliot*, pp. 270, 284, and *Cambridge Hist. Journal*, viii, pp. 15–16.

[3] *Op.* i, p. 314: 'Sed si homo alienigena, qui nec unum habet cognatum in Wallia tota, generosis et probis patriae viris sua per violentiam auferre presumit, hoc equidem dedecus non in personam tantum unius, sed *in genus totum* redundat'.

[4] *Ibid.*, p. 329: 'Quicquid autem super his fecerit, quia credo quod parum faciet nisi coactus, si vos tantum unanimes esse et sicut jurati sumus stare simul viderit, faceret certe quicquid facere de iure deberet; sicut in ultima synodo quando simul stetimus fecit'.

[5] *Ibid.*, p. 309f.

[6] Sarcastically, Giraldus quoted from the canonical demands on a bishop: '. . . sobrium, prudentem, ornatum moribus pudicis, doctorem, domui sue bene prepositum, non cupidum, non negligentem', *Op.* i, p. 322. Such demands are contained also in pontificals, cf. the 'Mainzer Pontificale', ed. C. Vogel and R. Elze, *Le Pontifical Romano-Germanique*, I, p. 194f.; cf. also M. Richter, 'Professions', p. 200f.

not touch on this subject, and it is unknown whether the dispute was ever settled. With the death of the bishop in July, 1198, Giraldus was faced with more important problems and greater issues.[1]

The letters which have been analysed would hardly justify the assumption that Giraldus' relationship with the canons of St. David's before the death of Bishop Peter was based on solid agreement. However, it would be unrealistic to assume that there was no agreement whatsoever between them. It would appear that Giraldus collected in the *Symbolum Electorum* in the first place the correspondence which was concerned with controversies, where he could appear as the righteous and conscientious cleric who attempted to defend his colleagues against unjust action from the bishop. Such letters had the additional advantage that Giraldus could display in them his literary still as well as his knowledge especially on legal issues. When attempting to win the trust of the chapter, Giraldus tried to widen the antagonism between the Welsh members of the cathedral chapter and the English bishop who was concerned mainly with his own profits and therefore could not easily make friends with his subordinates.[2] He may have reckoned on the growing drive for Welsh independence which can be discerned in the years after the death of Henry II. He must have succeeded, at least in part, to win the confidence of the chapter, and he was able to profit in this from his own family connections in the area as well as from the years in which he had been actively involved in the administration of the diocese or of the archdeaconry.

Although it is impossible to trace his development in these years with any accuracy, it is clear that Giraldus had changed his attitude towards Wales in the decade which followed his tour of the country in

---

[1] The chronology of the above mentioned letters is based on the following considerations: a reconciliation between Giraldus, Bishop Peter, and the chapter of St. David's, which has to be assumed to have occurred before G. entered the royal service (*Op.* i, p. 55f.), Dr. J. C. Davies dated 1197/98, *Ep. Acts*, i, p. 300. There is, however, a passage in the text which raises some difficulties: 'apud Meneviam in synodo, quam tenuit ultimam episcopus Petrus circa Pentecosten', *ibid.*, p. 55 [on the diocesan synods in the 12th century C. R. Cheney, *From Becket to Langton* (Manchester, 1956), p. 142ff.]. It would be difficult to relate this to the synod in 1197 which was held before the death of the Lord Rhys (28 April) while Whitsun in that year was celebrated 25 May. If we do not have to deal just with a mistake on the part of Giraldus, the text could refer to the synod of 1183 as the last one celebrated by Bishop Peter at St. David's. Miss Humphreys dates Letter No. xxxi, which is the most interesting one of the *Symbolum Electorum*, *c.* 1196, *op. cit.*, 238, without, however, referring to the excommunication of the Lord Rhys. The following dates are suggested here: Letter No. xxix: 1197; xxx: 1197; xxxi: (? January) 1198; xxxii: spring 1198.

[2] *Op.* i, p. 226: 'paucos in patria amicos inveniat, contra hostes ecclesiae non improvide prolem suscitat, ut suis saltem confidere possit, qui minime confidere meruit alienis'.

the entourage of Baldwin of Canterbury, and had lost part of his anti-Welsh bias. Such a modification of his attitude found its way, if only in minor points, into a revision of his *Itinerary through Wales*.[1] The two instances in which such a revision was introduced betray that Giraldus at that time had a deeper understanding and showed more sympathy for the needs of Wales and for the questionable blessings which the Norman advance brought to this country.

As far as evidence goes, Giraldus did not become, at that stage, a fervent supporter of the Welsh cause, but he was at least thoroughly dissatisfied with the way things went for him in England. He had made enemies in England who were such important men that any future advancement for him was virtually impossible. What England offered at that time, and what Wales could not offer to the same extent, were the facilities to study and an intellectual climate which was an indispensible precondition if Giraldus really wanted to become then what he claimed to be: a scholar and theologian, a man who was concerned with greater things and more vital issues than petty everyday ambitions.

Bishop–elect of St. David's.

The years 1199–1203 were the most eventful time in Giraldus' life. Elected bishop of St. David's in opposition to commands from England, he attempted to become archbishop and primate of Wales. During these years he turned into a fervent Welshman and became the mouthpiece of the grievances which the Welsh laid against England, accusing the representatives of the English church and monarchy of abusing their power towards Wales. This new image of Giraldus found its permanent form in the books which he wrote about these years and which are still responsible for much of the opinion held about him in general. Two books are exclusively dedicated to this period: the *De Invectionibus* which Giraldus begun at Rome at the request of the pope and completed later.[2] This book is a collection of documents of his suit as well as that of Bishop Bernard's of St. David's, of commentaries and reflections, and the fullest source-book for his dispute which exists. Of a different nature is the book which was written only towards the end of his life, the *De Iure et Statu Menevensis Ecclesiae*. The available material there had been transformed into a fictitious discussion between two people who argue all aspects of the dispute but in fact eulogize Giraldus all the time. It is the commentary of Giraldus on his suit, of a lesser value as far as historical documentation is concerned, but a

---

[1] Cf. *Op.* vi, pp. 15–16, 105, also Thomas Jones, *NLWJ*, vi, 1949–50, p. 144f.

[2] It was not completed before 1216, cf. *Speculum Duorum*, Introduction.

good psychological study of the author. Finally, the greatest part of Giraldus' autobiographical work, the *De Rebus a se Gestis*, is devoted to this time. The dispute stands so much in the foreground of the work, covering the whole of the (now lost)[1] Book Three with 238 chapters, that it is not quite correct to call the work an autobiography; the chapters on his youth are short and basically uninformative, and the years after 1203, Giraldus' defeat, are left out altogether. If one would classify the three works, they could justly be called the chronological (*De Rebus*), systematic (*De Invectionibus*) and psychological (*De Iure*) treatment of his election dispute.

Giraldus is the only historian to deal at great length with the controversy, and therefore his accounts have to be evalued very carefully: he seems to be reliable as far as documents are concerned, for in a few instances it is possible to check Giraldus' version against independent sources, notably the register of Pope Innocent III. His personal comments, which form the second element of the books, will be appreciated on a different level, but still are an invaluable body of material to study the problems involved in the case where two national opinions clashed. As sources for the intellectual side of the study of national grievances they assume a value in their own right. Giraldus' fight has not yet been described in full,[2] and the present study deals only with two aspects: the problems involved in his election and the political implications of his actions and plans.[3]

---

[1] 19 chapters of Book 3 only have been preserved in the single MS which now exists: BM Cotton Tiberius B xiii. But there is no reason to doubt whether Giraldus ever completed it [e.g. *Ep. Acts* i, p. 28, n. 168; Humphreys, *op. cit.*, p. 41; 'There would surely have been no need for the *De Iure* and the *De Invectionibus* to have been written if the *De Rebus* contained the whole story already. My opinion is that Gerald compiled the *De Rebus*, more as a collection of notes – its form is very disconnected – and afterwards used them for his other works, and while *the later part was never copied again*, the first part was kept . . .']. The manuscript was defective by the seventeenth century, but there is evidence that the work had been completed earlier, cf. *De Invect.*, vi, 1, p. 204: 'capitula . . . que quasi in calce libelli eiusdem conscripta reperiuntur'; cf. also *De Invect.*, iv, 2, p. 167, and *Op.* iii, p. 273. There are only incidental references to the time of its composition, which was certainly not before 1208, the year when Giraldus' relative Meiler fitzHenry ceased to be justiciar of Ireland, cf. *Op.* i, p. 7, c. xl; 'Qualiter archiepiscopus per Meilerium, Hiberniae *tunc* justiciarium, animum archidiaconi ad concordiam minus honestam frustra flectere tentavit'.

[2] The most detailed account to date is J. C. Davies, *loc. cit.*, and *Ep. Acts*, i, pp. 210–30. Both versions require some correction, while in the present study the point of departure is different.

[3] In questions of chronology, the author follows the table of content in the *De Rebus* which seems to be the most reliable guide. The chapters divide into the following groups: First journey to Rome: xvi–xxx; Return and sojourn in England and Wales: xxxi–liii; Second journey to Rome: liv–lxii; Second stay at Rome: lxii–lxxviii; Return to England and Wales: lxxix–clvii; Third journey to Rome: clviii–clxvi; Third stay at Rome: clxvii–ccv; Return to England and reconciliation with the archbishop: ccvi–ccxvi.

In order to understand the implications of Giraldus' dispute in Rome and his eventual failure to obtain recognition from the pope, it will be necessary to sketch some aspects of episcopal election more generally. The growing concern in ecclesiastical circles with the body of canon law in the twelfth century brought more clarity and precision in various aspects of Church government and administration. Much discussed, also, was the problem of the canonical elections of bishops, a topic which was dramatically fought out in the Investiture Contest between the papacy and the Empire. Yet while the Investiture Contest ended in 1122 as a political issue, final clarity was not brought into the problem of canoncial elections. It had been demanded by the Church that such elections should be free, but 'freedom' is a very imprecise and subjective term. The Concordat of Worms in 1122 attempted to guarantee freedom from lay control, while at the same time strengthening control by the higher circles of the hierarchy. This concept found a defender among the canonists, notably in Rufinus who held that a free canonical election meant an election which was reached in agreement between the electing body (theoretically clergy and laity of the diocese concerned, but in practice only confined to the cathedral chapter) and the elect, and which was ratified by the ecclesiastical superior, normally the archbishop who was at the same time the consecrating pontiff.

More radical as well as more far-reaching was the concept which was developed towards the end of the twelfth century by the great canonist Huguccio, a close friend and teacher of Pope Innocent III. Huguccio held that the third element of the concept of Rufinus was unnecessary, and that it was sufficient for a canonical election that agreement be reached between the electing body and the elect. In his system, the function of the archbishop was much more limited, amounting to no influence on the election proper, but instead being restricted to un-conditional consecration of the elect. It has been shown that Huguccio based his theory on the classical Roman concept of marriage by consent.[1] Both these opinions, that of Rufinus as well as that of Huguccio, were the result of private research into the vast body of ecclesiastical legislation. They carried some weight within the Church, but neither concept ever was applied in a pure form. In fact, the popes, in agreement with the concept of their office which was expressed in the term of *plenitudo potestatis*, claimed the right to interfere in ecclesiastical business at all stages, a right which, incidentally, was not challenged by any of the leading theological thinkers, thereby inclining in practice more towards the concept of Rufinus. Thus even the most extreme

---

[1] R. L. Benson, *The Bishop-Elect* (Princeton, N.J., 1968), p. 121ff.

claims for freedom of election meant no more than freedom within the restricting framework of the hierarchy of the Church.

The important role played by the Church in secular affairs was another limiting factor. The appointment to a bishopric was a matter of the greatest interest to the king as well as to the archbishop concerned, and the secular powers found means to defend their influence over new appointments, while the Church, involved in secular affairs as it was, never challenged this right of the secular princes in practice, although in principle intervention by the king was deplored. Thus in reality freedom of episcopal elections was not even tantamount to freedom from intervention by the secular powers.[1]

This last aspect can be studied particularly well in England. Both the insular position of the country and the determined policy of the Conqueror and his successors had achieved that in England episcopal elections in the twelfth century were at all times closely controlled by the Crown.[2] Freedom of canonical election in this framework meant freedom to chose from the candidates who had been approved by the king and the archbishop of Canterbury beforehand.

It is perhaps significant that England was the country in which the first full theoretical treatise on the election of a bishop was written. Lawrence of Somercote, canon of Chichester, wrote in 1254 a book which has been called by its editor *Tractatus (sive summa) Laurentii de Somercote de formis electionum episcoporum faciendarum*.[3] It is perhaps too ambitious to call the work a treatise. It consists mainly of a collection of documents which formed the standard correspondence in connection with an episcopal election, in this particular case taken from the cathedral archives and stemming from the election which had been held at Chichester in 1253.[4] The treatise is enlarged by a listing of the four

---

[1] In fact, Pope Innocent III acknowledged in 1200 that the indispensible elements in episcopal elections were: 'concors capituli, electio, petitio populi, *assensus principis*, votum tuum (i.e. the archbishop of Canterbury), suffraganeorum suffragia', *Decret. Greg. IX*, 1. 6. 20, quoted in Benson, *op. cit.*, p. 346, n. 13. It is found in a decretal letter to the archbishop of Canterbury. Cf. however, an earlier decretal letter (1187) by Pope Celestine III, *Decret. Greg. IX*, 1. 6. 14, where the role of the prince is less decisive, as it had been designed in the Concordat of Worms in 1122.

[2] The practice of episcopal elections had been formulated neatly in chapter xii of the Constitutions of Clarendon (1166): '...cum ventum fuerit ad consulendum ecclesiae, debet dominus rex mandare potiores personas ecclesiae, et in capella ipsius domini regis debet fieri electio assensu domini regis et consilio personarum regni, quas ad hoc faciendum vocaverit. Et ibidem faciet electus homagium et fidelitatem domino regi ... priusquam sit consecratus', Stubbs, *Select Charters*, 8th edition (Oxford, 1905), p. 140. See also Giraldus *Op*. iv, pp. 337–40.

[3] Alfred von Wretschko, ed., *Der Traktat des Laurentius de Somercote über die Vornahme von Bischofswahlen* (Weimar, 1907).

[4] *Ibid.*, p. 12.

different ways in which a bishop is to be elected, by inspiration, by compromise, by scrutiny, or by postulation.

Of particular interest are the various stages of correspondence which are described as the normal feature in an episcopal election. They show the extent to which such election was controlled by the king and by the archbishop of Canterbury. After the death of the bishop, the king had to be informed and was requested to issue a *congé d'élire*, i.e. a permission to proceed with a new election.[1] Then the canons, the electoral body, had to be summoned to the cathedral; every canon had to attend or to excuse his non-attendance, by which he lost his right to vote. Then the election was to be made with the consent of the archbishop (the elements of correspondence varied according to the mode adopted for the election). Since a bishop-elect had to do homage to the king before his consecration, a further controlling barrier was in existence. Finally, the archbishop of Canterbury, the consecrating pontiff, had the last word in his capacity to decide whether or not an elect would be consecrated.

Although Lawrence de Somercote's book dates only from the mid-thirteenth century, the documents preserved by Giraldus show that all the elements mentioned by Lawrence applied already half a century earlier. In fact, the system appears to have been complete as early as the first quarter of the twelfth century, as can be gathered from some documents which have been preserved elsewhere.[2] Thus by the end of the twelfth century, it was the accepted practice in England to proceed to episcopal elections only with the approval of the king and the archbishop, a practice which was tolerated by the papacy.

It is against this background that the implications of Giraldus' election have to be evalued. Crown and Canterbury had an interest in the appointment of the Welsh bishops which was perhaps even greater than in elections of English bishoprics since only parts of Wales by that time were under the control of the crown. Peter de Leia, bishop of St. David's, had died 16 July, 1198.[3] The archbishop of Canterbury, Hubert Walter, requested the chapter of St. David's to submit to his approval a list of

---

[1] According to the agreement of 1215 between King John and Pope Innocent III, the royal permission would be given in all cases unconditionally, cf. C. R. Cheney and W. H. Semple, *Selected Letters of Pope Innocent III*, NMT (London, 1953), no. 76, pp. 198–201, but in fact the king had held a real controlling function before that time and retained it later as well.

[2] Cf. the correspondence about the consecration of Gregory, bishop-elect of Dublin (1121), British Museum, Cotton MS Claudius Ev, f.255v, printed in James Usher, *Veterum Epistolarum Hibernicarum Sylloge* (Dublin, 1632), pp. 100–101.

[3] Annals of Tewkesbury, *Ann. Mon.*, i, p. 56. Giraldus wrote later in the *De Rebus* that Peter's death occurred 'in principio autumni', *Op.* i, p. 94.

candidates for the bishopric. By September[1] this list was complete. It included Giraldus de Barri, archdeacon of Brecon; Walter, abbot of St. Dogmael's; Peter, abbot of Whitland; and Reginald Foliot, canon of St. David's.[2] Reginald was the only Englishman among the candidates, and the fact that he was included at all was regarded by Giraldus merely as a tactical move of the chapter not to offend the archbishop by a purely Welsh list. Hubert Walter rejected all people who were Welsh, but in particular Giraldus, because of his affinity to the Welsh princes.[3] Instead, he suggested two of his followers, the Cistercian abbot Alexander and his physician Geoffrey de Henlaw, prior of Lanthony by Gloucester. The administration of the vacant diocese was conferred upon Geoffrey while the archbishop had already earlier rejected Giraldus who had been suggested by the chapter for this function.[4]

Giraldus, at that time still at Lincoln, had corresponded with the archbishop since the summer.[5] The tenor of these letters was that Giraldus showed no desire to become a bishop anywhere, and that even the offer of a bishopric in England or France would not induce him to give up his studies. In his own words: 'Other people may wish and run for bishoprics'.[6] Although such words found the warm support of Hubert Walter, it appears that both parties already were aware that they pretended a harmony and friendship which did not really exist. For while Giraldus praised the courage of the archbishop who so effectively used the spiritual and the material sword, such praise was implicitly a fundamental criticism of the fact that Hubert Walter held jointly prominent secular and spiritual offices and could not fulfil both his offices at the same time. Giraldus also strongly criticised the suggestions made by the archbishop for the bishopric of St. David's. He had been critical of regular clergy all his life, his controversy with William Wibert had widened this aversion, and now the archbishop suggested two monks as candidates in Wales, both of them English. Was a monk *ipso facto* unsuitable for the episcopal office, so much more if this was an Englishman for Wales. Adapting a phrase of St. Augustine, Giraldus wrote polemically: 'Sic forte malus monachus, bonus clericus; sic quoque malus Anglicus, bonus Wallicus; sic vilis et abjectus in Anglia, quia boni se ad haec non vigerunt cathedra digni in Wallia'.[7] This statement was made in

[1] 'parum ante festum S. Michaelis', *Op.* i, p. 94.

[2] *Ibid.*, p. 95. Reginald, a scribe of Bishop William de Vere of Hereford, had been made canon by his uncle Bishop Peter de Leia.

[3] *Ibid.*, pp. 96, 103.

[4] *Ibid.*

[5] *Op.* i, pp. 96–103; *Symbol. Elect.*, Letters no. xxv–xxviii.

[6] 'cupiant, inquam, et currant et cathedras scandant', *Op.* i, p. 99.

[7] *Op.* i, p. 301; Augustine, Ep. 60, 1, *CSEL*, 34, 1895, p. 221.

a letter of October, 1198, by which time the archbishop had made clear whom he would like as bishops in St. David's. Giraldus said that the chapter would never agree to elect a physician, a man who did not know Welsh and thus would not be able to perform his duties, except with the help of interpreters. Giraldus for his part suggested two other people; if it had to be somebody from England, one should appoint either the archdeacon of Worcester who knew Welsh[1] or the arch-deacon of Oxford, Walter Map, who was well acquainted with the customs of both peoples in Wales. He promised that he would give his support to either of them if the chapter were asked to choose between them.

From a slightly later stage of the proceedings another letter of Giraldus is preserved,[2] in which Giraldus replied to a summons of the arch-bishop. He apologized for not having been able to come, but said that he would agree to any election made unanimously by the chapter of St. David's with the permission of king and archbishop, as long as the chosen candidate would be suitable. It appears, therefore, that Giraldus, at this stage, accepted the normal English procedure of episcopal elections, which is an important point when we compare his later claim for free elections. As to the identity of the candidate to the Welsh dioceses, Giraldus demanded more than was commonly regarded as the essential features. He demanded that the bishop should accept freely and without complaint the poverty of his diocese, he should respect the customs of Normans and Welsh alike, he should reside in his bishopric, and finally, he should not accept the bishopric in order to try to be translated later to another, richer, see in England. As they stand, these demands had apparently not been fulfilled by the late bishop Peter de Leia, and in this respect Giraldus' demands are based on the painful experience of his bishopric. In addition to that, however, the demands are listed in a manner that Giraldus himself would have been the best choice for the vacant diocese, although he had accepted the poverty of the bishopric only very recently. He closed his letter with specifying once again that no regular canon should ever be elected.[3]

Down to this stage the election procedure had not produced any result: but the future antagonism was already foreshadowed. For one thing, Giraldus had been nominated from the beginning, perhaps even

---

[1] *Op.* i, p. 306. This man was not Peter de Leche (so, however, J. C. Davies, *loc. cit.*, p. 107, n. 10) who had died already in 1197, but was perhaps John of Brancaster who became arch-deacon *c.* 1199–1201, cf. *Hist. MSS. Comm.* 14th Report, App. pt. 8, p. 193.

[2] *Op.* i, pp. 102–05; 289–90.

[3] *Op.* i, p. 103: 'Excipimus autem omnem nigrae cucullae beluam. A monachis enim cunctis, et praecipue nigris, omnique huiuscemodi peste voraci ecclesiam nostram miseram . . . defendat Deus'.

in the first place, as he himself suggests. He had been nominated despite the fact that he had not appeared in St. David's, so there may well have been a group of canons there who would support his candidature and who also thought that he would have a chance of success. In his correspondence with Hubert Walter, Giraldus apparently showed no great desire for the bishopric, while also feeling no need to emphasize that he would not stand in an election. It is not possible to ascertain why Hubert rejected him so early and why he persisted in this attitude. Perhaps personal reasons played a dominant part, more than could be openly admitted. Giraldus had drawn a very unfavourable picture of Hubert in the *Life of Geoffrey of York*, and he had succeeded in the deposition of William Wibert as abbot of Biddlesden, while Wibert had been a friend of the archbishop. Other reasons may have moved Hubert Walter in the same direction. He knew Giraldus personally, and with his shrewd political insight he may have been able to assess that it would bring difficulties if Giraldus in fact was elected, that a bishop of St. David's called Giraldus de Barri would be an obstinate and unbending subordinate to his ecclesiastical superior, and that he could become dangerous as someone who had been disappointed in his ambitions in England.

Towards the end of the year, the chapter of St. David's received a summons from King Richard, who was in France at that time, to send a delegation of four canons to him who would be competent to perform the election in his presence. Since this letter did not reach St. David's in time, the justiciar issued a further summons for January, 1199.[1] At this stage the chapter of St. David's urged Giraldus to come to St. David's in person. His presence was desired so that they would not act contrary to the customs and become 'Welsh and rebellious'.[2] The situation had changed: by this time Giraldus had become the only candidate of the chapter; the canons who were sent to Giraldus assured him that they should elect nobody but him.[3] Giraldus finally met the emissaries of the chapter in London shortly before the beginning of Lent. When the justiciar insisted that any of the candidates who had been suggested by the archbishop should be chosen, they rejected this and sent one of their group, Elyodor fitzElyodor, to France to obtain from the king the *congé d'élire*. On their way to France they received the news of the King's death and therefore turned to Prince

---

[1] *Op.* i, p. 105, 107.

[2] *Ibid.*, p. 107.

[3] The manuscript produces here something of a puzzle: BM Cotton Tib. B xiii, f. 181d 'qui vos constanter putant et eligant. Si vero dominus rex . . .'; my interpretation: they should ask the king for his consent, and in case he should withhold it, they should elect him.

John, asking permission to elect Giraldus. While John did not issue the desired document at once, he as yet had no objection to the candidate Giraldus, but he insisted that the election should be made by some canons of the church in his presence. Giraldus in the meantime had returned from London to Lincoln but at once set out for France when asked to do so. A letter of the chapter of St. David's which he carried with him again claimed that he was the only candidate, and that the canons did not have the right to elect anybody but him.[1] But before the emissaries of St. David's had met the prince to perform their duty, John had returned swiftly to England and had been crowned on Ascension Day, 1199. When the canons approached him later, he refused to accept Giraldus on the advice of the archbishop of Canterbury.

The future of the bishopric of St. David's appeared to be again as open as it had been since the autumn of the preceding year. But in this situation Giraldus returned to St. David's, and it would appear that he was the driving force behind the following events. The canons of the cathedral were called together to attend a synod which was to be held on 29 June. When it met, it claimed to be a complete representation of the cathedral chapter. Some of the canons had not been able to attend, but they had sent either representatives or made known that they would accept the decisions of that gathering. Giraldus records that prolonged negotiations took place, but he fails to give any information about their content. As a result of the meeting, he was unanimously elected (*ipsum statim unanimiter eligentes*)[2] as the new bishop. The cathedral chapter took two further decisions: Giraldus was asked to travel to Rome in order to receive his consecration personally from the pope, thereby avoiding giving the oath to the archbishop of Canterbury not to pursue metropolitan ambitions for his church (without which promise the archbishop would never have consecrated him) and he was determined to ask the pope to make him archbishop of St. David's, and perhaps even primate.[3]

Giraldus' election had not taken place in the way which was the accepted practice in England. The chapter had at first tried to follow the normal procedure and to act in accordance with the customs of the realm, but events had taken a different way after it had become obvious that the choice of the chapter would not be acceptable to the king or

---

[1] *Op.* i, p. 110: 'quod magistrum Giraldum ... praecipue et prae aliis cunctis postulamus, et eum per illos duos vel tres canonicos ... eligimus'.

[2] *Op.* i, p. 111.

[3] *Ibid.*, 'supplicaverunt, quatinus Romam adeundo et perniciosam illam iuris ecclesiastici adjurationem evitando consecrationem suam a summo pontifice susciperet ... et dignitatem ecclesie sue metropoliticam Romae ... vendicaret'.

archbishop. Through their actions the clerics of St. David's had become what they had wished to avoid in the preceding year: 'Welsh and rebellious'. That they had not acted on the spell of the moment in choosing Giraldus is evident. In the short time between September and December 1198 the archdeacon of Brecon had become the only candidate of the chapter, having first been merely one among others. That this decision was reached while Giraldus was absent and in touch with his fellow canons only by means of letters seems to indicate that among the canons there must have existed a substantial faction which trusted him. The delay before the election in the summer of 1199 may have been due to the hestiation of some of the canons to act so patently against the customs of the kingdom, but it would appear that they were convinced that according to the law of the Church they had acted correctly.

Although Giraldus had two projects in mind when going to Rome, they were closely interrelated and required such an unusual step. If he was convinced that the bishop of St. David's should have metropolitan rank as they allegedly had had in the centuries before the Norman Conquest, then Giraldus' consecration as bishop of St. David's by the archbishop of Canterbury and the necessary profession of canonical obedience would make it rather more difficult to establish the right of independence from Canterbury. At the same time, the papacy was the only institution which could consecrate bishops other than the archbishops without violating the laws of the Church; the papacy also was the institution which decided when a bishopric should be raised to an archbishopric, but rarely did such a decision occur spontaneously, and the popes generally tried to come to a peaceful settlement of the issue before they gave it a final form. So Giraldus acted logically in his first steps after his election, and he seems to have been able to convince his electors of this logic.

It was, however, a different question to act according to the plans one wanted to pursue and to hope for their fulfilment. The decision in the case lay, on the surface, with the pope alone. Innocent III decided, in the end, against Giraldus, not, however, because Giraldus failed to convince him of the justification of his claim. It is conceivable that Giraldus may have succeeded in his plans had they not had potentially grave political consequences, and if the pope could have been free at that time to give a decision which was in opposition to the declared policy of the English crown. As it was, the pope in these years was involved in the disputed double election to the imperial office in Germany, and his favourite candidate then was Otto the Guelf, a nephew of the English king. So it would appear that the European political constellation at that time made the grant of an archbishopric for Wales as difficult as possible. On the surface, Giraldus did not succeed for a different reason. The archbishop of Canterbury claimed that his election had not been as canonically sound as was maintained, and he invented a story that there had been a double election at St. David's in 1199, so that both candidates would lose their eligibility. When Giraldus' election was declared invalid in 1203, the archbishop of Canterbury made sure that a candidate would be chosen who would bow to his authority.

While on the surface, the dispute was an Anglo-Welsh affair, by referring it to the Roman curia, the institution which claimed at that time the ultimate sovereignty over all affairs, the dispute assumed an international dimension. In addition, Giraldus' arguments which voiced the complaints and grievances of a national minority serve to supply information for the notion of the nation in general, while his aim, the establishment of an archbishopric in Wales, must be seen as one aspect of the wider spectrum of forces which aimed at a greater liberty and perhaps even sovereignty of Wales at the beginning of the thirteenth century.

The election at St. David's on 29 June, 1199, had long and profound repercussions on the Anglo-Welsh relations at the turn of the century. In the light of later events it turned out to be the last major effort of the church of St. David's in the Middle Ages to gain independence from Canterbury and is therefore of special interest. Since the archbishop of Canterbury later tried to alienate the electing body from their elect, it is possible to establish almost completely the list of people who were involved in the election, since they changed sides one by one. In 1291, the chapter of St. David's numbered altogether 22 prebends,[1] and the number may have been the same at the end of the twelfth century. Giraldus informs us that it consisted in equal proportions of English and Welsh people.[2] The following names have been preserved:

archdeacons: Giraldus de Barri (Brecon), Maurice (Cardigan),[3] Osbert (Carmarthen), and Pontius (St. David's / Pembroke).

canons: Asser, David fitzIthenard, Elyodor fitzElyodor, Gerardus (also dean of Pembroke), Henry fitzRobert, Henry (son of Robert

---

[1] *Taxatio Ecclesiastica P. Nicholai IV* (Record Commission, 1802), p. 274.

[2] *De Invect.*, p. 87: 'totidem fere Anglicos in ecclesia nostra canonicos habeamus quot Walenses'.

[3] The same in Le Neve, *Fasti Ecclesie Angl.*, i, p. 308, 313. Occasionally, Giraldus refer to Maurice as archdeacon of St. David's / Pembroke, *De Invect.*, p. 224, and refers even to himself as archdeacon of St. David's, *Op.* i, p. 289. Strictly speaking, there was no archdeacon of St. David's, but those of Brecon, Cardigan, Carmarthen, and Pembroke (which included St. David's).

fitzJonas), John,[1] (*?iuvunculus canonicus*[2]), Martin, Meiler, M. (son of the archdeacon Pontius), Philip (*presbyter canonicus*), Reginald Foliot, Robert fitzJonas, Samuel.[3]

other members: Galterius (*exmonachus*), Ithenardus (*decanus provincialis et vicecanonicus*), Joscelin (dean of St. David's[4]).

It would appear also that the heads of the religious houses in the diocese of St. David's had a vote in the episcopal election.[5] The following names are mentioned: Geoffrey de Henlaw, Prior of Lantony by Gloucester (the future bishop), Peter, abbot of Whitland, and Walter, abbot of St. Dogmael's. In addition, a few other names may be mentioned. These were later enemies of Giraldus who assumed a position of power by the protection of Geoffrey de Henlaw: John of Llanddew, who became a canon and later archdeacon, and a son of Master Martin, the canon, who was made a canon at a very young age (*puerum canonicaverit*).[6]

Giraldus claimed to have been elected unanimously by the chapter. It may be true that unanimity was achieved by the canons who were present in the course of the negotiations which immediately preceded the election, but it is also known that some of the canons were not present, and these people could later most easily form the nucleus of resistance against Giraldus. It is known that the canon Reginald Foliot had gone to France in order to obtain royal assent to his own election. He would hardly have voted for Giraldus. Similarly doubtful are the votes of a few other members of the electing body, old enemies of Giraldus like the dean Joscelin, the archdeacon Osbert, and the abbots of St. Dogmael's and Whitland, Walter and Peter. On the other hand, Giraldus himself attests that the future bishop, Geoffrey of Henlaw, was not unfavourable to him until he himself was elected bishop at the end of 1203; this is all the more remarkable, since Geoffrey had been nominated by the archbishop of Canterbury as early as September, 1198, as a candiate who would be acceptable to England.

---

[1] 'iuvenis', *De Invect.*, vi, 4, p. 208, perhaps identical with the *iuvunculus* of the following note.

[2] Cf. the preceding note.

[3] 'canonicus vetus', *De Invect.*, vi, 10, p. 212, 214, and *Op.* i, p. 325, 327, the father of Henry fitzRobert.

[4] This man had been deposed as administrator of the diocese by Giraldus in 1197.

[5] *Op.* i, p. 112: 'priori Lantoniae et conventui, prohibentes eis *tanquam membris* ecclesie Sancti David et intra ipsius diocesim consistentibus'; also *Op.* iii, p. 115 'quod vacantibus ecclesiis pontificalibus, convocatis abbatibus et prioribus conventionalibus ceterisque de confinio viris religiosis'. Cf. also Gratian, D.LXIII, c.35.

[6] *Speculum Duorum*, p. 252.

Less clear is the amount of support which Giraldus had from the
lay powers in Wales. For although the 'people' were, in theory, the
element which together with the 'clergy' should perform the elections,
their precise function was defined even less than that of the clergy. It
would appear that they could approve an election, but should they
disagree, their opinion would be overruled. The only exception to this
was the king. In the present case, it seems that Giraldus secured the
support of some lay magnates before he went to Rome, the extent of
which may perhaps be gathered from the people to whom the pope
wrote at the end of Giraldus' first stay at Rome. Giraldus later claimed
that initially he had behind him 'the votes of almost the whole of Wales'.[1]
In 1200 the pope sent letters to the magnates in Wales, *Lewelino et aliis
principibus Wallie*[2] and Ireland, *magnis et nobilibus viris Hibernie Meilerio
tunc iusticiario et aliis de genere suo*,[3] that is those people who were
prepared 'to restore the ancient dignity of the church and (thereby)
the rights (*honor*) of the whole of Wales'.[4] Innocent III furthermore
wrote to the Cistercian abbots in Wales and to the clergy and people
of the country,[5] but this may have been a routine way of dealing with
the election and need not indicate special support from these particular
circles. What may be significant is that no letters to the remaining two
Welsh dioceses, those of Llandaff and St. Asaph (Bangor was vacant),
have been preserved. It is known from other information that the clergy
of Llandaff did not support the St. David's case as strongly as they might
have done, and Giraldus may have known of their hostile attitude already
at that stage and not asked for support. On the whole, however, it would
appear that Giraldus had been able to secure support from a wide range
of Welsh society.

The interest in Giraldus' election and the ensuing dispute about its
recognition goes beyond the limitations of a normal episcopal election.
In the first place, the see of St. David's was not just another episcopal

---

[1] 'vota secum habuit Wallie fere tocius', *De Invect.*, vi, 2, p. 206.

[2] *De Invect.*, iii, 4, p. 149 and *Op.* i, p. 7, No. xxvi, and *Op.* iii, p. 184. Cf. also C. R. Cheney
and M. G. Cheney (edd.), *The Letters of Pope Innocent III concerning England and Wales*
(Oxford, 1967). No. 223, p. 38. The present author wishes to acknowledge with gratitude the
permission given by Mrs. Cheney and Professor Cheney to make full use of their book then in
proof stage.

[3] *De Invect.*, iii, 6, p. 150; *Op.* iii, p. 184; Cheney, *Letters*, No. 225. It is apparent from this
that the pope replied to those people whose support Giraldus had secured (presumably in
writing) before going to Rome. He mentions his journey to Ireland 'ubi cognatos suos Meilerium scilicet tunc regni iusticiarium aliosque proceres patriae magnos consulens et conveniens,
multam super aggressu laudem a cunctis et maximam manus auxiliatricis in re tanta promissionem
suscepit', *Op.* i, p. 112.

[4] *Ibid.*

[5] References Cheney, *Letters*, No. 224, 226; cf. *Op.* i, p. 7, No. xxvii, xxviii.

see but had emerged in the twelfth century as the centre of a strong opposition of the Welsh Church against Canterbury's old policy to subject all Welsh dioceses to her metropolitan rule. Both older tradition and recent policy made St. David's the only potential metropolitan see in Wales, and therefore the efforts of the archbishops of Canterbury to control episcopal elections there were even greater than in the other Welsh sees.

The election of Giraldus de Barri opened up once more this opposition to Canterbury's control which Archbishop Theobald had hoped to have checked effectively half a century earlier. If Giraldus, in 1199, was known not to be fully dedicated to the Welsh cause, his descent combined with an injured pride over what might have appeared to be an unjustified lack of reward by the English monarchy could well mould Giraldus into a dedicated Welshman. He had many potentials which singled him out for such a metamorphosis, notably disappointment in England, and a certain knowledge of legal procedure. Popular support from Wales for his task was likely to come forward, for the continuous English intrusion into Wales over the past century had given enough ground for complaints from the native population. Such grievances against England would naturally not be confined to political issues. The nature of English administration, where lay and ecclesiastical barons worked together for the monarchy and for their own interests, made it easy for people who wanted to criticise to find a good target in the representatives of the Church who, so it was said, abused their spiritual position for alien political ends. But it is not enough to confine one's considerations to such relatively obvious and determinable factors, and Giraldus certainly did not push his own election for these reasons. It is impossible to say in how far he sought political power rather than following his spiritual vocation, or in how far he believed that he had a chance of success in what he was attempting. Giraldus' personality remains enigmatic throughout the following years. He may have believed at the time of his election that he was following God's commands,[1] but perhaps this consideration was fabricated after his defeat. Such points, while they cannot be pursued, should at least be kept in mind when we deal in the following pages with the political aspects of Giraldus' election and its dispute in Rome.

Before his departure to the continent, Giraldus paid a short visit to Ireland to secure the support of his friends and relatives there. On his

---

[1] *Op.* i, p. 112: 'ut ad reformandum ecclesie sue statum pristinum patriaeque totius honorem, tanquam *propter hoc natus et a Domino datus*, se totum indubitanter et incunctanter applicaret'; similarly *De Invect.*, v, 15, p. 195: 'Hoc velis quod Deus vult, alioquin curvus es. In hac etenim opinione ... non solum ipse sed et patria fere tota ... tunc temporis erat'.

return to St. David's, he found letters from the justiciar and the archbishop of Canterbury commanding the election of Geoffrey, prior of Lanthony by Gloucester on the Sunday after 15 August as the new bishop. In case they would not do so, the archbishop threatened to consecrate this man without the consent of the cathedral chapter.[1] The chapter of St. David's replied that they had made their election, and that any further moves by the archbishop or his representatives would be illegal, and that they would appeal to Rome. Letters of the same content were also sent to Geoffrey de Henlaw.

Of immediate political relevance was a letter to Pope Innocent III in which the chapter described the election of Giraldus and set out to explain the unusual procedure of sending him to Rome for his consecration. This letter foreshadows the future arguments on the case, and for this reason a translation of excerpts will be given: '. . . We make known to Your Holiness that we have at length in our Church canonically and with one accord elected our archdeacon Master Giraldus. Wherefore since the archbishop and the officers of the king, with violent intrusion against our election and against our privileges, have desired to set over us a stranger, wholly ignorant of our native tongue and the customs of our country, and since from the oft refusal of our demands we found the will of the archbishop wholly contrary to us and could not approach him by reason of the snares that were on all sides set for us and above all desiring that an unlawful oath might not be extorted from our elect to the prejudice of the rights of our church, such as had been forced more than once on our prelates, we have therefore appealed to your protection and with one accord have sent to you, that you may confirm and consecrate him, our elect . . . And we entreat you earnestly with supplication that, deigning to lay the hand of consecration upon him you will of your fatherly love apply remedies to those matters . . .'[2] This letter skilfully strikes a balance between the legitimate and indeed canonical proceedings which brought about Giraldus' election, and the injustice and violence by the archbishops of Canterbury. What was to follow in the next years was merely an elaboration of these two themes. It is very likely that Giraldus himself was reponsible for the drafting of this letter.

Giraldus arrived in Rome at the end of November, 1199,[3] accompanied by two youths. Not long afterwards, there arrived an emissary from

---

[1] *Op.* i, p. 112f.

[2] *Op.* i, p. 113f. The translation is taken from H. E. Butler, *The Autobiography of Giraldus Cambrensis* (London, 1937), p. 159.

[3] *Op.* i, p. 119: 'circa festum Sti. Andreae' (30 November). *Op.* iii, p. 176 gives 'circa festum omnium Sanctorum' (1 November), but this was written much later and is perhaps incorrect.

the archbishop of Canterbury, carrying twelve copies of a letter against Giraldus, addressed to the Pope and some of the cardinals. Giraldus succeeded in getting hold of one of them at an early date, and so he gained precious time to prepare his defence. On January 7, 1200, Hubert Walter's letter was read out in the consistory, and Giraldus obtained permission to reply to it.[1] The two documents were programmatic statements of policy from both parties involved. Giraldus aimed at being consecrated by the pope and St. David's being made an archbishopric, Hubert Walter stated that Canterbury was the archiepiscopal see of the Welsh dioceses, a regulation which was very beneficial, and he intended to prove that Giraldus' election was invalid.

There are a few points in Hubert Walter's letter which must be singled out. The Welsh dioceses, so he said, were subject to Canterbury, as attested by papal privileges from Eugenius III (1145–53) onwards. Now a certain Welshman called Giraldus had been elected bishop of St. David's uncanonically, by three canons only. He had taken the name and authority of a bishop-elect without being confirmed by his archbishop. Hubert Walter argued that Giraldus had gone to Rome since he could not hope to have his (uncanonical) election confirmed at Canterbury. The archbishop stated further that, should Giraldus be consecrated by the pope, he would see in this an encouragement of his attempt to gain archiepiscopal dignity for himself. Hubert Walter ended his letter with a strong appeal to the pope to prevent this, if only for political reasons: '. . . [Giraldus] would thus to the best of his power sow the seeds of political dissension between the Welsh and the English for all time to come. For the Welsh being sprung by unbroken succession from the original stock of the Britons, boast that all Britain is theirs of right. Wherefore, if the barbarity of that wild and unbridled nation had not been restrained by the censure of the Church, wielded by the archbishop of Canterbury, to whom it is known that this race has thus far been subject as being within his province, this people would by continual or at least by frequent rebellion have broken from their allegiance to the King, whereby the whole of England must have suffered disquietude'.[2] Hubert Walter's letter, although it reads superficially very well, lacks conviction and persuasiveness. It revolves solely round

---

[1] Letter and Giraldus' reply *De Invect.*, i, 1–2, pp. 83–93.

[2] *De Invect.*, i, 1, p. 83–85. The translation of this and of Giraldus' reply in Butler, p. 166–182. The hostilities between England and Wales had their repercussions also on papal policy, perhaps due to the information provided by Giraldus, in a letter by Pope Innocent III to the bishop of Worcester: '. . . cum inter Anglicos et Wallenses sint inimicitiae manifestae et ad partes illas Anglicis periculosus sit transitus pro viarum periculis et gerrae, quae inter gentes illas frequens esse dinoscitur et continue', Migne, *PL*, ccxiv, col. 974f.; *Decret. Greg. IX*, 2, 28. 47; Cheney, Letters, No. 406, p. 66.

the argument that Canterbury's rule over the Welsh dioceses was good and justified, in such a way that he seemed to say: it is good because it is just, and it is just because it is good. Naturally, this was a very subjective point of view and would never be shared by the Welsh. He appealed to the pope's spiritual powers in an expressively political interpretation already in the opening sentence: 'The ordinance of divine providence has set you over nations and kingdoms that the wisdom of your solitude may according to the merits of each, tear out, destroy, dissipate and overthrow, build up and plant . . .'[1] It is understandable that the archbishop failed to give Giraldus a fair treatment.

Giraldus' reply to Hubert Walter's letter must be read in full to be appreciated. It is both witty and profound. It reveals the lack of soundness in the archbishop's argument and does not shrink from even personally counter-attacking Hubert Walter as an ambitious, politically preoccupied, greedy and vain personality. Yet while these points embellish Giraldus' statements and invectives, three particular issues may be singled out to show the point which we are trying to make.

(1) The political importance of English control over the Welsh bishops: Hubert Walter had spoken about the elect of St. David's as 'a certain archdeacon of the church of St. David's, Giraldus by name, a Welshman by birth (*nacione Walensis*)'. To this Giraldus replied: 'For he introduces it by way of insult and to do me a hurt, as if he were openly saying, 'Because he is born in Wales, he cannot be a prelate in Wales'. On which showing there should be no English appointed prelates in England, nor French in France, nor Italians in Italy. Very well, give them shepherds who are ignorant of the language, and you will find most excellent preachers'.[2] It is true that Hubert Walter had suppressed half the evidence about Giraldus to make his argument more effective, but Giraldus himself was not totally honest about his own stand when he said later: 'I am descended from both nations, from the princes of Wales and from the barons of the March, . . . and yet I hate injustice by whichever nation it be committed'.[3] His commitment to the cause of Welsh ecclesiastical freedom would naturally weaken his allegiance to England.

(2) Giraldus was certainly right in questioning the objectively beneficial effect for Wales of Canterbury's rule. He argued that Hubert Walter abused his spiritual power for political ends, 'as if the King of England

---

[1] Cf. Yves M. J. Congar, '*Ecce constitui te super gentes et regna* (Jer. 1. 10) in Geschichte und Gegenwart', *Theologie in Geschichte und Gegenwart* [Festschrift M. Schmaus, 1957], pp. 671–696.

[2] *De Invect.*, i, 2, p. 86; Butler, p. 171f.

[3] *Ibid.*, p. 91; Butler, p. 180.

with all his great forces could not subdue that little nation by the power of his material sword without borrowing the spiritual sword to aid him'.[1] He pointed out that the archbishop had rejoiced in having excommunicated Welsh soldiers who then would die in a state of ecclesiastical censure when fighting the English. 'But whether he (i.e., Hubert Walter) ought more truly to be called a good shepherd of his flock or rather a ravening wolfe, I leave as a matter of further inquiry'.

(3) While the two points which we have dealt with so far would have required from the pope an openly political decision on the St. David's election, Giraldus finally argued along a line which apparently was the concern of canon law alone: that of the terms of his election. He said: '. . . [Hubert Walter] refuses the name of canonical to this election which was made in a church that is the mother and womb of churches, with the consent of all and the applause of the whole people. Yet if four canons or six having been summoned to London with letters of ratification were forced by threats and spoliation of their property to elect his monk or physician or any other . . . he would, I believe, consider such an election to be just and canonical'.[2] To this Giraldus should have added that he himself had complied with the form of election which he here lamented, namely as long as he saw some chance of success for himself. According to the law of the Church as it was codified at that time, Giraldus could regard his election as canonical. Two objections, however, have to be raised against his argument: firstly, the preceding half century and especially the reign of Henry II had established in England the practice of episcopal elections along the lines lamented by Giraldus, and this development had been accepted by the popes as well; secondly Giraldus had described the law of the Church as it had stood by the time when Master Gratian had compiled his *Decretum*, but the law of the church had developed rapidly and in parts been modified considerably in the half century after Gratian, and among other aspects that of episcopal elections had been modified further.[3] Certainly Giraldus' case would not be decided by legalistic argumentation alone: if political considerations would be adduced, then Hubert Walter had the better chance of success. If we want to bring the archbishop's letter and Giraldus' reply to a common formula this would perhaps

---

[1] *Ibid.*; on the 'two swords' cf. Gratian's *Decretum*, C. xxiii, q.v, c. 20; C. xxiii, q.iv, c. 45, and C. xxxiii, q. ii, c.6; also Hartmut Hoffmann, 'Die beiden Schwerter im hohen Mittelalter', *Deutsches Archiv*, xx, 1964, p. 78–114.

[2] *De Invect.*, i, 2, p. 88; Butler, p. 175.

[3] Geoffrey Barraclough, 'The Making of a Bishop in the Middle Ages, the Part of the Pope in Law and Fact', *Catholic Historical Review*, xix, 1933–34, p. 275–319; esp. p. 309: 'The electoral system of the *Corpus Iuris Canonici* lasted in full vigour for hardly more than half a century'.

be that the subordination of the Welsh dioceses to the rule of Canterbury was analysed both from the English and Welsh point of view, while the legitimacy of this rule was as yet undecided. If it had been legally defined without any ambiguity, Hubert Walter would certainly not have failed to point this out.

The first reaction of the curia to this exchange of arguments was little encouraging to the Welsh cause. Still, Giraldus' claim that St. David's had been an archbishopric in the past was followed up in the papal records. When the current papal *provinciale* was inspected, it appeared that the Welsh dioceses formed a certain autonomous unit in themselves, since they were not listed under the rubric of the province of Canterbury.[1] Taken by itself, this evidence would not have amounted to any firm rule, but on the basis of this evidence Pope Innocent III allowed Giraldus to look up the register of his predecessors for any privileges which may have been granted earlier to the church of St. David's.[2] It was on this occasion that Giraldus found the letter which Pope Eugenius III had written to Archbishop Theobald of Canterbury in 1147 and which had apparently left the point of St. David's subjection undecided in principle. It would appear that only then did Giraldus learn any precise details about the activities of Bishop Bernard, and the document which he had found certainly encouraged him to follow up his claim further. Pope Eugenius' letter also impressed Innocent III more than the evidence from the *provinciale*, for when he was informed about this letter, he promised to set up a commission which should inquire into the relative claims of St. David's and Canterbury. On the basis of this wider evidence, Giraldus was allowed to draw up a memorandum about the history of Christianity in Wales.[3] This memorandum will have to be dealt with at some length because it forms the complementary part of Giraldus' reply to Hubert Walter's letter, and summarizes the current view held in Wales about the past history

[1] *Op.* iii, p. 165ff, cf. also *supra*, p. 49f.

[2] *Op.* i, p. 398.

[3] The chronology of the various events cannot be established with certainty. The chapter headings of the *De Rebus* give the following sequence: Letter of Hubert Walter, Giraldus' reply, register Eugenius III, promise of commission, search in the *provinciale*. The memorandum is not mentioned. The *De Jure* has after Giraldus' reply the *provinciale*, then a report by Giraldus of the various metropolitan moves by St. David's in the twelfth century (this seems fabricated since Giraldus had not yet found the letters from the pontificate of Eugenius III!), then the memorandum, a refusal to grant a commission, the register of Eugenius III, then the promise of a commission. The *De Iure* gives the events a dramatic touch! In agreement with *Haddan & Stubbs* i, p. 405, I assume that the memorandum was given early, perhaps in February. For a different opinion J. C. Davies, *Ep. Acts*, i, D. 320, p. 312. Early also Roger Howden, *Chronica, Op.* iv, pp. 103–05.

as it had been written down in the twelfth century in various forms, most clearly in Geoffrey of Monmouth's *History of the Kings of Britain* and in the various *Lives* of Saints, groups of sources well known to Giraldus.

The memorandum derives its information from three different groups of sources: (a) native Welsh tradition; (b) evidence taken from Bede; (c) evidence taken from the reform of the Church in the British Isles after the Norman Conquest. Giraldus combined in his argumentation what we know to be myth with historical facts, a combination which makes his account particularly interesting. (a) This is the story of the conversion of the Britons to Christianity in the second century,[1] the administrative subdivision into five provinces, namely of Wales with Caerleon, Kent with Canterbury, Mercia with London, Maximia with York, and Valentiana with St. Andrews as archbishoprics. The arrival of the pagan Saxons destroyed Christianity in England but could not extinguish it in Wales and Scotland. There followed the conversion of the Saxons under Pope Gregory I and the establishment of the arch-bishoprics of Canterbury with twelve suffragans and York with one suffragan bishop. The message of this part was that the Saxons (and their descendants, the English) were, as Christians, inferior to the Welsh.

Giraldus added to this a summary account of the history of the Welsh Church. Archbishop (St.) David transferred the archiepiscopal see from Caerleon to St. David's, and was succeeded in an unbroken succession by twenty-five archbishops. The last of them, St. Samson, fled in the time of Pope Gregory I to Brittany and settled at Dol. In the following centuries, Dol received the pallium which originally had been that of St. David's, but apart from that the prelates of St. David's enjoyed full archiepiscopal authority.

(b) Bede's *History* did not mention anywhere that the Welsh Church was subject to the English Church. On the contrary, what evidence he gave seemed to prove the opposite: Augustine, archbishop of Canterbury, tried to persuade the Britons to adopt the Roman way of calculating the Easter date and to help with the conversion of the Saxons, but the Welsh clergy refused both. 'If they thus refused to be helpers of Augustine, how much less did they want to be subject to him or his successors.'[2]

---

[1] For the references to the 'Lucius Legend' cf. C. N. L. Brooke, *loc. cit. (SEBC)*, pp. 240–42. The sequence of the documents referred to there will have to be altered, with the letter of the chapter of St. David's to Pope Honorius II in the first place, since there can be no doubt now that it is genuine (Richter, 'Canterbury's Primacy . . .'); furthermore, the same story is also told, with a Llandaff-bias, in *LL*, p. 88.

[2] *De Invect.*, ii, 1, p. 132: 'Si ergo Augustini renuerunt esse socii, multo minus sibi vel successoribus suis vellent esse subjecti'.

The seventh successor of Augustine, Laurentius, was equally unsuccessful in subjecting the Welsh Church. He called two synods where no British bishop was present. 'It is apparent from this that the Welsh Church was not at all subject to Canterbury, for if this had been the case, Bede, being an Englishman himself, would not have failed to mention it in his *History*.'[1]

(c) Until quite recently the Welsh Church had in fact been free from the English dominance. There were people still living who remembered it being subject to Rome alone, like the Scottish Church. Even the most recent development apparently worked in favour of St. David's. Had not the bishopric of Dol (Brittany) lost its pallium by a papal decision early in 1199?[2] Since Dol's pallium had originally come from St. David's, it should logically return there, 'cum omnia redire debeant ad sua initia'.[3]

Compared to the effort put by Giraldus into his case at Rome, the initial reaction of the papal curia was both tentative and cautious, not, however, altogether unfavourable. This was revealed when in the spring of 1200 Bonjohannes, an emissary from Canterbury, arrived with new information. He reported that shortly after Christmas, 1199, the canons of St. David's had elected Walter, abbot of St. Dogmael's, as their bishop, and that the king had accepted their choice. Pope Innocent declared this election null and void since it had taken place after Giraldus' appeal. Giraldus obtained the concession that the pope would appoint a certain sub-deacon, Philip, as head of a commission to inquire into the validity of the election of June, 1199. The pope also ruled that Giraldus should have the administration of the vacant diocese and wrote to the bishops of Lincoln, Durham, and Ely asking them to influence the archbishop of Canterbury to consecrate Giraldus while at the same time they should take care that the candidate should not be compelled to give an oath in prejudice of the rights of his church.[4] If this could not be done, Giraldus should return to Rome.

When Giraldus left Rome in summer, 1200, the prospects in his case were not hopeless, but far from promising. The pope had conferred to him the administration of the diocese[5] and had also written letters of recommendation to the Welsh princes, the heads of the Cistercian

---

[1] *Ibid.*, p. 133.

[2] Cf. E. Durtelle de Saint Saveur, *Histoire de Bretagne* (Rennes, 1935), i, p. 170; Potthast, *Reg. Pont.*, i, nos. 635–636, 721–724.

[3] *Op.* iii, p. 176.

[4] Roger Howden, *Chron.*, p. 106.

[5] *De Invect.*, ii, 1, p. 147.

houses, and more generally to the clergy and people of Wales.[1] Giraldus took the number of letters which the pope wrote as an indication of a favourable attitude,[2] but he would appear to have been blinded by numbers while underestimating the extent of Roman bureaucracy. A clearer indication of the Pope's personal opinion concerning the issue may perhaps be gathered from two other letters. He wrote to King John saying that Giraldus had not done anything in Rome to the disadvantage of the realm;[3] he also admonished Hubert Walter to treat Giraldus mildly and generously in order to avoid unnecessary strain and to be able to preserve the rights of Canterbury undiminished.[4] Thus it would appear that Innocent III had not yet decided which party to support, although the letter to the archbishop of Canterbury was rather more favourable to the *status quo* in the English Church.

Giraldus' subsequent sojourn in England and Wales between the autumn of 1200 and the spring of 1201 remains dark in details since the principal source for this period, *De Rebus a se Gestis*, is lost except for the chapter headings. What can be gathered from them, however, indicates some very dramatic and drastic developments. They suggest in the first place a strong effort by the king and the archbishop to intimidate the chapter of St. David's and Giraldus himself[5] as well as his relatives.[6] Then the archbishop apparently tried to divide the chapter of St. David's by favouring the election of Peter, abbot of Whitland, who could count on a number of relatives among the canons of St. David's.[7] Some of his former friends, influential people like Meiler fitzHenry, the justiciar of Ireland, and William of Braose, now turned against Giraldus.[8] It must have been a great consolation and a much-needed

---

[1] *Ibid.*, iii, 4–6, p. 149ff.

[2] *Ibid.*, p. 150: 'ex quibus evidens esse potest quanto proposuerit tunc papa studio Menevensem ecclesiam promovere'.

[3] *De Invect.*, iii, 8, p. 151f.: 'nichil unquam proponeret, quod in iniuriam sublimitatis regie redundaret', and '[non] honori regio in aliquo derogasset'.

[4] *Ibid.*, iii, 9, p. 152: 'ut eum in gratia tua receptum ita tractare studeas, in spiritu lenitatis iudiciorum strepitum evitando, ut et ipsum ad devotionem ex hoc invitare valeas, et iura Cantuariensis ecclesie tuis temporibus illibata conservare'.

[5] *Op.* i, p. 7f., nos. xxxiii–xxxvi, xlii, xlix, lii.

[6] Perhaps it is reading too much into a headline (chapter l) when suggesting that Philip de Barri had been excommunicated.

[7] *Op.* i, p. 8, no. xlviii; *De Invect.*, i, 4, p. 96: 'ut per primum schisma faceret in genere meo, per alterum vero in capitulo'. Relatives of Peter of Whitland who at first supported Giraldus but later turned against him were the canons Martin and Samuel, *Op.* iii, p. 219, also *De Invect.*, i, 7, p. 107f.

[8] *Op.* i, nos. xxxv, xl.

encouragement to the bishop-elect in this quickly deteriorating situation to find at St. David's further documents dealing with the metropolitan activities of Bishop Bernard.[1]

On the other hand, Hubert Walter appears to have shown a genuine interest to come to an agreement with Giraldus, and perhaps he would have been prepared to consecrate him now bishop of St. David's if Giraldus had given up the metropolitan claim.[2] Hubert Walter chose his relative Gilbert Glanvill, bishop of Rochester, as his man to work out the compromise; but the proposal came to nothing. This may have been the reason why the archbishop now took stronger measures. He went to Wales personally to negotiate with the chapter of St. David's.[3] Early in 1201, at a meeting at Gloucester, the canons of St. David's gave evidence before many bishops and abbots that they had never elected Giraldus.[4] At Rome, the elect maintained later that they had been forced into this testimony either directly or indirectly.

It is tantalizing to have only the barest outlines of an embryonic alliance between King John and Giraldus at that time. It would appear that John for a short time turned away from Hubert Walter and offered to support Giraldus in his metropolitan claim.[5] The king appears, however, to have returned very quickly to his traditional line and issued a statement to the effect that he had never given his consent to Giraldus' election nor would do so in future.[6] So when Giraldus went back to Rome in the spring, 1201, the situation had not changed essentially. It had become apparent that the chapter of St. David's could be intimidated to speak against him, but whether such evidence would have a lasting result remained to be seen.

Giraldus' second visit to Rome in spring and summer 1201 did not decide his case, nor did it bring any substantial progress in either direction. What was discussed can be summarized briefly. Two people from England, a certain Andrew as proctor of the archbishop of Canterbury, and Reginald Foliot, canon of St. David's, as proctor of the chapter of St. David's and of Walter, abbot of St. Dogmaels', spoke against Giraldus.

---

[1] *Ibid.*, nos. xlv–xlvii.

[2] *Op.* i, p. 8, no. lvii; *De Invect.*, i, 4, p. 99. There Giraldus states referring to the situation of 1201: 'me pluries sollicitare presumpsit, iam si vellem cornutus incederem'.

[3] Cf. C. R. Cheney, *Hubert Walter*, p. 110.

[4] *De Invect.*, i, 4, p. 98; *Op.* i, p. 8, no. lviii; cf. *infra*, Appendix II, no. 1, the letter of Hubert Walter to Bishop Gilbert.

[5] Cheney, *Hubert Walter*, pp. 105f., 136; *Op.* i, p. 8, no. lviii: 'Qualiter archidiacono rex super causa status promovenda auxilium promisit, sed statim archiepiscopo sibi pacificato sententiam mutavit'.

[6] *Rot. Chart.*, i, 100b (ed. T. D. Hardy): 'quod electioni archidiaconi de Brekeinou Geroldi in pastorem ecclesie Menevensis nunquam assensum praebuimus neque praebemus'.

Their new version of the proceedings at St. David's in 1199 ran to the effect that Walter had been elected bishop twice, once before Giraldus' own election and once afterwards.[1] This new version could not impress the pope, but it was not taken as improving Giraldus' chances. Innocent III ruled instead that a new hearing of the dispute should take place on 1 November, 1202; he promised to give a final decision on that occasion. It was also decided that on the third hearing the hitherto neglected problem of the metropolitan status of St. David's should be discussed, provided that Giraldus still had the whole chapter of St. David's or at least the majority of the canons on his side[2]. Innocent favoured Giraldus in so far as he ruled that at the next meeting the archbishop of Canterbury should be present personally,[3] and that he should help the elect of St. David's to meet the expenses of his previous journeys to Italy. Giraldus was once again assured that in the meantime he should keep the administration of the vacant bishopric. Yet despite the poor performance of Hubert Walter's proctors Innocent III quite clearly wrote favourably to the archbishop: 'we do not want to diminish your position and rights but rather to preserve them fully, yet we do not intend to do anything against his rights which have come before us for examination, if he has any in this affair'.[4]

The way in which Giraldus had been treated by the archbishop of Canterbury in the previous two years, together with the undiplomatic performance of the proctor Andrew produced one new result: Giraldus spoke in Rome as a fervent Welshman against the English, and the way in which he voiced the national prejudices of the Welsh against the English shows that by this time he had fully identified his own cause with the cause of Welsh freedom.[5] The antagonism was reduced to the most basic level, an English–Welsh confrontation. A few quotations may illustrate this point: 'How has he [Andrew] the face to venture to set the English nation above ours or even to compare it? For the English are the most worthless of all people under heaven; for they have been subdued by the Normans and reduced by the law of war to permanent slavery ... The English in their own land are the slaves of the Normans

---

[1] *Op.* iii, 191ff.

[2] *Ibid.*, p. 194.

[3] *Op.* iii, p. 195: 'sciens quippe archiepiscopum in Anglia testium copiam ad quidlibet asserendum habere posse, ex cautela et industria hoc statuendum esse'.

[4] *De Invect.*, iii, 12, p. 154: 'sicut ius tuum nolumus impediri, sed integre tibi pocius intendimus reservare, sic ius illius *si quod habet in causa*, que ad nostrum pervenit examen, nolumus deperire'. Cf. also Cheney, *Letters*, p. 55f., esp. no. 345, printed here for the first time.

[5] *De Invect.*, i, 4, p. 93: 'In nos et gentem nostram crebris invectionibus coram vobis impudenter invehitur ...'; 'genti nostre Britannice gentem Anglicanam preferre ausus est vel et conferre, puta nationum omnium, quae sub coelo sunt, vilissimam ...'

and of all slaves the most worthless, while in our land we have no cowherds, shepherds, cobblers, skinners, mechanics, or cleansers of our sewers, save English only ... But our British race, now known by the false name of Welsh, is, like the Romans, sprung from Trojan blood, and defending its freedom both against Norman and Saxon with ceaseless rebellion, and have to this very day shaken the yoke of slavery from their necks. Wherefore let Andrew cease to compare slaves with freemen, the wretched with the great, the vile and abject with the noble and brave ...'[1]

Giraldus also attacked Hubert Walter personally, charging him with greed, ambition, unscrupulous behaviour and even heresy. The attack had grown out of proportion and blinded Giraldus for the limitations which the archbishop's office implied by virtue of its position in the kingdom. Thus when attacking Hubert Walter he only described from the subjective angle of a Welsh churchman the position and policy of an English archbishop who claimed the spiritualities of any vacant bishoprics for himself, the temporalities for the king. Giraldus outlined the unfortunate situation in which the Welsh Church was because Canterbury tended to make predominantly political appointments to the bishoprics in Wales: 'It is with this design that they are wont in Wales to set over us dumb dogs that cannot bark, since they are ignorant of our language and have no desire to do so, seeing that just as they persecute our bodies owing to the inborn hatred that divide our nations, so also they have no care for our souls'.[2] Giraldus ended his speech with the heroic assertion that as long as he lived he would not refrain from making difficulties for the archbishop, until the Welsh Church would enjoy again its ancient and due liberty.[3] In this bold spirit he ended his second visit to Rome.

During the next few months the negotiations in Wales and England decided the fate of Giraldus' election and his wider ambitions, so that when finally he returned to Rome it was almost certain that the pope would decide against him. This happened because King John showed a keen interest in the outcome of the election dispute and threw in his weight with the archbishop; he agreed with Hubert Walter that Giraldus should never become bishop or archbishop, and they together had all the practical power at their disposal to deprive Giraldus of popular support even in the face of papal commands to the contrary effect. King

---

[1] *Ibid.*, p. 93f, Butler, pp. 209–211.

[2] *Ibid.*, p. 98, Butler, p. 217; the phrase *canes muti non valentes latrare* occurs in Isaiah 56, 10.

[3] *Ibid.*, p. 105: 'nunquam domino suo deerit vexatio, quamdiu vixero, donec ecclesia nostra solita et debita gaudeat libertate'.

John was well aware that Innocent III was rather restricted in his own diplomatic moves even if he had favoured Giraldus and Welsh ecclesiastical independence. The pope was at that time deeply involved in the other election dispute of greater concern to the papacy: in 1198 two men, Philip of Swabia, and Otto of Saxony, had been elected kings of Germany, and the pope eagerly grasped the opportunity to decide whose election should be recognized. His decision was dictated by practical political consideration and by the awareness of the valuable precedence he would set if he could examine the two candidates and choose between them. Pope Innocent clearly favoured Otto, a nephew of King John, for political reasons, although Philip's claim was more sound, and he could not afford to alienate John from supporting him in this great issue by granting ecclesiastical independence to Wales.

John would not tolerate that Innocent III had ordered Giraldus to administer the *temporalia* of the vacant see, a royal privilege which had been painfully established by the Crown and was guarded jealously. He therefore condemned the pope's decision in strong terms.[1] John declared everybody who would support Giraldus an enemy of the Crown, Giraldus himself a traitor. The same language was used by the justiciar, Geoffrey fitzPeter, in a letter to the abbot of Whitland in 1201: Giraldus was 'an enemy of the Lord King, working openly against the dignity of the Crown, and encouraging the Welsh to plot against the king'.[2] Everybody who wanted to maintain his income in future had to declare himself openly and unambiguously against Giraldus.

In view of this concerted pressure from England it was little more than a moral boost that all the Welsh princes now unanimously declared their support for Giraldus. Maelgwn and Rhys, sons of the Lord Rhys, openly indentified themselves with the aim of Giraldus' election and the quest for the metropolitan status of St. David's. They declared that everybody who would act against this would be their enemy. Llywelyn ab Iorwerth, prince of Gwynedd, offered double compensation to everybody who would suffer material loss from the English Crown for their conviction, and he announced to take under his protection those who would be exiled in England. For the Crown now devised stronger means to deprive Giraldus of his support. Whereas the previous policy had been to attract some canons into the royal camp by bribes

---

[1] *Rot. Lit. Pat.*, ed. T. D. Hardy, i 3b (17 Dec. 1201): 'in damnum et dispendium dignitatis corone nostre presumit usurpare, quod nos nulla ratione salva dignitate nostra sustinere possumus vel debemus'.

[2] *Op.* iii, p. 201.

and promises, open pressure was now put onto the last faithful followers of Giraldus. The justiciar deprived the canons of St. David's who still stood out for their elect of their income. All of them appear to have been Welshmen. Giraldus named especially the archdeacon Pontius, his son Maurice, Robert fitzJonas, Henry fitzRobert, Meiler, G., Samuel and Asser.[1] This was done in open defiance of the pope's commands not to do anything to alienate the supporters of the elect of St. David's by any means,[2] but the pope had no means of enforcing his will.

The bishops of Ely and Worcester, appointed by Innocent III to head a commission to inquire into the status of St. David's, held a meeting with Giraldus and representatives of the cathedral chapter of St. David's in the autumn of 1202. Giraldus complained about the way in which the pope had promised him freedom of action and the manner in which this had been disregarded by the justiciar and the archbishop. The cathedral chapter was represented by four canons: two Englishmen and enemies of Giraldus of long standing, Osbert and Reginald Foliot, and two Welshmen, relatives of Peter, abbot of Whitland, and for this reason no fervent supporters of Giraldus either, Martin and Samuel. When questioned about their attitude towards the metropolitan claim of St. David's they replied that the election of a bishop would have to be settled first. By this attitude they undermined the strong basis on which Giraldus had stood in the past: that the episcopal election and the metropolitan claim should be tackled simultaneously. It was even more disappointing to Giraldus to hear on that occasion that the whole of the chapter of St. David's allegedly never had elected him. This pronouncement caused the bishop of Ely, a man who was generally well disposed towards Giraldus, to ask him why he had undertaken all the trouble in order to free his ungrateful colleagues from suppression. In his reply, Giraldus made a rather moving statement of great ethical depth: 'As you know', he said, 'a benefit differs according as it consists in liberty, liberation, or liberality. The first and second can be conferred upon the unwilling, the third never. For I can emancipate my slave and set my captive free from prison, however unwilling he may be. But I cannot give my moral code to anyone, unless he is willing to accept it'.[3] He added to this: 'the result of this corruption is in truth most wonderful: for here we have Welsh canons who used to rejoice in the honourable liberty that originally was theirs, and now, like the whole of their race, refuse to be snatched from the servitude and subjection which now oppresses them, even if the boon be proffered by a stranger, whoever

---

[1] Op. iii, p. 214f.

[2] De Invect., iii, nos. 2, 10–16, pp. 148, 152–57.

[3] Op. iii, p. 222; Butler, p. 246, mistranslates 'codicem meum' as 'a book of mine'.

he be and whatever the circumstances, not to speak of their refusal to be liberated by one of their own brothers who with such diligence and toil fights on behalf of the body of their own church. It is not so amazing in the case of the English, long since reduced to servitude, which by now has become almost a second nature, if they refuse to depart from their habitual state of slavery . . .'[1] For the last time the proud Welshman had spoken, but already in this passage one can perceive that he had been as greatly disappointed by the Welsh as he had earlier been by the English.

Giraldus tried in vain to win the support of the Oxford school of law for his case. Hubert Walter had acted more quickly and secured help from the more experienced people. Giraldus had to be satisfied with a lawyer who was not yet well know.[2] But even he was convinced by then that he would have to compromise in certain respects if he wanted to gain anything for himself, for St. David's, and Wales. In this situation he put a plan before the bishops of Ely and Worcester in September, 1202. He began by elaborating once again the past history and dignity of the church of St. David's. The see had held archiepiscopal status at all times in the past, even if for some centuries without a pallium for its archbishops. He now suggested that it should remain an archbishopric, but under the primatial jurisdiction of Canterbury.[3] This is the only place where Giraldus stated quite unambiguously what he had originally wanted to secure: the status of archbishop *and* primate of Wales, equal in rank with the primate of England and the primate of Ireland. Had he succeeded in this, he would indeed have unified the Welsh bishoprics and elevated them to a status of a national church. Medieval Welsh history might have taken a different direction! According to the suggested compromise, an archbishop of St. David's under the primacy of Canterbury would have had to concede a certain administrative and jurisdictional influence to Canterbury in Wales, while at the same time such a semi-autonomous status would have done justice to Wales as a country whose people differed from England in language, law and customs. It would have done justice also to the political situation as it stood before the Edwardian conquest. Giraldus even offered to renounce his election in case his plan would be accepted, as long as another suitable candidate would become archbishop at St. David's.

[1] *Op.* iii, p. 223; *De Invect.*, v, 21, p. 201f.; Butler, p. 246f.

[2] *Op.* iii, p. 228. Cf. S. Kuttner and E. Rathbone, 'Anglo-Norman Canonists of the Twelfth Century', *Traditio*, vii, 1949–51, pp. 279–358, at p. 324, n. 23. It is there dated incorrectly 1198–99.

[3] *De Invect.*, vi, 1, pp. 162–64.

Hubert Walter refused to accept or even consider this compromise, although several people tried to persuade him to do so. From his point of view he was certainly right: Canterbury would have been the losing partner while Giraldus would have gained the substance while giving way over a high-sounding title. Acceptance by Hubert Walter would have amounted to the renunciation of his archiepiscopal power in Wales which his predecessors had held *de facto* since the time of Anselm. In addition to that, there was little chance that the pope would decree against Canterbury at that time. On the other hand, the concession which Giraldus was prepared to make was as great as he could make one if he wanted to gain the substance of his plan. A true compromise was not possible over this issue.

When Giraldus left England for Rome under the greatest difficulties in November 1202, he knew that he was defeated. The only evidence he could produce this time was a letter in which all the major Welsh princes, Llywelyn ab Iorwerth of Gwynedd, Madog of Powys, Gruffydd, Maelgwn, Rhys and Maredudd of Deheubarth, pledged their support for him.[1] The letter was apparently drawn up by Giraldus himself and reiterated the well-known arguments and grievances: the Welsh Church (*ecclesia Walensica*)[2] had been subjected to Canterbury without papal permission. The archbishops saw no harm in imposing as bishops on the Welsh sees men who knew neither language nor customs of the country. Canonical elections had given way to forced appointments. The alien bishops did not feel any attachment to their diocese, alienating shamelessly Church property and working only for their own material benefit. More grave than any material loss, however, was the perverted way in which they used their power for secular advantages: in case of war, when English people attacked Wales, the country was put under the interdict and the princes excommunicated together with their people, although they only fought to protect their own country and freedom (*qui pro patria nostra solum et libertate tuenda pugnamus*).[3] The princes

---

[1] According to Lloyd, *History*, ii, p. 627, n. 73, this letter belongs to 1200, but because of its content it can quite safely be set in 1202; cf. *Op.* i, p. 15, no. clxix.

[2] *De Invect.*, ii, 1, p. 131. This terminology replaces the earlier one used by Giraldus: *ecclesia Wallie* and underlines a new self-consiousness. It was coined after the term *ecclesia Anglicana* which was used in the twelfth century, cf. Charles Duggan, 'From Conquest to the Death of John', *The English Church and the Papacy in the Middle Ages*, ed. C. H. Lawrence (London, 1965), p. 108. Cf. also Denis Hay, 'The Church of England in the later Middle Ages', *History*, 53, 1968, pp. 35–50, at p. 35, 47ff.

[3] *Op.* iii, p. 244–46, at 245; cf. G. Post, *Studies*, p. 437ff., Kantorowicz, *King's Two Bodies*, p. 251ff.

concluded their appeal by requesting the pope to renew the primacy of St. David's in Wales.[1]

The massive support of the Welsh princes for Giraldus perhaps did not improve his chances of success. It is conceivable, on the contrary, that when it became apparent that the St. David's election produced a total confrontation between England and Wales, on a scale hitherto unprecedented, the pope had no choice but to stand by Hubert Walter and King John who mobilized the influence of the German king Otto IV.[2] The negotiations lasted three months altogether. Although Hubert Walter did not appear personally in Rome, he had as his proctors both Welshmen and Englishmen. From St. David's appeared the canons Reginald Foliot, Osbert, and Philip; a canon from Llandaff, Ifor, was introduced as a canon of St. David's although he apparently had never seen the place.[3] Other people mentioned by Giraldus were two monks, Roger and Golwenus, and a member of the archbishop's *familia*, John of Tynemouth. Giraldus alleged that just as they themselves had been bribed by the archbishop, so they bribed the pope and the cardinals.[4] On his first vist to Rome he had boasted that while other people tried to make friends at the Roman curia by distributing money, he himself brought his own books as presents ('*Praesentant vobis alii libras, sed nos libros*')[5] but he had miscalculated which gifts would win better friends.

The last negotiations dealt with the alleged double election of St. David's in 1199. Giraldus believed that he could make quite clear that his enemies had been spreading lies, but the pope gladly grasped the opportunity to evade giving a decision in principle and instead pronounced on a question of procedure. On 15 April, 1203, Pope Innocent III quashed the elections of both Giraldus and Walter, abbot of St. Dogmaels.[6] It was no more than the last stubborn resistance of a defeated man when Giraldus declared that he would continue to

---

[1] *Op.* iii, p. 246: 'Quoniam ante illorum trium, qui nunc ultimo fuerunt, tempora ecclesia Menevensis primatiae Walliae totius sedes fuerat, sicut et antiquitus, metropolitana, sanctae Romanae scilicet ecclesiae solum obnoxia'. Again we see the strong emphasis on archbishopric *and* primacy!

[2] *Op.* iii, p. 267.

[3] He pretended to be a canon of St. David's, but when asked about the position of the cathedral he said it was situated on top of a hill, *Op.* iii, p. 248.

[4] Giraldus claimed that the last negotiations in Rome cost the archbishop, 11.000 marks, *Op.* iii, p. 264.

[5] *Op.* i, p. 119.

[6] *Op.* iii, pp. 267–68; Cheney, *Letters*, no. 468.

fight for the status of St. David's as archdeacon of Brecon. The pope magnanimously promised a new commission, consisting of people from the province of York and therefore less biased, if Giraldus could produce good evidence that the chapter of St. David's had been forced to withdraw their support from him.[1] This was not more than a gesture by the pope, for how could Giraldus have produced such evidence without the co-operation of the canons? Even if he would succeed in this, the promise of a commission was non-committal and was never brought to the test.

Innocent III announced his decision in a letter to the bishops of Ely and Worcester, and he urged them to supervise the overdue election of St. David's. A suitable person should be elected within two months and then consecrated at Canterbury by his archbishop (*per metropolitanum proprium*). The pope also urged the two bishops to make sure that the new bishop of St. David's should not undergo any obligation which could jeopardize the status of St. David's.[2] This pronouncement was indeed a success for Giraldus,[3] in principle at least, for the pope either had no means to enforce this regulation or he did not apply them. The form in which previous bishops of St. David's had been forced into this obligation had been practiced although it was uncanonical. The pope also remained silent about the question of whether Canterbury's metropolitan right would in future exist *de iure*, although his decision about the consecration of the new bishop, as it stands, clearly indicates that the consecration of previous Welsh bishops by Canterbury had not created a legally sound right over Wales by the English primate.[4]

Pope Innocent was not unfriendly to Giraldus personally. He absolved him from his obligation to go on crusade,[5] and declared that the archbishop of Canterbury had to pay a considerable sum of the expenses in the election dispute. He gave his approval to some measures taken by the bishop-elect in the previous three years by re-iterating the sentence of excommunication against Nicholas Avenel and W. fitzMartin who had intruded into Giraldus' benefices of Llanwda and Mathry,[6] and

---

[1] *Op.* iii, p. 271.

[2] *De Invect.*, iv, 4, p. 172; Cheney, *Letters*, p. 79, no. 479; Migne, *PL*, ccxv, col. 70: 'ne idem archiepiscopus aliquam ab eo recipiat caucionem, propter quam prosequi nequeat causam status ecclesie Menevensis'.

[3] *Ibid.*, iv, 5, p. 172f.; iv, 9, p. 177: 'multiplex laboris Giraldi commendatio', and *passim*.

[4] M. Richter, 'Professions', p. 212.

[5] *De Invect.*, iii, 18, p. 158f.

[6] *Ibid.*, iii, 20, p. 160; Cheney, *Letters*, no. 490.

by confirming the conferment to benefices of three people who seem to have been the last faithful followers of Giraldus: Philip, Ithenard, and John.[1]

Giraldus had been assured that his election had not been cancelled because he was personally unsuitable for the episcopal office.[2] He cherished some slight hope of being nominated once again. The list of nominations submitted by the chapter of St. David's included Giraldus, and the abbots Walter and Peter. The fact that Giraldus was mentioned as a possible candidate once again was a grave provocation of the archbishop and the king. But the canons of St. David's were quickly convinced that they could not afford to do this. So Giraldus was substituted on the list by Reginald Foliot,[3] but none of them was elected in the end. The king felt it once more necessary to pronounce clearly against Giraldus who had worked against the Crown's prerogative in episcopal appointments. In September, 1203, John declared that Giraldus was an enemy of the realm 'who strives towards a diminishing of the dignity of the king and to upset the peace of the realm'.[4]

The new bishop of St. David's was Geoffrey de Henlaw, formerly prior of Lanthony by Gloucester and the first choice of Hubert Walter.[5] He was consecrated, as the pope had ordered, by the archbishop of Canterbury[6] on 7 November, 1203, at Westminster, having first given the customary profession of canonical obedience.[7] It is not quite clear whether on this occasion he was compelled to abjure any metropolitan ambitions for himself.[8] In fact the consecration of Geoffrey as bishop of St. David's sealed the final subjection of the Welsh bishops to the archiepiscopal jurisdiction of Canterbury.

---

[1] *Ibid.*, iii, 21–23, pp. 160–62; Cheney, Letters, no. 491–93.

[2] *Ibid.*, iv, 7, p. 173. Thus, according to canon law, he could be nominated again, cf. *Decret. Greg. IX*, 1, 6. 12.

[3] *Op.* iii, p. 298f.

[4] *Rot. Lit. Pat.*, ed. T. D. Hardy, i, 34a (11 Sept. 1203): 'qui in damnum et dispendium dignitatis regiae et pacis regni perturbationem anhelat'.

[5] Letter to the archbishop of Canterbury by the chapter of St. David's concerning Geoffrey's consecration *infra*, Appendix II, no. 2.

[6] Cf. C. R. Cheney, *Hubert Walter*, p. 63 and n. 3.

[7] For Geoffrey's profession cf. *infra*, Appendix II, no. 3. Different dates are given for his consecration in Giraldus, *Op.* iii, p. 321 (7 December) and the same in the Annals of Waverley, *Ann. Mon.*, ii, p. 255. A more detailed discussion of this and the following will be found in Giraldus, *Speculum Duorum*, Introduction.

[8] Giraldus later maintained that Geoffrey had given his oath jeopardizing any metropolitan claim of St. David's already before the confirmation of his election. So when the bishops of Ely and Worcester warned him on the day of his consecration not give the oath, it was too late, cf. *Op.* iii, p. 345.

The defeat of Giraldus went further than this failure to become bishop or archbishop. In summer, 1203, he still had declared that he would fight for the metropolitan status of St. David's, but at the end of the year he formally abandoned this ambition. Two leading members of Hubert Walter's *familia*, both eminent canonists, Honorius, archdeacon of Richmond[1] and John of Tynemouth[2] worked out an agreement between Giraldus and Hubert Walter. Giraldus now pledged fullest possible support for Canterbury against any metropolitan claim of St. David's. He promised: 'In whatever position I shall be I shall never raise the issue of the status of the church of St. David's against the church of Canterbury, nor shall I give counsel or help to anybody else who would like to raise it, but I shall oppose, as much as I can, anybody who would raise it, in order to protect the liberty and the dignity of Christ Church, Canterbury'.[3] There can be little doubt that the archbishop of Canterbury had to make considerable concessions to Giraldus to obtain this full submission. One of them was certainly his approval of a transaction by which Giraldus' nephew, also called Giraldus de Barri, was to succeed his uncle in the archdeaconry of Brecon. It was a highly uncanonical procedure to pass on a major ecclesiastical position in a family, but it can be explained as an exchange for the obligation which Giraldus undertook. Hubert Walter finally secured a reconciliation between Giraldus and King John early in 1204.[4] While Giraldus faithfully kept his promise not to do anything for the status of St. David's, John seems to have had the intention of encouraging a revival of this dispute when he felt provoked and annoyed by the election of a new archbishop of Canterbury in 1206, Stephen Langton. But the issue had been finally closed in 1203.

The metropolitan claim thus disappeared with Giraldus' abdication as its champion. This underlines the very personal importance it assumed in his life, but what is known about it comes mainly from the champion himself who gave it a publicity which was perpetuated – although for different reasons–for a long time afterwards. In this respect, the evaluation of the historian by John of Salisbury applies to Giraldus as a political figure in a double way: 'Eadem est asini et cuiusvis imperatoris post modicum tempus gloria, nisi quatenus memoria alterutrius scriptorum

---

[1] Cf. Kuttner-Rathbone, *loc. cit.*, p. 340f.

[2] *Ibid.*, p. 317ff; also Cheney, *Hubert Walter*, p. 164–66; also Cheney, *English Bishops' Chanceries* (Manchester, 1950), pp. 12–15; on both also *Op.* iii, p. 323.

[3] The charter is printed in full *infra* Appendix II, no. 4.

[4] *Rot. Lit. Pat.*, ed. T. D. Hardy, i. 37b (5 January, 1204).

beneficio prorogatur'.[1] Against this may be set the comment of Gervase of Tilbury on the lack of success by the Welsh Church in freeing herself compared to the successful venture by the Scottish Church. The consolation and compliment of John of Salisbury's is counterbalanced by this statement which is both realistic and cynical: 'Sic ergo dum ludit in humanis Romana potentia rebus, hunc humiliat, et hunc exaltat, hunc Argum facit, illum Polyphemat, utinam haec sit mutatio dexterae excelsi!'[2]

IV.—POSTSCRIPT.

Any assessment of the importance of Giraldus Cambrensis stems from an evaluation of his own writings, as has been shown in the preceding pages. In order to come to a just appreciation of the author, it is imperative to determine as accurately as possible at what stage of his eventful and exciting career the author wrote a certain book or treatise. For if this aspect is neglected, there is always a danger of mis-judging his personality, a danger which stems to a great extent from the author's own intentions: already during his life-time he created a legend about his career and achievements; the sheer quantity of material concerning the dispute over the St. David's election pushes this issue into the foreground. While it is true that this was the most important political event in his life, it is equally clear that his election to the see of St. David's was not the climax of an unwavering dedication to the cause of Welsh independence. On the contrary, Giraldus only became a fervent Welshman after his hopes for a more attractive career in England had been destroyed. This may account for much of the radicalism and single-mindedness which were expressed by this ambitious and vulnerable man.

The historian will have to be careful not to be misguided by the available material. The danger of misjudgement can be great with a personality as vivid and outspoken as Giraldus was in his works. Most of the books which he wrote may have remained quite unknown in the Middle Ages. Not only would the evidence of the surviving manuscript copies have to be taken into account – most of his works survive in a single manuscript only, and these copies are almost invariably contemporary or nearly contemporary with his life – but the information provided in his works reached only a very small section of medieval society. From the author himself we know of the way in which he made known his Irish works, namely by reading from them to invited audiences, at one time in

---

[1] *Policraticus*, ed. C. C. Webb, i, p. 13.

[2] *Otia Imperialia*, ed. G. W. Leipnitz (Hannover, 1707), p. 918.

Oxford, at another time to Archbishop Baldwin on the tour of Wales. Whether any of his other books were then widely known is difficult to say. The reading public in general was very small, and in Wales, where his books would have found perhaps a greater number of interested people than elsewhere, it was even smaller than in England. There is, on the other hand, no indication at all whether an oral tradition about Giraldus grew up around his fight for an archbishopric.

In addition, most of his writings were of a rather too special and personal nature to become very popular in his own days. The exception to this are the books on Ireland and Wales which are his greatest achievement, but even they had a considerable impact only when they appeared in print for the first time in the early seventeenth century. Even then their appeal was limited to the specialist or to the patriot. Giraldus never became as popular as either Bede or Geoffrey of Monmouth.

Giraldus lived long enough to see great changes in the political life of Wales. He was born in the age of Owain Gwynedd and the reign of King Stephen, and he died in the age of Llywelyn Fawr and during the minority of Henry III. The Welsh princes made a considerable contribution to the unification of North Wales and eventually the whole of Wales. In the political field, however, it was the thirteenth century rather than the twelfth which brought Wales near unification.[1] The history of the Welsh Church followed a different pattern. There the desire for independence from England followed closely on to the reform movement and had virtually come to an end in the middle of the twelfth century. Bishop Bernard of St. David's was the great reformer of the Welsh Church and also the man who did most to gain independence for a 'national' church in Wales. The gap between his efforts and those of Giraldus was too wide to create a continuity in their identical efforts.

Yet the two reform movements in pre-Edwardian Wales, the ecclesiastical and the political one, were separated one from the other not only in time but also in space. Church reform came from an area which was held all the time under close control by the Normans for strategic and political reasons. The bid for ecclesiastical independence therefore always lacked effective political backing. There can be little doubt that the failure to establish an archbishopric made a political unification of Wales by the princes much more difficult.

While Giraldus was unable to modifiy substantially the course o₁ Welsh history in the Middle Ages, posterity will gratefully acknowledge the information which his books provide about a country otherwise of marginal interest to the educated class. Giraldus gained his insight

---

[1] See now M. Richter, 'The political and institutional background to national consciousness in medieval Wales', forthcoming (*Historical Studies*, Dublin 1977).

by the education which he received outside Wales; his thoughts and ideas are set firmly in the mainstream of European tradition, especially in the values set by the classical and the patristic age. This is why he could later describe his native country in a way which was understood outside. In describing Wales in terms which had been set by the medium in which he was educated, he could bring out quite clearly those features of Welsh society which struck the observer as unusual while they would be taken for granted by the native Welshman. Thus in a way his cosmopolitan education was a precondition for his greatest literary achievements.

And yet his contribution is essentially a personal one. In fighting for an archbishopric for Wales he was the person who made this ecclesiastical issue one of political importance. While not all his followers may have seen the issue in this radical light, they flocked to his support when he persuaded them to follow him, thereby not only giving him greater strength but also transforming the issue into a popular national cause. Giraldus, the man of cosmopolitan background and with a sound education could mould the issue into its most radical and rudimentary form: it became the outcry of one nation against suppression by its neighbour. In this he was not understood by all his Welsh followers to many of whom material loss and personal discomfort became soon the more important criterion of behaviour, but his principal antagonists, the king and the archbishop of Canterbury, understood Giraldus and reacted accordingly.

Welsh history in the Middle Ages is the history of a country which was slowly being conquered and reshaped by a strong and determined neighbour. Few great personalities stand out who attempted to stem this development, but certainly Giraldus must be named side by side with the two Llywelyns and Owen Glyn Dŵr. The greatness of three of these lies in their political ideas and actions. Giraldus, however, will be remembered for his individual contribution. His career full of set-backs and without eventual fulfilment in public life moved him to write copiously about himself and the country in which he was born. Giraldus is the greatest writer in Latin whom Wales has ever produced. It is mainly in this sense that he will be appreciated as Giraldus Cambrensis.

APPENDIX I

The correspondence about the metropolitan claim of Bishop Bernard.

A Calendar.

under Pope Honorius II (1124–30)

1   The chapter of St. David's to Pope Honorius II. Request to renew the metropolitan dignity of St. David's as it had been before the arrival of the Normans in Wales.
    (no date) – *Auctoritatis uestre excellentie.*
    Found by Giraldus in 1200 in St. David's (copy),
    Giraldus, *De Invect.*, ii, 10, pp. 143–6; *Ep. Acts*, i, 249–50, calendared.

2   The pope's reply.
    Mentioned only *De successione episcoporum et gestis eorum uidelicet Bernardi et Dauid secundi*, ed. M. Richter, *BBCS*, xxii, 1967–8, p. 248.

under Pope Innocent II (1130–43)

3   Bernard, bishop of St. David's, to Pope Innocent II. The first personal approach of the pope by the bishop with the request to renew the metropolitan dignity of his cathedral.
    (no date, ?1136–38). – *Apud clementem iudicem.*
    Found by Giraldus in 1200 in St. David's (?copy),
    Giraldus, *De Invect.*, ii, 7, pp. 141–2; *Ep. Acts*, i, 259, calendared.

4   The pope's reply.
    Mentioned only, cf. no. 2.

5   Owain (Gwynedd) and Cadwaladr, princes of North Wales, to Bernard, bishop of St. David's. The princes complain to the bishop that Theobald, archbishop of Canterbury, consecrated Meurig to the see of Bangor, an act which had violated the metropolitan dignity of St. David's. They promise to support the bishop in his metropolitan claim.
    (no date, ?1140) – *Notum sit uestre potestati.*
    Giraldus, *De Invect.*, ii, 9, 12, pp. 142–3; 146–7; *Ep. Acts*, I, 259–60, calendared.

6   King Stephen and Ranulph, Earl of Chester, to Bernard, bishop of St. David's. Mandate to consecrate (Richard, *recte:*) Gilbert to the see of St. Asaph.
    (?1140/41) Mentioned only, Giraldus, *De Invect.*, p. 141.

under Pope Lucius II (1144–45)

7   Bernard, bishop of St. David's, to Pope Lucius II. Request to renew the metropolitan dignity of his cathedral.
    (1144, February / May). Mentioned only, Giraldus, *De Invect.*, 136–7.

8   Letter(s) to Pope Lucius II (?from North Wales), supporting Bernard's metropolitan claim.
    (1144, February / May). Mentioned only, cf. no. 7.

9 Pope Lucius II to Bernard, bishop of St. David's. Promise to set up a commission to inquire into the metropolitan claim of St. David's.

Lateran, 2 id. Maii (1144), – *Fraternitatis tue literas.*

Giraldus, from the original (bull), *De Invect.*, ii, 3, 136–7; *Op.* iii, 197; *Ep. Acts*, i, 260, calendared.

under Pope Eugenius III (1145–53)

10 The chapter of St. David's to Pope Eugenius III. Report of the metropolitan position of St. David's in the pre-Norman period. Protest against the consecration of three Welsh bishops by the archbishop of Canterbury. Request to grant Bernard, bishop of St. David's, the pallium.

(?1145) – *Magnam nobis spem.*

Giraldus, *De Invect.*, ii, 6, 139–41; *Ep. Acts*, i, 262–3, calendared.

11 Robert, bishop of Hereford, to Pope Eugenius III. Report of the traditional subordination of the bishops of Wales to the archbishops of Canterbury. Request to confirm this against the claim of Bernard, bishop of St. David's.

(?1145–6) – *Cum in omnibus.*

Original (seal lost) Canterbury Cathedral, Dean and Chapter Archives, Chart. Ant., D 108. Attested copy Oxford, Bodleian Library, MS Tanner, 127, f. 340. *Ep. Acts*, i, 264; Holtzmann, *Papsturkunden*, ii, 14, calendared. For print cf. no. 12.

12 Robert, bishop of Bath, to Pope Eugenius III. As no. 11.

(?1145–6) – *Cum in omnibus.*

Original (seal) Canterbury Cathedral, Dean and Chapter Archives, Chart. Ant., C 136

Haddan & Stubbs, i, 353; *Ep. Acts*, i, 264; Holtzmann, *Papsturkunden*, ii, 14, calendared.

13 Nigel, bishop of Ely, to Pope Eugenius III. As no. 11.

(?1145–6) – *Cum in omnibus.*

Original (seal) Canterbury Cathedral, Dean and Chapter Archives, Chart. Ant., D 107; *Ep. Acts*, i, 264; Holtzmann, *Papsturkunden*, ii, 14, calendared.

14 Robert, bishop of Exeter, to Pope Eugenius III. As no. 11.

(?1145–6) – *Cum in omnibus.*

Original (seal lost) Canterbury Cathedral, Dean and Chapter Archives, Chart. Ant., C 137. *Ep. Acts*, i, 264, Holtzmann, *Papsturkunden*, ii, 14, calendared.

15 Henry, bishop of Winchester, to Pope Eugenius III. He informs the pope that Bernard, bishop of St. David's, in past years acted like a suffragan of Canterbury.

(?1145–6) – *Expedit omnibus.*

Original (seal) Canterbury Cathedral, Dean and Chapter Archives, Chart. Ant., C 134; Voss, Lena, *Heinrich von Blois, Bischof von Winchester*, Berliner Historische Studien, no. 210 (Berlin 1932), 176–7; M. Richter, 'Professions', 203–4. *Ep. Acts*, i, 264; Holtzmann, *Papsturkunden*, ii, 14, calendared.

16 Everard, formerly bishop of Norwich, to Pope Eugenius III. He has heard that Bernard, bishop of St. David's, refuses obedience to the archbishop of Canterbury and claims for himself the right to consecrate the bishops in Wales. But Everard can confirm that all the bishops in Wales are lawfully Canterbury's suffragans. A controversy over diocesan boundaries between the bishops of St. David's and Llandaff was negotiated before the common proper archbishop. Request to deny Bernard's metropolitan claim.

> (?1145–6) – *Miror qua fronte.*
> Attested copy, Oxford, Bodleian Library, MS. Tanner 127, f.339.
> Holtzmann, *Papsturkunden*, iii, no. 60, p. 186 f.; *Ep. Acts*, i, 264, calendared.

17 Pope Eugenius III to Theobald, archbishop of Canterbury. Until autumn, 1148, the time when the metropolitan claim of St. David's is to be considered again, and decided, Bernard, bishop of St. David's, shall be subject to Theobald ' as his proper archbishop' (*tanquam proprio metropolitano*).

> Meaux, 3 Kal. Julii (1147) – *Uenerabilis frater noster.*
> Giraldus, *De Invect.*, ii, 2, 135–6; *Op.* iii, 180–1; Howden, *Chron.* iv, 105.
> *Ep. Acts*, i, 261, calendared.

18 Pope Eugenius III to the chapter of St. David's. As no. 17.

> Meaux, 3 Kal. Julii, 1147.
> Mentioned only, Giraldus, *De Invect.*, p. 136; *Op.* i, p. 8, no. xlvi.

19 Bernard, bishop of St. David's, to Simeon, archdeacon of Bangor. Request to testify to the dignity of St. David's at the Council of Rheims (spring, 1148).

> (?1148, spring) – *Nos et omnis ecclesia nostra.*
> Giraldus, *De Invect.*, ii, 8 and 11, pp. 142, 146; *Ep. Acts*, i, 265, calendared.

APPENDIX II

SELECTED DOCUMENTS

I

Hubert Walter, archbishop of Canterbury, reminds Gilbert Glanvill, bishop of Rochester, of a meeting at Gloucester (20 January, 1201, cf. *De Invectionibus*, i, 4, p. 98) *where the chapter of St. David's had given evidence never to have elected Giraldus (de Barri) their bishop. Request to notify the pope by writing that this evidence had been given without pressure.* no date (*c.* 1201).

Canterbury, Dean and Chapter Muniments, Eastry Correspondence, Group vi, no. 1. (seal lost). Cf. *Ep. Acts*, i, D 335.

H(ubertus) dei gratia Cantuariensis archiepiscopus, tocius Anglie primas, venerabili in Christio fratri G(ileberto) eadem gratia Roffensi episcopo salutem in domino. Bene recolit, sicut credimus, vestra fraternitas qualiter canonici Menevensis ecclesie apud Gloccestr' convenerunt ibique in nostra vestraque necnon et quorundam fratrum et coepiscoporum nostrorum et etiam multorum abbatum presentia super facto electionis Geroldi archidiaconi de Brecghenio requisiti spontanea voluntate et absque ulla coactione iurati dixerunt se nunquam eundem Geroldum elegisse. Unde quia memoratus Geroldus in audientia domini pape non est veritus asserere quod iidem canonici ea que ibi dixerunt dixere coacti, rogamus fraternitatem vestram quatinus, sicut novistis, eosdem canonicos spontanea voluntate et absque ulla coactione ea dixisse que ibi sub iuramento sunt protestati, ita ad convincendum ipsius Geroldi mendacium literis vestris patentibus domino pape significare velitis quod spontaneum fuerit eorundem canonicorum testimonium et non extortum vel coactum. Valete.

Endorsement: Domino Roffensi episcopo pro ecclesia Menevensi.

2

The chapter of St. David's thanks Hubert Walter, archbishop of Canterbury, for confirming the election of Geoffrey de Henlaw and requests his episcopal consecration.
no date (1203)

Canterbury, Dean and Chapter Muniments, Chartae Antiquae, C 105 (seal lost). Cf. *Ep. Acts*, i, D 378.

Reverentissimo domino et patri H(uberto) dei gratia Cantuariensi archiepiscopo, tocius Anglie primati, capitulum Menevensis ecclesie salutem et devotam obedientiam. Super eo quod desolationi ecclesie nostre relevande paterna pietate propensius intendistis et electionem venerabilis viri Gaufridi electi nostri confirmastis, sanctitati vestre multiplices gratiarum exsolvimus actiones, instanter postulantes ut una cum venerabilibus dominis suffraganeis vestris manus ei consecrationis imponere dignemini. Bene valeat sanctitas vestra.

Endorsement: deprecator. Littere capituli Menevensis ecclesie pro Gaufrido electo consecrando ab archiepiscopo Huberto Cantuariensis ecclesie.

3

Geoffrey de Henlaw, bishop-elect of St. David's, promises canonical obedience to Hubert Walter, archbishop of Canterbury, before his consecration.   7 November, 1203.

Canterbury, Dean and Chapter Archives, Chartae Antiquae, C 115, no. 70. Personal signature of the elect. Cf. *Ep. Acts*, i, D 381; *Canterbury Professions*, no. 144, p. 61.

Ego frater Galfridus Menevensis ecclesie electus et a te, reverende pater Huberte sancte Cantuariensis ecclesie archiepiscope et tocius Britannie primas, antistes consecrandus, tibi et omnibus successoribus tuis canonicam obedientiam me per omnia servaturum promitto.

Ego Galfridus subscribo

Endorsement: Hec professio facta est vii idus No(vembris) in capella sancte Katerine apud Westmonasterium astantibus et cooperantibus W(illelmo) Lund' episcopo, G(ileberto) Roffensi, W(illielmo) Lincoln', Hen(rico)[1] Exoniensi, Malg(erio) Wigorn', Mauricio Corcacensi.

4

Giraldus de Barri, formerly archdeacon of Brecon, promises in the presence of Hubert Walter, archbishop of Canterbury, nine bishops and other lay and ecclesiastical dignitaries of England and Wales, neither to raise the metropolitan claim of St. David's in future personally nor to help others to do so, but instead to defend the legal position of Canterbury. He also promises not to undertake anything to receive absolution from this obligation.

no date (late 1203–1204)

Early fifteenth century copy, Canterbury, Dean and Chapter Muniments, Register A, f. 73v, no. 215. Listed in J. C. Russell, 'Dictionary of Writers of Thirteenth Century England', *Bulletin of the Institute of Historical Research, Special Supplement No. 3*, p. 37.

Carta Geroldi Breghen' archidiaconi'[2] quod numquam movebit litem etc.

Omnibus Christi fidelibus ad quos presens scriptum pervenerit, Geroldus quondam archidiaconus de Breghen' salutem in domino. Noverit universitas vestra quod cum auctoritate domini pape me tunc temporis archidiacono de Breghen' et procurante causam adversus venerabilem patrem Hubertum Cantuarien(sem) archiepiscopum et ecclesiam suam Cant(uariensem) <que> super <statu>[3] ecclesie Menevensis mota fuisset, tandem manifeste considerans me quod inceperam circa causam eandem nullatenus posse optinere, in presencia prenominati H(uberti) Cant(uariensis) archiepiscopi et quorundam coepiscoporum suorum, scilicet W(illelmi) Lundon(iensis), G(ileberti) Roffen(sis), H(ereberti) Sar(esberiensis), E(ustacii) Elien(sis), H(enrici) Exoniens(is), S(avarici) Bathoniensis et Glaston(iensis), J(ohannis) Norwicens(is) et M(algerii) Wigorn-iens(is), J' de Cer(tesia) et de Walth(a)m abbatum, et quorundam aliorum magnorum

---

[1] *MS* Her.

[2] *MS originally* archiepiscopi.

[3] < > *not in MS.*

virorum et prudentum, presente eciam saniore parte capituli Menevensis ecclesie et consenciente, prosecucionem predicte cause renunciavi in totum, firmiter promittens me numquam, in quocumque statu fuero, questionem super statu ecclesie Menevensis contra ecclesiam Cantuariensem moturum, et non solum eam alii movere volenti consilium vel auxilium non prestiturum, verum eciam cuicumque eam moventi pro libertate et dignitate ecclesie Christi Cantuariensis tuenda me pro viribus meis oppositum, adiecti eciam ponam quingentarum marcarum, quam si forte veterem suscitavero vel novam super statu ecclesie Menevensis questionem adversus ecclesiam Cantuariensem inchoavero vel eam moventi consilium vel auxilium impendere vel eam moventi me non opposuero, me predicto Cantuariensi archiepiscopo vel eius pro tempore successori, tactis sacrosanctis evangeliis, iuravi soliturum antequam idem archiepiscopus vel eius qui pro tempore fuerit successor, super questione status ecclesie Menevensis teneatur respondere et ad coarhercionem super solucione predicte pene faciendam me iurisdictionem predictorum, Lundon(iensis) et Elien(sis) episcoporum vel eorundem successorum, remota appellacione et contradictione subiecti. Sub eodem eciam iuramento promisi quod huiusmodi promissionis pene vel iuramenti absolucionem per me vel per alium nullatenus postulare curabo. Et hoc presenti scripto et sigilli mei apposicione protestor. Hiis testibus, magistro Simoni de Siwell thes(aurario) Lychesfelden(si), magistro Johanne de Tynem(ue), magistro Roberto de Balbo, Geraldo filio Philippi archidiacono de Breghen', magistro Michaele de Ryngefeld, Rogero de Basyngham, Roberto de Bristoll' et aliis multis.

SELECT BIBLIOGRAPHY

MANUSCRIPTS CITED

CAMBRIDGE, Corpus Christi College, MS 400

CANTERBURY, Dean and Chapter Archives
    Chartae Antiquae
    Eastry Correspondence
    Register A

LONDON, British Museum
    Cotton MSS
      Claudius E v
      Cleopatra E i
      Julius D x
      Tiberius B viii
      Vespasian A v
      Vitellius E v
    Additional MS 17 004
    Harley Roll A 3

VATICAN CITY, Biblioteca Apostolica Vaticana
    Cod. Reg. Lat. 470

PRINTED SOURCES

Anglo-Scottish Relations, 1174–1328, Some Selected Documents, ed. by E. L. G. Stones (London 1965)

Annales Monastici, ed. by H. R. Luard, 5 vols. (RS 36, 1864–69)

Brut y Tywysogyon (*Red Book of Hergest Version*), ed. by Thomas Jones, Board of Celtic Studies, History and Law Series xvi (Cardiff 1955)

Canterbury Professions, ed. by Michael Richter, with a palaeographical note by T. J. Brown, Canterbury and York Society, vol. lxvii (Torquay, 1973)

Cartularium Prioratus S. Johannis Evangelistae de Brecon, ed. by R. W. Banks (London 1884)

The Cartulary of Worcester Cathedral Priory, Register I, ed. by R. R. Darlington, Pipe Roll Society N.S. 38 (London 1968)

Chronica Rogeri de Houedene, ed. by William Stubbs, 4 vols. (RS 51, 1868–71)

Concilia Magnae Britanniae et Hiberniae, ed. by David Wilkins, 4 vols. (London 1737)

Councils and Ecclesiastical Documents relating to Great Britain and Ireland, ed. by A. W. Haddan and W. Stubbs, 3 vols. (Oxford 1869–73)

' " Cronica de Wallia" and Other Documents from Exeter Cathedral Library MS 3514', ed. by Thomas Jones, *BBCS*, xii, 1948, pp. 27–44.

Eadmeri Historia Novorum in Anglia, ed. by M. Rule (RS 81, 1884)

Episcopal Acts and Cognate Documents Relating to Welsh Dioceses, 1066–1272, ed. by J. C. Davies, *HSCW Publications* 1, 3, 4 (1946–48) (incomplete)

Giraldi Cambrensis Opera, ed. by J. S. Brewer, J. F. Dimock, G. F. Warner, 8 vols. (RS 21, 1861–91)

Giraldus Cambrensis, De Invectionibus, ed. by W. S. Davies, *Y Cymmrodor* xxx, 1920.

Giraldus Cambrensis: Speculum Duorum or A Mirror of Two Men, ed. by Yves Lefèvre and R. B. C. Huygens, English Translation by Brian Dawson, General Editor Michael Richter, Board of Celtic Studies, History and Law Series xxvii (Cardiff 1974)

Henrici archidiaconi Huntendunensis Historia Anglorum, ed. by T. Arnold (RS 74, 1879)

The Historians of the Church of York and its Archbishops, ed. by J. Raine, 3 vols. (RS 71, 1879–94)

Ioannis Saresberiensis Policratici sive de nugis curialium et vestigiis Philosophorum Libri viii, ed. by C. C. I. Webb, 2 vols. (Oxford 1909)

Hanes Gruffydd ap Cynan, The History of Gruffydd ap Cynan, ed. by A. Jones (Manchester 1910)

Hugh the Chantor, The History of the Church of York, 1066–1172 ,ed. by Charles Johnson (London 1961)

The Latin Texts of the Welsh Laws, ed. by H. D. Emanuel, Board of Celtic Studies, History and Law Series xxii (Cardiff 1967)

The Letters and Charters of Gilbert Foliot, ed. by Dom A. Morey and C. N. L. Brooke (Cambridge 1967)

The Letters of John of Salisbury, ed. by W. J. Millor, H. E. Butler, C. N. L. Brooke, vol. 1 (London 1955)

Le Liber Censuum, ed. by P. Fabre, L. Duchesne and others, 3 vols. (Paris 1910–52)

Liber Eliensis, ed. by E. O. Blake, Camden Third Series xcii (London 1962)

Littere Wallie, ed. by J. G. Edwards, Board of Celtic Studies, History and Law Series v (Cardiff 1940)

Materials for the History of Thomas Becket, ed. by J. C. Robertson and others, 7 vols. (RS 67, 1875–85)

Monasticon Anglicanum, ed. by W. Dugdale, revised edition, 6 vols. in 8 pts. (London 1817–30)

De Nugis Curialium, ed. by E. S. Hartland, Cymmrodorion Record Series ix, 1923

Orderici Vitalis Historiae Ecclesiasticae Libri Tredecim, ed. by A. le Prevost, 5 vols. (Paris 1838–55)

Otia Imperialia, Gervase of Tilbury, ed. by G. W. von Leibnitz, Scriptores Rerum Brunsvicensium vol. 1, 1707

Papsturkunden in England, ed. by Walther Hotzmann, 3 vols., Abhandlungen der Gesellschaft der Wissenschaften zu Göttingen, Phil.-hist. Klasse, Neue Folge (Berlin 1930–52)

Polychronicon Ranulphi Higden monachi Cestrensis, ed. by C. Babington and J. R. Lumby, 9 vols. (RS 41, 1865–66)

Le Pontifical Romano-Germanique du Dixième Siècle, Le Texte, I, ed. by C. Vogel et R. Elze, Studi e Testi 226 (Città del Vaticano 1963)

The Psalter and Martyrology of Ricemarch, ed. by H. J. Lawlor, vol. 1 (London 1914)

Radulfi de Diceto decani Lundoniensis Opera Historica, ed. by W. Stubbs, 2 vols. (RS 68, 1876)

Registrum Epistolarum Fratris Johannis Peckham, ed. by C. T. Martin, 3 vols. (RS 1894)

Sacrorum Conciliorum Collectio Nova, ed. G. D. Mansi, 1748ff.

Rhigyfarch's Life of St David, ed. by J. W. James (Cardiff 1967)

Selected Letters of Pope Innocent III Concerning England (1198–1216), ed. by C. R. Cheney and W. H. Semple (London 1953)

'De Successione episcoporum et gestis eorum, uidelicet Bernardi et David Secundi', ed. by M. Richter, *BBCS*, xx, 1967, pp. 245–49.

The Text of the Book of Llan Dâv, ed. by J. G. Evans and J. Rhys (Oxford 1893)

Der Traktat des Laurentius de Somercote über die Vornahme von Bischofswahlen, ed. by A. von Wretschko (Weimar 1907)

Veterum Epistolarum Hibernicarum Sylloge, ed. James Usher (Dublin 1632)

Venerabilis Bedae Historiam Ecclesiasticam . . ., ed. by Charles Plummer, 2 vols. (Oxford 1896)

The Vita Wulfstani of William of Malmesbury, ed. by R. R. Darlington, Camden Third Series xl (London 1928)

Willelmi Malmesbiriensis monachi de Gestis Regum Anglorum libri quinque, ed. by W. Stubbs, 2 vols. (RS 90, 1887–89)

SECONDARY WORKS

ANDERSON, A. O., *Early Sources of Scottish History AD 500–1286*, 2 vols. (Edinburgh 1922)

BARRACLOUGH, G., 'The Making of a Bishop in the Middle Ages. The Part of the Pope in Law and Fact', *Catholic Historical Review*, 19, 1933–34, pp. 275–319.

BARROW, G. W. S., 'King David I and the Honour of Lancaster', *EHR* 70, 1955, pp. 85–89.

BENSON, R. L., *The Bishop-Elect* (Princeton, N.J. 1968)

BERGES, Wilhelm, *Die Fürstenspiegel des hohen und späten Mittelalters*, Schriften der MGH 2, second edition (Stuttgart 1952)

BIERBACH, Karl, *Kurie und nationale Staaten im früheren Mittelalter (bis 1245)* (Dresden 1938)

BÖHMER, Heinrich, *Kirche und Staat in England und in der Normandie im XI. und XII. Jahrundert* (Leipzig 1899)

BÖRSTING, Heinrich, *Das Provinciale Romanum* (Münster 1936)

BOWEN, E. G., *Saints, Seaways, and Settlements in the Celtic Lands* (Cardiff 1969)

BOWEN, E. G., *The Settlements of the Celtic Saints in Wales* (Cardiff 1956)

BUTLER, H. E., 'Some new Pages of Giraldus Cambrensis', *Medium Aevum* iv, 1935, pp. 143–152.

BUTLER, H. E., *The Autobiography of Giraldus Cambrensis* (London 1937)

CHADWICK, N. K. ed., *Studies in the Early British Church* (Cambridge 1958)

CHARLES, B. G., *Non-Celtic Place-names in Wales* (London 1938)

CHENEY, C. R., *English Bishops' Chanceries, 1100–1250* (Manchester 1950)

CHENEY, C. R., *From Becket to Langton* (Manchester 1956)

CHENEY, C. R., *Huber Walter* (London 1967)

CHENEY, C. R., and CHENEY, M. G., edd., *The Letters of Pope Innocent III (1198–1216) Concerning England and Wales* (Oxford 1967)

CONGAR, Y. M. J., '*Ecce constitui te super gentes et regna* (Jer. 1. 10) in Geschichte und Gegenwart', *Theologie in Geschichte und Gegenwart* [Festschrift M. Schmaus 1957], pp. 671–696

CRONNE, H. A., 'The Honour of Lancaster in Stephen's Reign', *EHR* 50, 1935, pp. 670–680.

CURTIUS, E. R., *Europäische Literatur und Lateinisches Mittelalter*, 6th edition (Bern-München 1967)

DARLINGTON, R. R., 'Ecclesiastical Reform in the late Old English Period', *EHR* 51, 1936, pp. 385–428

DARLINGTON, R. R., 'The Norman Conquest'. A Lecture (London 1963)

DAVIES, J. C., 'Giraldus Cambrensis, 1146–1946', *Arch. Camb.* 99, 1946–47, pp. 85–108; 256–280

DAVIES, Wendy, '*Liber Landavensis:* its construction and credibility', *EHR* 88, 1973, pp. 335–51

DAVIES, Wendy, 'The Consecration of Bishops of Llandaff in the Tenth and Eleventh Centuries', *BBCS* 26, 1974–5, pp. 53–73

DAVIES, W. S., 'Giraldus Cambrensis: Speculum Duorum', *Arch. Camb.* 83, 1928, pp. 111–134

DAVIS, R. H. C., *King Stephen* (London 1967)

DÖLGER, F., *Regesten der Kaiserurkunden des Oströmischen Reiches*, 5 vols. (München-Berlin 1924 ff.)

DOUIE, D. L., *Archbishop Geoffrey Plantagenet and the Chapter of York*, St Anthony's Hall Publications No. 18 (York 1960)

DOUIE, D. L., *Archbishop Pecham* (Oxford 1952)

DUCKETT, Sir George, 'Evidences of the Barri family of Manorbier and Olethan', *Arch. Camb.* 5th series 7, 1891, pp. 190–208; 277–296

DURTELLE DE SAINT SAVEUR, E., *Histoire de Bretagne*, 2 vols. (Rennes 1935)

EDWARDS, J. G., 'The Normans and the Welsh March', *Proc. Brit. Acad.* 42, 1956, pp. 155–177

EMANUEL, H. D., 'An Analysis of the Composition of the *Vita Cadoci*', *NLWJ* vii, 1951–52, pp. 217–27

FUNKENSTEIN, Amos, *Heilsplan und natürliche Entwicklung* (München 1965)

GOTTLOB, Theodor, *Der kirchliche Amtseid der Bischöfe* (Bonn 1936)

GRAUS, Frantisek, 'Die Entstehung der mittelalterlichen Staaten in Mitteleuropa', *Historica* x, 1965, pp. 5–65

GRIFFITHS, M. E., *Early Vaticination in Welsh with English Parallels*, ed. by T. Gwynn Jones (Cardiff 1937)

HANNING, R. W., *The Vision of History from Gildas to Geoffrey of Monmouth* (New York 1966)

HAY, Denis, 'The Church of England in the later Middle Ages', *History* 53, 1968, pp. 35–50

HAYDEN, Mary T., 'Giraldus Cambrensis', *Studies* xxiv, 1935, pp. 90–100

HOFFMANN, Hartmut, 'Die beiden Schwerter im hohen Mittelalter', *Deutsches Archiv* 20, 1964, pp. 78–114

HOLDSWORTH, J. C., 'Visions and Visionaries in the Middle Ages', *History* 48, 1963, pp. 141–153

HUGHES, Kathleen, *The Church in Early Irish Society* (London 1966)

HUMPHREYS, Dorothy, 'Some Types of Social Life as shown in the works of Gerald of Wales', B.Litt. thesis, typescript (Oxford 1936)

HUYGENS, R. B. C., 'Une lettre de Giraud le Cambrien à propos de ses ouvrages historiques', *Latomus*, 26, 1965, pp. 90–100

JAFFÉ, Philipp, *Regesta Pontificum Romanorum*, 2nd edition, 2 vols. (Lipsiae 1881–88)

JARMAN, A. O. H., 'The Legend of Merlin'. An Inaugural Lecture (Cardiff 1960)

JONES, Thomas, 'Gerald the Welshman's "Itinerary through Wales" and "Description of Wales": An Appreciation and Analysis', *NLWJ* vi, 1949–50 pp. 117–148; 197–222

KANTOROWICZ, E. H., *The King's Two Bodies* (Princeton, N.J. 1957)

KIRN, Paul, *Aus der Frühzeit des Nationalgefühls* (Leipzig 1943)

KNOWLES, Dom D., *The Episcopal Colleagues of Archbishop Thomas Becket* (Cambridge 1951)

KNOWLES, Dom D., 'Some Enemies of Gerald of Wales', *Studia Monastica* 1, 1959, pp. 137-41

KURZE, Dietrich, 'Nationale Regungen in der spätmittelalterlichen Prophetie', *Historische Zeitschrift* 202, 1966, pp. 1–23

KUTTNER, S., and RATHBONE, E., 'Anglo-Norman Canonists of the Twelfth Century', *Traditio* vii, 1949–51, pp. 279–358

LAPIDGE, Michael, 'The Welsh-Latin Poetry of Sulien's Family', *Studia Celtica* viii-ix, 1973–74, pp. 68–106

LAWRENCE, C. H., ed., *The English Church and the Papacy* (London 1965)

LEGGE, D. M., 'Anglo-Norman and the Historian', *History* 26, 1941, pp. 163–175

LLOYD, J. E., *A History of Wales*, 2 vols. (London 1911)

LLOYD, J. E., *The Story of Ceredigion* (Cardiff 1937)

LLOYD, J. E., 'Wales and the Coming of the Normans', *Cym. Trans.* 1899–1900, pp. 122–179

MAGOUN, F. P., 'Giraldus Cambrensis on Indo-Germanic Philology', *Speculum* 1, 1926, pp. 104–109

MARTIN, F. X., 'Gerald of Wales, 1146–1223, Norman Reporter on Ireland', *Studies* 58, 1969, pp. 279–292

MISCH, Georg, 'Die autobiographische Schriftstellerei des Giraldus Cambrensis', *Geschichte der Autobiographie*, II, ii, 2 (Frankfurt 1962)

MOREY, Dom A., *Bartholomew of Exeter, Bishop and Canonist* (Cambridge 1937)

MOREY, Dom A., and BROOKE, C. N. L., *Gilbert Foliot and his Letters* (Cambridge 1965)

NELSON, L. H., *The Normans in South Wales 1070–1171* (Austin, Texas 1966)

NICHOLL, D., *Thurstan, Archbishop of York 1114–1140* (York 1964)

OTWAY-RUTHVEN, A. J., 'The Constitutional Position of the Great Lordships in South Wales', *Tr. RHS*, 5th series, 1958, pp. 1–20

PARRY, Thomas, *A History of Welsh Literature*, translated by H. I. Bell (Oxford 1955)

POOLE, R. L., *Lectures on the History of the Papal Chancery* (Cambridge 1915)

POWICKE, F. M., 'Gerald of Wales', *BJRL* xii, 1928, pp. 389–410

POST, Gaines, *Studies in Medieval Legal Thought* (Princeton, N.J. 1964)

REES, W., *An Historical Atlas of Wales* (London 1951)

RICHTER, Michael, 'Canterbury's Primacy in Wales and the First Stage of Bishop Bernard's Opposition', *JEH* xxii, 1971, pp. 177–189

RICHTER, Michael, 'Professions of Obedience and the Metropolitan Claim of St. David's', *NLWJ* xv, 1967–68, pp. 197–214

RICHTER, Michael, 'The *Life of St David* by Giraldus Cambrensis', *WHR*, iv, 1968–69, pp. 381–386

RICHTER, Michael, 'The First Century of Anglo-Irish Relations', *History* 59, 1974, pp. 195–210

RICHTER, Michael, 'The political and institutional background to national consciousness in medieval Wales', *Historical Studies* (Dublin 1977)

RODERICK, J. A., 'The Feudal Relations between the English Crown and the Welsh Princes', *History* 37, 1952, pp. 201–212

RUSSELL, J. C., *Dictionary of Writers of Thirteenth Century England*, Bulletin of the Institute of Historical Research, Special Supplement No. 3, 1936

RYAN, Mary T., 'The Historical Value of Giraldus Cambrensis' *Expugnatio Hibernica* as an account of the Anglo-Norman Invasion of Ireland' M.A. thesis, typescript (University College Dublin 1967)

SALTMAN, A., *Theobald, Archbishop of Canterbury* (London 1956)

SCHNITH, Karl, 'Betrachtungen zum Spätwerk des Giraldus Cambrensis *De Principis Instructione*', Festiva Lanx (München 1966), pp. 53–66

SHAW, I. P., 'Giraldus Cambrensis and the Primacy of Canterbury', *Church Quarterly Review* 48, 1949, pp. 82–101

SOUTHERN, R. W., *St Anselm and his Biographer* (Cambridge 1963)

SOUTHERN, R. W., 'The Canterbury Forgeries', *EHR* 72, 1958, pp. 193–226

SOUTHERN, R. W., 'The Place of Henry I in English History', *Proc. Brit. Acad.* 48, 1962, pp. 127–169

STENTON, F. M., *Anglo-Saxon England*, 2nd edition (Oxford 1947)

STRAYER, J. R., 'Defense of the Realm and Royal Power in France', *Studi in onore di Gino Luzzatto* (Milano 1949)

TANGL, Michael, *Die päpstlichen Kanzleiordnungen 1200–1500* (Innsbruck 1894)

TAYLOR, R., *The Political Prophecy in England* (New York 1911)

VASILIEV, A., 'Manuel Comnenus and Henry Plantagenet', *Byzantinische Zeitschrift* 29, 1929–30, pp. 233–44

VOSS, Lena, *Heinrich von Blois, Bischof von Winchester*, Berliner Historische Studien 210 (Berlin 1932)

WILLIAMS, E. A., 'A Bibliography of Giraldus Cambrensis', *NLWJ* xii, 1961–62, pp. 197–240

WILLIAMS, Glanmor, 'Prophecy, Poetry and Politics in Medieval and Tudor Wales', *British Government and Administration*, Studies presented to S. B. Chrimes, ed. by H. Hearder and H. R. Loyn (Cardiff 1974), pp. 104–116

WILLIAMS, Glanmor, *The Welsh Church, from Conquest to Reformation* (Cardiff 1962)

WILSON, R. M., 'English and French in England', *History* 28, 1943, pp. 37–60

WRIGHT, J. K., '*The Geographical Lore of the Time of the Crusade* (New York 1925, reprint 1965)

NOTE: A full bibliography of Giraldus Cambrensis has appeared in the edition of *Giraldus Cambrensis, Speculum Duorum*, pp. lxix-lxx.

INDEX

Abraham, bishop of St. David's, 34
Adam, abbot of Evesham, 88
Adam, bishop of St. Asaph, 5
Adam du Petit Pont, 5 n.1
Adrian IV, pope, 28
Albinus, canon of Hereford, 88
Alexander, Cistercian abbot, 99
Alexander, archdeacon of Bangor, 68
Alexander III, pope, 26, 53
Andrew, Canterbury's proctor in Rome, 116–117
Anselm, archbishop of Canterbury, 24, 30, 35
archbishop, office of, 2, 24–5, 39, *passim*
archdeacon, office of, 90
Armagh, bishop of, *see* Malachy
Arthen, son of Sulien, 34
Arthur, king, 75, 76
Asser, canon of St. David's, 104, 120
Atselin, bishop of Rochester, 36
Augustine, missionary, 41–2

Baldwin, archbishop of Canterbury, 7, 64, 68, 84, 94, 128
Bangor, archdeacon of, *see* Alexander, Simeon; bishops of, *see* Adam, David, Hervey, Meurig; diocese of, 13, 25, 35; vacancy at (1161–75), 53–4; offered to Giraldus, 85
Barri, de family of, *see* Giraldus, Giraldus jr., Philip, Robert, Walter, William
Bath, bishop of, 46
Bede, 60, 63, 113–4, 128
Bernard, bishop of St. David's (1115–1148), 3, 14, 15, 16, 24, 25, 31, 32, 33, 34, 35, 36, 57, 94, 128, 130–2; metropolitan claim of, 8, 22, 36–7, 38–52; – , used by Giraldus, 112, 116
Biddlesden (Bucks.), Cistercian monastery, 84; *see also* William Wibert
bishop, election of, 96–7, 111; *see also* Huguccio, Lawrence de Somercote, Rufinus
Bohemia, 43 n.2
Bonjohannes, 114
Braose, William de, 91, 115.
Brecon, archdeacons of, *see* Giraldus, Giraldus jr.
Brefi, synod of, 45
Britons, their descent, 67

Cadoc, St., 13, 14, 15, 35 n.1
Cadwaladr, 31, 44, 75, 130
Caerleon, archbishopric at, 113
Calixtus II, pope, 14, 24, 25, 41 and n.3

Canterbury, archbishops of, *see* Anselm, Baldwin, Hubert Walter, John Pecham, Lanfranc, Ralph d'Escures, Richard of Dover, Stephen Langton, Theobald, Thomas Becket, William of Corbeil; forgeries, 25, 39; professions, 23, *passim*
Cardigan, archdeacons of, *see* David fitzGerald, Ieuan, Maurice
Carmarthen, archdeacon of, *see* Osbert
Celestine III, pope, 26, 56, 91 and n.6, 97 n.1
Cencius, 49
Ceri, 4–5
Chester, bishopric of, 25, 35
Chichester, bishop of, 46; canon of, *see* Lawrence de Somercote
crusade, preached in Wales (1188), 7; *see also* French, Latin
Cum Universi, papal bull, 26, 27
Cymry, meaning of, 67 n.4

Daniel, son of Sulien, archdeacon of Powys, 34, 35 39
David, St., 13, 14, 33, 40, 113; Life of, *see* Giraldus, works; Rhigyfarch
David I, king of Scotland, 32, 37
David, bishop of Bangor, 31 44 n.3
David fitzGerald, archdeacon of Cardigan, subsequently bishop of St. David's (1148–1176), 4, 8, 48, 54, 55
David fitzIthenard, canon of St. David's, 104
Dinefwr, 74
Dol, archbishopric of, 113, 114
Dublin, bishops of, 27
Dubricius, St., 14, 15, 33, 40
Durham, bishopric of, 25; *see also* Ranulf

Eadmer, historian, 31
Edward I, English king, 67, 79, 81
Eleutherius, 40
Ely, bishops of, 46, 120, 121, 124; *see also* Hervey
Elyodor fitzElyodor, canon of St. David's, 101, 104
English, assessed by Giraldus, 117–8; language, 68–9
Eugenius III, pope, 8, 28, 36, 44–8, 109, 131–2; register of, 48–49, 112
Everard, bishop of Norwich, 46 and n.1, 47, 132
Exeter, bishop of, 46

Falaise, treaty of (1174), 26
Ferns, bishopric of, offered to Giraldus, 6
Flemings in Wales, 4, 18–21; *see also* Rhos
Folet, Ralph, canon of Hereford, 88 n.4
Foliot, Ralph, canon of Hereford, 88, 92 n.2

Foliot, Reginald, canon of St. David's, 99, 105; *see also* Reginald

Foliot, William, precentor of Hereford, 88 and n.4

French language, 68–9, 90

Galterius, 90, 105

gens, 21, 60–61

Geoffrey de Henlaw, prior of Llanthony, subsequently bishop of St. David's (1203–1214), 91 n.2, 99, 105, 108, 125, 133, 134

Geoffrey of Monmouth, 11, 63, 67, 75, 113, 128

Geoffrey fitzPeter, justiciar of England, 119

Geoffrey Plantagenet, archbishop of York, 27, 86; *see also* Giraldus, works, Vita Galfridi

Gerald of Windsor, 4

Gerard, archbishop of York, 23

Gerard Pucelle, bishop of Coventry, 8

Gerardus, dean of Pembroke, canon of St. David's, 104

Germany, double election (1198), 103–4, 119.

Gervase of Tilbury, 50, 127

Gilbert, bishop of St. Asaph, 36, 130

Gilbert Foliot, bishop of London, 47 n. 2, 48 n.1, 56, 68 n.8

Gilbert Glanvill, bishop of Rochester, 116, 133

Gilbert of Limerick, 25, 27, 28

Gildas, 63

Giraldus de Barri [Giraldus Cambrensis], characterisation of, 2, 3, 10–11; life of, 4–10; refuses bishoprics in Wales and Ireland, 87, see *also* Bangor, Ferns; hopes for bishopric in England, 87; relations with St. David's, 4, 5, 6, 88–93; elected bishop, 102; election quashed, 123; metropolitan ambitions abandoned, 121, 126, 134–5; attitude towards the English, 121; attitude towards Wales and the Welsh, 3, 19, 76–7, 117; linguistic abilities, 69; works of, De Invectionibus, 9, 38, 61, 94; De Iure et Statu Menevensis Ecclesiae, 9, 61, 94; De Rebus a se Gestis, 9, 61, 95; De Vita Galfridi Archiepiscopi Eboracensis, 86, 101; Gemma Ecclesiastica, 61; Irish works, 6–7, 11, 62, 76 n.2, 92 n.1; Speculum Duorum, 10, 62 n.1; Symbolum Electorum, 88, 93; Vita Sancti Davidis, 35 n.1, 40–41, 60 n.6, 61; Welsh works, 2, 7, 11, 61–66, 81–82, 92 n.1; *see also* Barri, de, family of; Hereford; Ireland; Lincoln, Paris

Giraldus de Barri jr., archdeacon of Brecon, 9 n.5, 69, 126

Glamorgan, 17

Glasgow, bishops of, 24, 26, 39

Golwenus, monk, 123

Gratian, Master, on bishops' elections, 111

Gregory I, pope, 41

Gregory of Caerwent, 30 n.5

Gruffydd ap Cynan, 30, 31, 44, 50

Gruffydd ap Rhys, 73

Henry I, English king, 4, 18, 19, 21, 24, 31, 33, 35, 38, 42, 73

Henry II, English king, 7, 19, 26, 28, 52, 55 and n.1, 63, 72, 74, 84, 93, 111; view of the Welsh, 79; linguistic abilities, 68 n.8

Henry, canon of St. David's, 104

Henry of Blois, bishop of Winchester, 36, 37, 46, 52, 131

Henry of Huntingdon, 60

Henry fitzRobert, canon of St. David's, 104, 120

Hereford, bishops of, 15, 46; Giraldus at, 7, 88, 90

Herewald, bishop of Glamorgan, 14, 32

Hervey, bishop of Bangor, subsequently of Ely, 30

Honorius II, pope, 15, 40, 43, 45, 48 and n.3, 130

Honorius, archdeacon of Richmond, canonist, 126

Hubert Walter, archbishop of Canterbury, 7, 56, 86, 98–126, 133; on the Welsh, 109

Hugh, bishop of Lincoln, 7

Hugh, dean of Hereford, 88

Huguccio, canonist, concept of canonical election, 96

Ieuan, son of Sulien, 34, 39

Ifor, canon of Llandaff, 123

Innocent II, pope, 15, 25, 42, 43, 44, 46, 130

Innocent III, pope, 8, 43 n.2, 49, 50, 95, 103.

interpreter, 68

Ireland, contacts with Wales, 13; metropolitan ambition of, 27–8; characteristics of the Irish, 78–9; Giraldus in, 6, 9, 107

Ithenardus, rural dean, canon of St. David's, 105, 125

John, English king, 6, 8, 9, 85, 102, 115, 116 and n.5

John, canon of St. David's, 105, 125

John of Brancaster, archdeacon of Worcester, 101 n.1

John of Llanddew, archdeacon, canon of St. David's, 105

John Pecham, archbishop of Canterbury, 79–80, 81

John of Salisbury, 28, 79

John of Tynemouth, canonist, 123, 126

Joscelin, rural dean, 90, 105

Kambria, meaning of, 67

Kells, synod of (1152), 28

Lanfranc, archbishop of Canterbury, 22, 23, 26, 27, 28

Latin language, used in preaching, 68

Laudabiliter, papal bull, 28

Lawrence of Somercote, canon of Chichester, 97–8

lechlavar, 72

Lifris, 14, 35 n.1

Limerick, bishop of, 27; *see also* Gilbert of Limerick

Lincoln, bishop of, 46; *see also* Hugh, Robert; chancellor of, *see* William de Montibus; Giraldus at, 7, 9, 88, 99–101

lingua, 60–61; *see also* English, French, Latin, Welsh language

Llandaff, bishops of, *see* Nicholas, Uctred, Urban; canon of, *see* Ifor; diocese of, 13–16, 106, 132; bishopric of, offered to Giraldus, 85

Llanddewi Brefi, synod of, 41

Llanthony, 63, 79, 99; prior of, *see* Geoffrey de Henlaw

Llywelyn ab Iorwerth, 17, 106, 119, 122, 128

London, bishop of, *see* Gilbert Foliot

Longchamp, William of, 86

Lucius II, pope, 44, 130–131

Madog, prince of Powys, 122

Maelgwn ap Rhys, 119, 122

Malachy of Armagh, 42 n.2

Malvern, 88

Map, Walter, archdeacon of Oxford, 88, 100

Maredudd ap Rhys, 122

Martin, canon of St. David's, 105, 115 n.7, 120

Mathry, prebend of Giraldus', 91, 124

Matilda, empress, 32, 35, 36, 46, 60

Maurice, archdeacon of Cardigan, 104, 120

Meiler, canon of St. David's, 105 120

Meiler fitzHenry, justiciar of Ireland, 95 n.1, 106, 115

Merlin, 72–3, 75, 76

Meurig, bishop of Bangor, 31, 34, 36, 50, 130

natio, 1, 3, 43, 57, 60–1, 82

Nennius, 63

Nest, 4

Nicholas, bishop of Llandaff, 33

Nicholas Avenel, 124

Norwich, bishop of, *see* Everard

Osbert, archdeacon of Carmarthen, 91, 104, 105, 120, 123

Otto IV, German king, 103, 119, 123

Owain Gwynedd, 31, 32, 44, 53, 128, 130

Oxford, archdeacon of, *see* Map

Padarn, St., 13, 14, 45

Paparo, papal legate, 28

Paris, Giraldus at, 4, 6

patria, 58–60, *passim*

Patrick, St., 42

Pembroke, 4, 17, 19; archdeacon of, *see* Pontius; dean of, *see* Gerardus; *see also* Flemings

Pencadarn, prophecy of, 74

Peter, abbot of Whitland, 99, 105, 115, 120, 125

Peter de Leche, archdeacon of Worcester, 92 n.2, 100 n.1

Peter de Leia, bishop of St. David's(1176–1198), 5, 6, 7, 55, 56, 85, 98, 100; relations with Giraldus, 89–93

Philip, canon of St. David's, 105, 123, 125

Philip de Barri, brother of Giraldus, father of Giraldus jr., 4, 6, 21 n.3, 89, 115 n.6

Philip of Swabia, German king, 119

Pontius, archdeacon of Pembroke, 104, 120

Powys, archdeacon of, *see* Daniel, son of Sulien

propaganda, political, 71–5

provinciale, 2, 49–50, 112

Ralph d'Escures, archbishop of Canterbury, 24, 31, 33 n.4, 35, 39, 41 and n. 3, 47

Ranulf, bishop of Durham, 24

Reginald Foliot, canon of St. David's, 116, 120, 123, 125

Rheims, council of (1119), 14, 24, 39; (1148), 50, 54, 132

Rhigyfarch, son of Sulien, 14, 34, 39; his Life of St. David, 33, 35, 39, 41, 45, 63

Rhos, Flemings in, 18–21

Rhys ap Gruffydd (the Lord Rhys), 72, 74, 84, 91, 93 n.1; *see also* Maelgwn ap Rhys

Rhys ap Rhys ap Gruffydd, 119, 122

Richard I, English king, 7, 63, 84, 85 n.8, 86, 101

Richard of Dover, archbishop of Canterbury, 56

Robert de Barri, brother of Giraldus', 4

Robert de Chesney, bishop of Lincoln, 54

Robert fitzJonas, canon of St. David's, 105, 120

Rochester, bishops of, *see* Atselin, Gilbert Glanvill

Roger of Howden, 12, 56

Rufinus, canonist, concept of canonical election, 96

St. Andrews, bishopric of, 26

St. Asaph, bishops of, *see* Adam, Gilbert; diocese of, 13, 25, 35–7, 106

St. David's, bishops of, *see* Abraham, Bernard, Geoffrey de Henlaw, Peter de Leia, Sulien, Wilfred; chapter of, *see* Asser, David fitzIthenard, Elyodor fitz-Elyodor, Gerardus, Henry fitzRobert, Henry, Ithenardus, John, Joscelin, Martin, Meiler, Philip, Reginald Foliot, Robert fitzJonas, Samuel; letter by the chapter to Innocent III, 108; deny to have elected Giraldus, 120; diocese of, 13, 17; metropolitan claim of, 3, 6, 8, 17, see also Bernard, Giraldus

St. Dogmael's, abbot of, see Walter

Samson, St., 15, 42, 45, 113

Samuel, canon of St. David's, 105, 115 n.7, 120

Scotland, church of, 25-7

Simeon, archdeacon of Bangor, 44 and n.3, 50, 132

Stephen, English king, 31, 36, 38, 46, 50, 52, 54, 128, 130

Stephen Langton, archbishop of Canterbury, 7, 126

Sulien, bishop of St. David's, 14, 34; family of, see Arthen, Daniel, Ieuan, Rhigyfarch

Teilo, St., 14, 15, 45, 61

Theobald, archbishop of Canterbury, 8, 28, 31, 32, 33, 36, 37, 44 n.4 45, 47, 48, 50, 52, 54, 55, 107, 130, 132

Thomas, archbishop of York, 23, 24

Thomas Becket, archbishop of Canterbury, 53, 54

Thurstan, archbishop of York, 24, 25, 27, 36, 39

Uctred, bishop of Llandaff, 33, 36

Urban, bishop of Llandaff, 14, 15, 24, 32, 33, 43, 47, 48 n.3, 49, 51

Wales, Irish influence in, 13; geopolitical assessment of, 13; political fragmentation of, 3, 17-28;

Welsh Church, 2, 13-24; attitude of Giraldus towards, 77, 92; see also Henry II, Hubert Walter; Welsh customs, 3, 70-1; Welsh, meaning of, 67; Welsh language, 3, 67-8; necessary for bishops in Wales, 100, 108, 118, 122; Welsh people, individuality of, 3, 57; see also Flemings; Giraldus, Welsh works

Walter, abbot of St. Dogmael's, 99, 105, 114, 116, 123, 125

Walter de Barri, brother of Giraldus, 4

Waterford, bishop of, 27

Whitland, abbot of, see Peter

Wilfred, bishop of St. David's, 34, 35

William the Conqueror, 19, 22

William I, Scottish king, 26, 27

William de Barri, father of Giraldus', 4

William of Corbeil, archbishop of Canterbury, 15 n.4, 25, 36, 38 and n.1

William of Malmesbury, 19, 39

William de Montibus, chancellor of Lincoln, 62

William de Vere, bishop of Hereford, 88, 99 n.2

William Wibert, 84, 85, 87-8, 99, 101

Winchester, bishop of, see Henry of Blois

Worcester, archdeacons of, see John of Brancaster, Peter de Leche; bishops of, 120, 121, 124

York, archbishops of, see Geoffrey Plantagenet, Gerard, Thomas, Thurstan; metropolitan controversy with Canterbury, 23-5.